Political Economy of Islam

Series Editors
Hossein Askari
George Washington University
Washington DC, USA

Dariush Zahedi
University of California
Berkeley, CA, USA

All Middle Eastern countries, with the exception of Israel and Lebanon, profess Islam as their state religion. Islam, whether simply in words or in fact, is woven into the fabric of these societies, affecting everything from the political system, to the social, financial and economic system. Islam is a rules-based system, with the collection of rules constituting its institutions in the quest to establish societies that are just. Allah commands mankind to behave in a fair and just manner to protect the rights of others, to be fair and just with people, to be just in business dealings, to honor agreements and contracts, to help and be fair with the needy and orphans, and to be just even in dealing with enemies. Allah Commands humans to establish just societies, rulers to be just and people to stand up for the oppressed against their oppressors. It is for these reasons that it said that justice is at the heart of Islam. In the same vein, the state (policies) must step in to restore justice whenever and wherever individuals fail to comply with divine rules; government intervention must enhance justice. This series brings together scholarship from around the world focusing on global implications of the intersections between Islam, government, and the economy in Islamic countries.

More information about this series at
http://www.palgrave.com/gp/series/14544

Hayat Alvi

The Political Economy and Islam of the Middle East

The Case of Tunisia

Hayat Alvi
US Naval War College
Newport, RI, USA

Political Economy of Islam
ISBN 978-3-030-17052-3 ISBN 978-3-030-17050-9 (eBook)
https://doi.org/10.1007/978-3-030-17050-9

This Palgrave Macmillan imprint is published by the registered company Springer Nature Switzerland AG
The registered company address is: Gewerbestrasse 11, 6330 Cham, Switzerland

The views in this book are those of the author and are not representative of their affiliation.

Preface

In January 2011, I sat at the edge of my seat while watching events unfold in the unprecedented protest movement leading to the Jasmine Revolution in Tunisia. From my living room in New England, I was awestruck with how resolute the Tunisian people remained in the face of security forces. Having studied the Middle East and North Africa (MENA) region for decades, I knew that the odds against the protestors were insurmountable. Yet, they succeeded. Not only that, they also inspired the rest of the region to do the same: topple ruthless authoritarian dictators who, for decades, have cheated the people from the rewards of their labor, education, and endurance in dealing with economic hardships and violent repression.

I visited Tunisia during the dictator Ben Ali's era in fall 2003. Then, I visited after the revolution, in March 2012 and again in July 2017. The differences have been remarkable, and the resilience of the Tunisian people has been noticeable. Most of all, their determination to preserve Tunisia's nascent democracy by means of engaging in dialogue, negotiations, and compromises at various levels, including the highest levels of national political leadership, and maintaining peaceful, non-violent transitions, has been exceptional. The Tunisians witnessed what happened in Libya, Egypt, Syria, and Yemen, with violent chaos and civil conflict causing shocking destruction and casualties. Tunisians have been steadfast in keeping the peace in their country, and Tunisia stands as a model of democracy and non-violent change, which are truly unprecedented in the MENA region.

I have come across plenty of people from the MENA region, especially the oil-rich Persian Gulf Arab states, who have tried to discredit Tunisia's democratization efforts. They have even sullied Mohamed Bouazizi's name. Bouazizi is the young Tunisian man who lit himself on fire out of desperation in the face of gross corruption and abuse of power, and by so doing, he sparked the Jasmine Revolution. Most regimes, including the monarchies, in the MENA region detest the concept of democracy, because it rattles the status quo power structures and economic benefits that they have been enjoying for decades and generations.

As I write, the horrific disappearance and murder of the renowned Saudi journalist Jamal Khashoggi in the Saudi Consulate in Turkey has dominated the news headlines and shocked the world of journalism. Realistically, this case is just the tip of the iceberg regarding the regimes' hatred for democracy, freedoms, human rights, the free press, women's empowerment, gender equality, and the international norms and values that promote them. They also hate any scrutiny of their actions. This is the sad reality even in the twenty-first century.

In post-revolution Tunisia, we see the opposite direction, one in which freedoms and rights, press freedoms, government scrutiny, women's empowerment, and national dialogue in the spirit of non-violent discourse—which has won Tunisian civil society and labor unions the Nobel Peace Prize (2015)—are the prevalent values and processes in the newborn democracy. The most striking characteristic in modern Tunisian politics is the sincere effort of the secularists and Islamists to be civil toward each other, regardless of their deep-rooted differences, and to remain engaged in the national dialogue.

Similarly, it is highly impressive to see how focused the Tunisian civil society and activists are on the post-revolution national priorities, which comprise of improving the economy, especially to provide jobs for the desperate educated youth; fighting corruption; and ensuring security at the local and national levels. Tragically, Tunisia has suffered from some terrorist attacks, and thousands of Tunisians joined the Islamic State (IS) in Syria and Iraq during its peak. Fortunately, these have been the exceptions rather than the rule.

Tunisia has not presented itself as the "perfect" model of Arab democracy, but it deserves to be seen as an important source of lessons from which the rest of the MENA region should learn. Tunisia faces daunting challenges, but the people are not deterred. There is no going back.

Tunisia has a unique history, during the early Islamic period as well as during French colonialism. It has always stood out as unique, different, and unwilling to be merely compliant, whether to France or to the rest of the Arab and Muslim world. For that, Tunisia has always been impressive, and, perhaps, it is the main reason Tunisians dance to their own tunes, as they should, even if it means revolution.

Newport, RI, USA Hayat Alvi

Acknowledgments

I am very indebted to a long list of scholars and assistants, activists and journalists, Islamists and secularists, and feminists, in Tunisia and the United States, who have assisted me in this most important project. Included in my list are Alina Yurova and Mary Fata at Palgrave, who have been very patient and most helpful during my writing and publishing process. In Tunisia, Mouna al-Khazami at the CSID office has been an outstanding assistant and scheduler of my interviews.

All of the interviewees for this book project are worthy of my deepest gratitude: Dr. Radwan Masmoudi, Souad Goussami Hajji, Lotfi Hajji, Ali Ayadi, Hatem Abidi, Fatma Kamoun, and Meherzia Labidi. Without their cooperation and warm reception, I would not have succeeded in this project. These individuals are also treasures of firsthand knowledge and information. Their insights are indispensable.

I am also grateful to the Arab Center for Research and Policy Studies (CAREP), which graciously allowed me to attend their July 2017 conference in Hammamet.

Finally, I wish to express gratitude to my dearest friends in New England and family members, who have cheered me on and provided crucial moral and emotional support.

Louisa May Alcott once said, "I want to do something splendid… Something heroic or wonderful that won't be forgotten after I'm dead… I think I shall write books."

Thank you for helping me in this endeavor.

Praise for *The Political Economy and Islam of the Middle East*

"Hayat Alvi analyzes the Tunisian Revolution within the broader context of less successful movements elsewhere in the Arab world since 2011, suggesting Tunisia as a model for emulation. Based on my own experience of twelve years in Tunisia, including annual visits since the Tunisian Revolution, I find Professor Alvi's analysis clear and persuasive. Her book shows a deep understanding of both the country and the area and a firm command of the literature and social science theory. It will appeal to a broad audience of both specialists and generalists."

—Laurence O. Michalak, Former Vice-Chair, *Center for Middle Eastern Studies, University of California, Berkeley, USA*

"Following the revolutions of the 2011 Arab Spring, the Middle East and North Africa (MENA) region has experienced some of the most profound divisions in its history. With this excellent book, Alvi offers a fresh look at a complex interplay between political Islam and political economy of the region, with a special emphasis on Tunisia. Timely and relevant, this book does a superb job in explaining the intricate legacies of Tunisia's Jasmine Revolution."

—Lasha Tchantouridzé, Professor, *Norwich University, USA*

"Professor Alvi's fascinating analysis of modern Tunisia offers intriguing insights into the only state to achieve a delicate balance of democracy and Islamic values in the Post-Arab Spring world. With exceptionally clear analysis, Alvi guides the reader through a comprehensive synthesis of Tunisia's on-going political, economic, and human rights concerns. The result is a most valuable addition to our understanding of the impact of repression, reformation, and post-revolutionary societal change in the Arab world."

—Frank C. Pandolfe, Vice Admiral, *U.S. Navy (ret.)*

"Dr. Alvi makes a seminal contribution to understanding a region which is still undergoing profound change. Where the cards will eventually fall, no one knows. But this critical work certainly helps us make sense of the journey."

—Azeem Ibrahim, Research Professor, *Strategic Studies Institute, US Army War College, USA*

"The Arab uprisings that spread across much of the Arab world in 2011 started in a place that was seemingly unlikely to inspire Arab revolution: Tunisia. Since then, Tunisia has been touted as a relative success story, even as recent developments have raised some doubts about its trajectory. Strikingly, Tunisia's transition has been largely non-violent. What explains this? In this thoughtful, well-informed book, Hayat Alvi expertly credits the inclusive nature of the dialogue across civil society and the political system. She grounds the conversation in analysis of Tunisia's political economy, and powerfully addresses the challenges of the gender issue across the secular-religious divide. Highly recommended."

—Shibley Telhami, Anwar Sadat professor for Peace and Development, *University of Maryland, and Non-Resident Senior Fellow at the Brookings Institution, USA*

"After initiating the Arab Awakening in 2011, Tunisia has courageously sustained forward progress in a way that neighboring countries in the MENA region have not. How? Dr. Alvi's book brings us into the center of Tunisia's political economy, and the at times difficult balance between secularists and Islamists, as they jointly attempt, through civic dialogue, to forge a path out of Tunisia's recent history of corruption and abuse of power. The complexity of contemporary Tunisia requires a multidisciplinary and multi-leveled approach, which Alvi deftly provides, helping us more fully understand this precarious moment of hope."

—Daniel Cowdin, Professor, Religious Studies, *Salve Regina University, USA*

"With passion and sound academic logic, Professor Hayat Alvi argues that the social transformation in the relatively smaller but diverse Tunisia can be an ideal role model for the wider Arab world primarily because of Tunisian resilience on the age-old but long-forgotten social-bonding or *Asabiyya*. Inclusiveness advocated by the Tunisian Islamists would continue to inspire the broader region as did the Jasmine Revolution which unleashed the Arab awakening."

—P. R. Kumaraswamy, Professor, *Centre for West Asian Studies (CWAS), Jawaharlal Nehru University, and Honorary Director, Middle East Institute, New Delhi, India*

"Tunisia's relative success in transitioning away from strongman rule to a more democratic framework makes it stand out in the Arab world. Alvi's political economy approach to explaining these important developments marks an important advance that transcends the emphasis in press accounts on personalities and stereotypes."

—Juan Cole, Richard P. Mitchell Collegiate Professor of History, *University of Michigan, USA*

Contents

List of Figures

List of Charts

List of Maps

List of Tables

CHAPTER 1

Introduction

He who finds a new path is a pathfinder, even if the trail has to be found again by others; and he who walks far in advance of his contemporaries is a leader, even though centuries may pass before he is recognized as such and intelligently followed.
—Ibn Khaldun

Ibn Khaldun was a renowned fourteenth-century Tunisian historian, philosopher, and sociologist, whose observations about Arab, North African, and Middle Eastern social and leadership structures still resonate today. His theories reflect the social bonds, struggles, and tensions between religion and politics that persist in modern-day Tunisia as well as throughout the Middle East and North Africa (MENA). His mapping of historical cycles deserves attention in the post-2011 Arab Awakening MENA region. From these historical observations, one can see that certain patterns run through the region. Such patterns pertain to socioeconomic and resource deficiencies; authoritarianism in political and religious institutions; iden-

The original version of this chapter was revised. The name of the first president of Tunisia has been corrected from Ghannouchi to Moncef Marzouki in this revised version. A correction to this chapter can be found at https://doi.org/10.1007/978-3-030-17050-9_9

H. Alvi, *The Political Economy and Islam of the Middle East*, Political Economy of Islam,
https://doi.org/10.1007/978-3-030-17050-9_1

tity politics and the need for bonding based on tribal, ethnic, sectarian, and national classifications; marginalization of women and minorities; and yearning for reconstructing the "Golden Age" of past empires and Islamic civilization.

For Ibn Khaldun, the Golden Age "was the time of Mohammed and the first four caliphs. He looked back with huge nostalgia for when things were simpler and people didn't wear fancy clothes, and they didn't eat expensive meals."[1] Ibn Khaldun expressed disdain for the "city-state" and the urban scene. He preferred the rural nomadic setting, where, according to his theories, social bonding drives politics, economics, trade, security, and survival—in general, *life*. He referred to the social bonding as *Asabiyyah*. The MENA region's political economy has long been based on the desert culture and way of life and has evolved from them. In fact, "The German travel writer Wilfred Thesiger describes how [*Asabiyyah*] develops in the desert because you're heavily dependent on each other to survive. But it's not just *esprit de corps*, it's also *elan vital*, a drive to conquer, supplement that with religion and you're just about unbeatable."[2]

Fast forward to the twenty-first century, and it is clear that not much has changed in the MENA region. Moreover, rather than bonding and unity, the region has never been more divided along political, socioeconomic, and religious fault lines. Asabiyyah is what the people in the MENA region may have aspired to achieve throughout generations, but due to centuries of authoritarianism and religious schisms, the goals of social bonding at a larger scale have remained unrealized. The problems of authoritarianism, illiteracy and undereducation, and marginalization of women persist and have continued to plague the region well into the modern era.

For instance, if we examine the groundbreaking 2002 report entitled the *Arab Human Development Report (AHDR) 2002*, we see that nothing much has changed in the Middle East and North Africa (MENA) region in political economy terms even after the earthshaking 2011 Arab Awakening uprisings and revolutions. The *AHDR 2002*, which followed the model of the annual *United Nations Human Development Report*, serves as a significant marker to analyze the MENA region's political economy even today.

The report encompasses the political, economic, and sociocultural variables of Arab states in the Middle East. The conclusions of the *AHDR 2002* are described in three "deficiencies" based on these findings: (1) deficiencies in freedoms and rights, and the preponderance for authoritarian rule in the region; (2) deficiencies in a knowledge-based society, that is, concerning literacy and education standards, and intellectual productivity in the form of patents, book publishing and translations of books, and research and development and innovations; and (3) deficiencies in women's empowerment.[3]

The twenty-first century continues to pummel the MENA region's economies, politics, and societies with continuous, seemingly implacable challenges. This book examines the comparative traits and components of political Islam along with the political economy of the MENA region since the 2011 Arab uprisings and revolutions, as well as the secular and religious ideologies affecting and shaping societies. This book also provides a special case study analysis of Tunisia since its 2011 "Jasmine Revolution." While most of the MENA countries suffer from political and economic problems and deficiencies, in some cases manifesting themselves in violent conflicts, Tunisia has mostly maintained stability throughout its post-revolution transitions, notwithstanding some serious obstacles and tribulations. Tunisia is the "outlier," or the anomaly in the region. The reasons behind its uniqueness in securing political and economic stability—*however fragile*—require examination and elucidation.

While the three major deficiencies continue to plague the MENA region since 2002, the Republic of Tunisia, with approximately 11 million people, has initiated a fearless internal regime change through the 2011 Jasmine Revolution, demanding freedoms, rights, economic opportunities, justice, and, most importantly, dignity. In the process of post-revolution transformation (i.e., evolution), Tunisia has implemented anti-corruption action plans, economic and foreign direct investment (FDI) initiatives, and political and electoral developments and transitions in the face of daunting challenges to the country's stability and security. Tunisia has also secured a substantial measure of democracy, which it has not experienced in its past and which remains elusive throughout the MENA region. Tunisia has achieved these goals, albeit with degrees of success, because of (a) the Tunisian people's commitment to dialogue, negotiations, and compromise in the domestic political processes; (b) the emergence and functions of a vibrant civil society, which could not operate freely and openly under the dictatorship; and (c) lessons learned from the democracy failures and violent repression in Egypt, Bahrain, Libya, Syria, and Yemen, the latter three of which have precipitated into bloody civil conflicts.

Tunisia's 2011 Jasmine Revolution provided the inspiration and impetus for other countries in the MENA region to follow its example and carry out uprisings and revolutions within their own settings. The 2011 uprisings caught on like dominoes throughout the region. However, democratization efforts have been far from successful in other countries, mainly because of the violent repression against pro-democracy movements at the hands of preexisting political elites, the military (in the case of Egypt and Syria), and remnants of the previous regimes. Civil society in these other countries has not been allowed to flourish, and democracy as a concept in and of itself has been vilified by both secular and religious forces, even though the latter has opportunistically sought empowerment through elections in post-revolution political systems (e.g., the case of the Muslim Brotherhood in Egypt and Libya; the Salafist party in Egypt; and the case of Ennahda in Tunisia). The post-2011 regimes and political institutions in Egypt, Syria, Libya, and Bahrain have sought to maintain the *status quo ante*, mainly because these regimes and political elites have benefited greatly from the pre-2011 economic, political, and security systems and apparatuses. Their systems have included extreme corruption, violent repression with torture, and long-term detentions of political and human rights activists as well as journalists, and boundless appetites for power through authoritarian rule. Wherein the protestors have demanded rule of law, accountability and transparency, observance of basic human rights, the freedoms and right to political representation, and access to education and economic opportunities, the regimes in the MENA region have delivered the opposite.

In fact, the notion of self-imperialism, or *auto-imperialism*, is what various MENA regimes and political elites have been inflicting on their respective countries. Auto-imperialism is a modern take on the traditional concept of imperialism, but instead of foreign forces pursuing imperial economic and political advantages in developing countries, the governments and regimes of a given state are pursuing "conquest" by means of military, security apparatuses, socioeconomic and political forces, and overall "dominion" over others, in this case one's own populace.

According to *Oxford*'s traditional definition of imperialism, it connotes "the dominion brought by way of the conquest, imperialism is in substance a form of large-scale political organization as old as recorded history. Varying both in terms of territorial expanse and formal institutional organization, all imperialism entails a fundamental political inequality between the imperial nation and its various subject nations or tribes."[4] The political and economic inequality imposed on a state's subjects (i.e., population, especially the underprivileged) is the regime's objective in auto-imperialism. This is achieved through corruption, violent repression and authoritarianism, and, not surprisingly, the three principal deficiencies that the *AHDR 2002* has outlined. Auto-imperialism is something that Tunisia has been trying hard to eliminate from its political and economic domains, while the governments in the rest of the MENA region, for the most part, strive to implement auto-imperialistic policies, because they gain significant advantages from doing so.

Moreover, following the 2011 uprisings, various Islamist parties have claimed to represent the people's interests, promised social justice and equity, and presented their religious platforms as compatible with democracy. However, political Islam has not proven to deliver on its post-2011 promises. In this area, Tunisia has also illustrated an exception to the rule with the actions and decisions of Ennahda, the Islamist party led by Rachid al-Ghannouchi, which are analyzed in detail.

Nevertheless, the political economy of the MENA region continues to decline. The preponderance of conflicts and wars, and the humanitarian crises arising from them, also contribute to political and economic stagnation. Natural disasters and climate change exacerbate these realities, especially in the form of water and food insecurity and basic human insecurity. Refugees and internally displaced persons (IDPs) proliferate throughout the region due to the combination of violent conflicts, economic despair, and human insecurity. Hence, many aspects of the *AHDR's (2002)* assessment of the MENA region's political economy remain true today. Where the regional actors should have made great strides in political and economic development since 2002, and especially following the 2011 uprisings, they have failed to make progress for their respective countries. In fact, the status quo elements of authoritarianism, corruption, violent repression, and suppression of democracy, freedoms, and rights persist throughout the MENA region (Map 1.1).

Map 1.1 Map of North Africa and the Middle East. (Source: Perry-Castañeda LibraryMap Collection, University of Texas at Austin http://legacy.lib.utexas.edu/maps/africa.html)

The Political Economy of the Middle East and North Africa

In order to set the stage for this analysis, relevant concepts and terms must be addressed and defined. Among the concepts and terms to address is political economy.

What is political economy? According to the School of Oriental and African Studies (SOAS), political economy examines

> how political forces influence the economy and economic outcomes. However, the interactions run both ways and political economy is interested in both. Thus, it is economic activity that generates the resources that are required to sustain political activity, for example, election campaign expenses. Moreover, whilst policy might lead to a certain economic activity prospering, this success in itself can generate a political constituency with an interest in maintaining the economic activity, because a sizeable number of people now benefit from it.[5]

Politics and economics are interdependent; what happens in one affects the other. This requires sound political and economic policies and good governance that positively affect the public simultaneously in diverse sectors including education, health systems, employment, technology, infrastructure, investments, trade, secure financial institutions and systems, currency value, equitable income/wealth distribution, and sustainable economic growth. All of these variables need to adjust for population growth and resource scarcities. In the mostly desert climates of the MENA region, water source is the most critical issue, and where there might be water insecurity, food insecurity is likely. Predictions indicate that climate change is not going to be kind to the MENA region, and that would only worsen regional stability and security. Hence, we see that all of these elements and variables are interconnected. Governance, then, is the crucial factor that could make or break a state's economy and interconnected variables. Thus, the health of the political economy of the MENA region lies in the hands of policy-makers, and so far, their track record has been far from stellar.

In fact, the causal factors leading to the 2011 uprisings and revolutions have pertained primarily to socioeconomic deficiencies, which, through interdependence with politics, translate into poor governance and imprudent policy-making along with gross mismanagement and stifling corruption. As Melanie Cammett et al. emphasize in *A Political Economy of the Middle East*, "As implied by the slogan 'Bread, freedom, and social justice,' which protestors chanted on Avenue Bourguiba, in Tahrir Square, and elsewhere in the region, both economic and political issues were central concerns."[6] The scholars add that both direct and indirect causal factors of the 2011 uprisings involved the following:

> Insufficient job creation, labor market pressures exacerbated by the youth bulge, the mismatch between educational systems and labor market needs, the declining quantity of water and rising dependency on food imports, the continuing decay of the public sector, the mixed record of economic liberalization, a growing housing crisis in urban areas, and the rise of political Islam across the region.[7]

Political Islam (also referred to as "Islamism") is another term that needs defining. In general, Islam does not separate religion and politics. The power and pull of (divine) religious ideology applying itself to (human) political governance are the drivers for political Islamist movements, parties, and platforms. These are not new phenomena, but following the 2011 Arab Awakening revolutions, Islamist parties sought to take advantage of new political participation in the "democratization" processes of certain countries.

Typically, once empowered, Islamism and Islamist political leaders tend to focus on socioreligious policies, such as women's dress codes, corporal and capital punishments, "Islamizing" codes and laws of the country, gender segregation in public spaces, Islamic curricula in schools, and the like. Therefore, their focus and priorities during the fragile stages in transitioning politics indicate misplaced priorities. While Islamist decision-makers should be focusing their priorities on socioeconomic development, political restructuring, financial stability, economic health and security, trade relations, food and water security, quality education and health care, infrastructure improvements, conflict resolution, and, most importantly, jobs for the youth, they instead tend to miss these priorities and are more preoccupied with their plans to "Islamize" society and politics. These approaches and strategies of Islamist leadership, which remains preoccupied with religious policies rather than the pragmatic issues pertaining to the country's pressing political economy issues, are recipes for failure.

The political economy analysis of the MENA region also posits that, for any means of stability to sustain itself in a state, the situational factors presuppose conflict resolution and/or peace to be in place. These variables are far from the reality in the MENA region, which has suffered from diverse forms of violence and conflicts for decades, and which has a reputation for being one of the most conflict-prone and conflict-ridden regions of the world. In addition, the MENA region has the reputation for some of the highest numbers of weapons purchases and for a seemingly never-ending regional arms race. That does not bode well for conflict resolution and peace, which in turn does not bode well for the MENA region's political economy.

Correspondingly, the MENA region has served as a theater for global powers to engage in their respective "Great Game" competitions; plus, the regional actors are gravely disunited, despite appearances and rhetoric promoting Arab unity; and non-state actors, including terrorist organizations like the Islamic State (IS) and Al Qaeda, proliferate throughout the region. Each terrorist organization exacerbates the environment of conflict and insecurity with its own violent political, territorial, and ideological agendas. Mixed into this climate is the existence of "hybrid" actors, like the Lebanese Hezbollah and Hamas in Gaza, which have the characteristics of non-state actors but with some degree of political legitimacy.

The political economy analysis must address the issues pertaining to MENA political leadership, because it is the leadership of a country that can make or break it economically and otherwise. That is never truer than in the MENA region, which constitutes sub-regions enjoying tremendous oil wealth and prosperity; other sub-regions suffering from high rates of poverty, unemployment, high population growth that is not sustainable by existing resources, and water and food insecurity; while a few countries suffer from ongoing wars, conflicts, and terrorist threats, with impending threats of spillover to non-conflict areas. Economic class differences and gaps within and between states are growing, and the political leaders are lagging far behind in addressing these dire crises, which could easily trigger greater instability and insecurity.

The MENA region has a number of hotspots for black market activities and financial hubs that serve both legitimate and illicit actors and agendas. Oil politics continues to dominate the Gulf Arab state economies, and with the decline in oil prices in recent years, these economies have suffered declining revenues, causing them to scramble to diversify their economic systems and financial deficits. However, they still continue to pour hundreds of millions of dollars into their respective militaries and in weapons purchases mainly from the Western powers. Conflict areas such as Iraq, Syria, Yemen, Northern Sinai, and Libya have robust black markets and trafficking networks, including in human/migrant trafficking, as well as in goods and weapons. These add fuel to the humanitarian crises already causing major stresses on local economies.

Refugee, internally displaced persons (IDPs), and migrant flows have increased since the 2011 Libya campaign followed by the Syrian civil war and the rise of Islamic State of Iraq and Syria (ISIS; also the "Islamic State") in Syria and Iraq. As numerous studies have shown, primarily women and children suffer the most from these humanitarian crises.

The political economy of the MENA region encompasses diverse sectors, factors, and forces that often pit governments against public interests and welfare in the former's efforts to benefit from the system at the latter's expense. That has been the status quo of the "Old Guard" regimes and political elite. The 2011 Arab Awakening that gripped the MENA region shook the Old Guard structures and systems and, in some cases, replaced them. But, it is only in Tunisia that we see a glimmer of sustainable democracy and, thus, hope. Therefore, it is imperative to examine why Tunisia is the best MENA model to follow in the post-2011 revolution era.

Tunisia: The Best Model

The political economy of the MENA region and the special case study of Tunisia provide insight into the similarities, complexities, and some differences between regional actors. These perspectives also elucidate why Tunisia presents the best model, comparatively, for the rest of the region to follow in terms of commitment to non-violent change and determination to disallow a "counter-revolution" back to the "Ben Ali era" of dictatorship and all-encompassing corruption. Tunisia's Islamist party, Ennahda, has remained committed to political dialogue and compromise, which also sets it apart from its counterparts promoting political Islam in the MENA region.

Despite its transitional difficulties and challenges, post-revolution Tunisia serves as an ideal model for the MENA region to follow. No other post-2011 Arab Awakening country has experienced peaceful political transitions. Yet, Tunisia is a special case in providing balance and non-violent processes for political negotiations and compromise between secularists and Islamists, which is an anomaly in MENA countries. These processes have been undertaken with the expressed purpose of domestic political and economic security and stability through democratization.

Many of the causal factors behind Tunisia's Jasmine Revolution pertain to the country's socioeconomic health and status. Under Zine al-Abidine

Ben Ali, Tunisia suffered terribly from high unemployment, a corresponding youth bulge, high rates of university graduates who faced joblessness and economic stagnation, gross corruption that penetrated all levels of society, and deficiencies in the rule of law. In other words, if you were a young Tunisian and a university graduate, you were not likely to find a job, marry, and start a family, and in practically every economic sector you faced no recourse from corruption. If you complained, you faced threats of imprisonment, torture, and no means of protection. Most of the countries in the region have similar systems and characteristics. That is why the 2011 Arab Awakening uprisings spread so swiftly throughout the region.

Since the 2011 revolution, the Tunisian people have been determined to overhaul the political, judicial, and economic systems. This case study focuses on Tunisia's political economy and assesses its strengths and weaknesses years after the revolution. The study, based on field research, examines the country's economic indicators, development and progress, trade relations, employment rates, and other relevant indicators that measure economic health. Comparative analyses are provided between Tunisia and post-revolution political economies and security situations in other regional actors. Threats that terrorism poses to Tunisia's tourism industry are also explored. Implications of these variables for the overall MENA region are analyzed.

Amartya Sen's "Social Choice Theory" is applied as the theoretical framework in this study. The theory posits that without freedoms and rights for individuals to make personal choices, an economy will not develop and progress adequately. While Comparative Democratization and Revolution Theories as well as a comparative analysis of political Islam are also relevant to the study, the primary theoretical framework applied in the Tunisia case is Sen's Social Choice Theory.

Conclusions about Tunisia's political economy outlook for the near and distant future are presented. Implications of the post-revolution Tunisian political economy for the region, as well as for Tunisia's European trade partners, are also presented. Particular focus on the post-revolution status of corruption in Tunisia is examined, since it has been one of the principal causal factors behind the revolution. Finally, linkages are identified between Tunisia's political and economic health and development, which also encompass rule of law issues, such as human rights, freedoms, transparency, and due process. All of these variables are interconnected and account for the causal factors of the 2011 revolution. Hence, it is crucial to approach a study of Tunisia's economy from a political economy level of analysis. If Tunisia's post-revolution economic health and status have not improved, and have failed to eliminate corruption, reduce high rates of unemployment, and implement rule of law effectively and fairly, then Tunisia will only go back to square one. The situation for other post–Arab Awakening revolution and uprising countries—Libya, Egypt, Yemen, and Syria, for example—is far more precarious and ominous.

Theoretical Framework

The political economy level of analysis in this book applies the Developmental Theory of Amartya Sen, recipient of the 1998 Nobel Prize in Economic Sciences. His *Social Choice Theory* posits that without freedoms there will be no socioeconomic progress, and hence, individuals and society cannot progress if they are not granted the freedoms to make choices.

Dr. Sen combines elements of philosophy and economics with the premise that "ethics and a sense of common humanity" contribute to social justice and equality.[8] In addition, Dr. Sen's freedom-based theories of development are predicated on the "removal of repressive states."[9] In fact, "Achievement of development is thoroughly dependent on the free agency of people."[10] The formula for this is that political freedoms allow for economic security; social opportunities allow for economic participation; and economic facilities allow for personal abundance and public resources.[11] Dr. Sen's theory has

> contributed to important paradigm shifts in economics and development—away from approaches that focus exclusively on income, growth and utility, with an increased emphasis on individual entitlements, capabilities, freedoms and rights. It has increased awareness of the importance of respect for human rights for socioeconomic outcomes—challenging the proposition that growth should take priority over civil and political rights, while highlighting the role of human rights in promoting economic security, and the limitations of development without human rights guarantees.[12]

Specifically, Sen's theory encompasses the power of agency afforded to women in the context of "survival advantages." Examples of survival advantages, which the above variables for women's well-being, in particular, tend to facilitate, include lower fertility rates and lower mortality rates of children. Given Tunisia's long tradition of embracing and supporting secularism and women's rights, these variables and principles are extremely important. Hence, gender equality and gender rights are indispensable for Tunisia's political and economic success.

It is also important to reiterate that Dr. Sen's freedom-based theories of development are predicated on the "removal of repressive states."[13] Clearly, one cannot enjoy political, economic, and personal freedoms and rights in a repressive and corrupt system. According to Dr. Sen, "Freedom is central to the process of development for two distinct reasons"—they are (1) the evaluative reason: that is, "assessment of progress has to be done primarily in terms of whether the freedoms that people have are enhanced"; and (2) the effectiveness reason: "Achievement of development is thoroughly dependent on the free agency of people."[14] The formula for this is, as mentioned, that political freedoms facilitate economic security; social opportunities allow for economic participation; and economic facilities enhance personal abundance and public resources.[15]

If authoritarian and repressive governments want their countries to develop socioeconomically and progressively in the modern, competitive globalized world, then they must realize that these goals cannot be achieved without individual freedoms and rights. As Dr. Sen says, "Freedoms are not only the primary ends of development, they are also among its principal means."[16] The regimes and societies in the Middle East and North Africa have yet to embrace these realities. Everything comes down to personal choices, that is, the freedom for individuals to make choices in society. Free agency of individuals is critical to the processes of development, progress, and modernization for society as a whole.

Dr. Sen articulates the "real conflict" in traditional cultures and societies (as found pervasively in the MENA region), which can impede freedoms of choice; they revolve around the following core factors:

1. The basic value that the people must be allowed to decide freely what traditions they wish or not wish to follow; and
2. The insistence that established traditions be followed (no matter what), or, alternatively, people must obey the decisions by religious or secular authorities who enforce traditions—real or imagined.[17]

The above two points explain the deeply rooted tensions between individuals and societies, and the latter and governments and religious establishments. In all such categories, women and girls are the primary targets of control and restrictions on their choices and freedoms. This is the case in both "secular" and religious contexts, as far as repressive governments and religious clerics are concerned.

Hypothesis

The main hypothesis of this analysis states: because Tunisia's civil society and political system have engaged in inclusive dialogues and negotiations, democratic transition processes have been non-violent, hence providing the MENA region with a positive example (or model) of post-revolution transformations.

The dependent variable for this study is ***national dialogue for non-violent conflict resolution***. The independent variables include commitment to democracy, inclusiveness in sociopolitical and economic activities (vs. exclusiveness), and institutional corruption (vs. rule of law).

Democracy, Secularism, and Islamism

Another paramount marker for this study consists of the findings in the groundbreaking *Arab Human Development Report 2002: Creating Opportunities for Future Generations*, (AHDR 2002), which presents three key challenges for the Middle East region: (1) the lack of a knowledge-based society, (2) the prevalence of authoritarian governments that suppress freedoms and rights, (3) the lack of empowerment of women. The *AHDR 2002* and Dr. Sen's Social Choice Theory are interconnected as they apply to the Middle East and North Africa (MENA), as the region has long been known for severe repression, resulting in restrictions and violations of human rights, as well as constricting individual and societal choices. Trends in educational and intellectual deficiencies (i.e., lack of a knowledge-based society); repressive and entrenched authoritarianism; and gender inequalities (especially restrictions on women's choices) that have contributed to lack of socioeconomic progress are evident. Therefore, Dr. Sen's Social Choice Theory and the premises and findings of the *AHDR 2002* are complementary. However, Dr. Sen's Social Choice Theory is considered the primary theoretical framework, with supportive data applied from the 2002 AHDR's findings.

Democracy Theory is also relevant in this study and is given reference on a contextual basis. For the MENA region, the contexts involve predominantly Arab ethnic and linguistic identities, Islam as the dominant religion with Sunni Islam as the principal sect, although certain demographics indicate Shi'a Muslims as constituting national majorities (e.g., Bahrain, Iran, and Iraq) and significant national minority populations. Most of the regional political systems are either monarchies or pseudo-democracies but in reality they function as autocratic/authoritarian dictatorships. Tunisia is a notable exception to these descriptions. The three non-Arab countries in the MENA region, Israel, Iran, and Turkey, have unique traits of degrees of electoral democracy, but for the purpose of this book the focus of the study is the predominantly Arab countries. In general, democracy has remained an elusive fantasy rather than a reality in the MENA countries even following the 2011 Arab Awakening.

Democracy, by definition, excludes the idea of dynastic rule, which is exactly what "Presidents for Life" in the Arab countries have been endeavoring to cement into their respective systems. In the process, minority groups and women have been marginalized, if not completely repressed, and elections are often rigged and manipulated. Symbolic quotas of political representation in parliaments for either an ethnic or a religious minority group and/or women do not adequately constitute true democratic frameworks. The absence of real civil and human rights, civil society, and judicial autonomy also undermine any hint of democracy.

Democratic Theory aligns well with this study because it argues for freedoms, rights, choices, and inclusiveness for success in political and socioeconomic development and progress,[18] and that, in turn, directly aligns with Amartya Sen's Social Choice Theory. Therefore, Democratic Theory is given relevant reference in the analysis, while Sen's theory formulates the primary theoretical framework. Sen's theory presupposes that the principles of democracy are applied to allow freedoms and rights, without which an economy cannot progress. Democratic Theory scrutinizes a country's commitment to democracy and democratic principles, how a country and its public define democracy, and

> when and why democracy is morally desirable are often rooted in empirical observations concerning the ways in which democracies have actually been known to function. In addition to a basic commitment to democracy as an object of study, most theorists agree that the concept *democracy* denotes some form or process of collective self-rule.

> Important questions arise: who constitutes the people and what obligations do individuals have in a democracy? What values are most important for a democracy and which ones make it desirable or undesirable as a form of government? How is democratic rule to be organized and exercised? What institutions should be used and how? Once instituted, does democracy require precise social, economic, or cultural conditions to survive in the long term? And why is it that democratic government is preferable to, say, aristocracy or oligarchy?[19]

Democracy scholar Philippe Schmitter breaks down the components of democratic transition from autocratic rule to a realistic democracy, describing the process as starting with

> The rule of one person (or small group of persons) to the rule of the people (or to that segment of the people possessing equal political rights as citizens). In the former, the government consists of a political elite clearly demarcated from and not accountable to the population; in the latter, either there is no elite and citizens govern directly or they govern indirectly through agents chosen by them, but who only rule *pro tempore* and depend periodically on their explicit consent. As the result of such a change in regime, there should be a complete change of elite personnel and structure. Moreover, the ensuing governing elite (or non-elite) is expected to pursue different policies benefitting different segments of the population.[20]

In most cases of the post–Arab Awakening MENA countries, the political elite personnel may have been removed, but the structures have remained intact. The case of Tunisia provides insight into the democratization process and political structures following the 2011 Jasmine Revolution.

Furthermore, as Guillermo O'Donnell points out, democracy is in perpetual crises, because it is "constantly redirecting its citizens' gaze from a more or less unsatisfactory present toward a future of still unfulfilled possibilities. There is in these crises something that belongs to what is best and most distinctive about democracy. For the crises underline democracy's intrinsic mix of hope and dissatisfaction, its highlighting of a lack that will never be filled. The capacity for hope is the great capacity of democracy, one which under the right circumstances can and should nourish other, more specific capacities that may promote improvements in democratic quality."[21] That constant hope in improvements in Tunisia's political and economic development is a paramount driver of democratic transition, and now that Tunisians have considerably more freedoms and rights, they are able to push the card further without the violent repression of the past. The push and pull between the political economy forces, and between the government and governed, constitute the "perpetual crises" for the nascent democracy. Tunisians might take these tensions to the edge, but they are determined not to allow the situation to collapse into violent chaos, like in Egypt, Libya, Yemen, and Syria. Still, Tunisia's democratic transition is an ongoing, and at times painful, process. It embodies the quintessential "evolution after revolution."

Moreover, theoretical discourse about the concepts of "secularism" and "Islamism" (also referred to as "political Islam") must be applied to this analysis. The struggle between secularism and Islamism following Tunisia's Jasmine Revolution illustrates the core ideological issues and challenges embodied in the process of defining the post-revolution national identity, values, and principles of the Republic of Tunisia (in Arabic, *Al Jumhuriyah at-Tunisiyah*). The Islamist political movements in Tunisia had long been violently repressed and forced underground. Following the 2011 revolution and the dawn of democracy, the floodgates of Islamist political prisoners, Islamist returnees from exile, and Islamist activists opened with full force. They inevitably clashed with the diehard secularists, who fervently wish to preserve the integrity of Tunisian secularism, as the republic's founding father, Habib Bourguiba, had established and intended for the country's future. The battleground for both of these ideological camps has encompassed the politics and political system, institutions, elections, political appointments, civil society, and the process of rewriting Tunisia's constitution following the 2011 revolution. It has also involved demands for reforming the Tunisian judicial system and embracing and implementing fundamental principles of rule of law.

What is Tunisian secularism? Elizabeth Shakman Hurd sheds light on the answer to this increasingly complicated question, as the post-revolution era has produced a bizarre, albeit relatively effective, concoction between secularism and Islamism in Tunisia. In an April 2012 article published in *Al Jazeera*, Dr. Shakman Hurd explains that

> At the time of Tunisia's independence from France in 1956, President Bourguiba pursued an aggressive secularization program aimed at entrenching his power and currying favor with Western allies. His government sought to imitate Western secularist models by marginalizing Islam. *Shari'a* (Islamic law) courts were abolished, the *Zaytouna* (a renowned center of

Muslim learning) closed, headscarves banned, and the *ulama* (body of Islamic scholars) debilitated.

> … In Tunisia secularization was a state-imposed political project associated with the marginalization of Tunisian history and traditions. Different trajectories of secularization carry different political and religious histories into the present.[22]

During the Bourguiba years, not all Tunisians agreed with or embraced his forced secularization policies and "enforced privatization of Islam," as Dr. Shakman Hurd describes it.[23] As a result, the first democratically elected president in post-revolution Tunisia was Moncef Marzouki, who appointed the Islamist party's representative, Hamadi Jebali, as prime minister. Rachid al-Ghannouchi returned from exile and founded the Ennahda ("Renaissance") Party, consisting of an Islamist platform and ideological foundation. Ennahda began as the "Islamic Tendency Movement," and Ghannouchi became its leader.[24] According to the *BBC News*:

> Originally inspired by the Muslim Brotherhood in Egypt, Ennahda advocates a more overtly Islamic identity and society for the country.
>
> Rumors that it was receiving campaign funds from the Gulf – denied by the party – fueled anxiety among some largely urban, secularist Tunisians. They fear the party could be vulnerable to the influence of more conservative currents or change its tune once in power.[25]

Ghannouchi is "now widely viewed as a moderate, reform-minded Islamist"[26] who contends that all Tunisian people can survive peacefully within a moderate vision of Islam which can be compatible with democracy:

> Our vision of Islam is a moderate one and since 1981… we have declared that we accept democracy without any restrictions and we accept the decision of the people whether they come with us or against us.
>
> We accept the notion of citizenship as the basis of rights, so all citizens are equal whether they are Islamist or not Islamist.
>
> He also stressed that Ennahda accepts gender equality, enshrined in Tunisia's Personal Status Code under Mr. Ben Ali, as 'an acceptable interpretation within Islam.'[27]

Still, these developments did not sit well with Tunisian secularists. Despite Ennahda's claims that the new moderate Islamist-based democracy in post-revolution Tunisia can be identical to the "Turkish model," with the Islamist Justice and Development Party (AKP) in power under Recep Tayyip Erdogan's rule, Tunisia's secular activists have

> held regular demonstrations to voice fears about losing the status they achieved under former President Habib Bourguiba – who criticized the wearing of the Islamic headscarf and once appeared on television during the [month of] Ramadan drinking orange juice.
>
> Thanks to the French-inspired secular tradition that he promoted and Mr. Ben Ali continued, Tunisians as well as tourists have generally been able to drink alcohol openly, and women at beaches and swimming pools commonly wear bikinis.
>
> While this might provoke some, the importance of mass tourism to Tunisia's economy, the determination of a vocal group of liberals, and the commitments from Ennahda will all make it harder to change.[28]

While post-revolution Tunisia has harbored the potential for exacerbating the secular-religious divide, in reality the Tunisian people and leadership have made a remarkable achievement. Various political parties have sought reconciliation rather than confrontation and conflict, and the potent example of violent chaos and counter-revolution in Egypt only made Tunisians more determined not to allow the same thing to happen in their country, which triggered the "Arab Awakening" and inspired the whole region. The results of the fall 2011 elections in Tunisia—the first ever open, fair, and democratic elections—saw Ennahda earn 40 percent (89 seats) of the Constituent Assembly. At the time, the top three parties earning most of the seats, along with Ennahda, included the CPR, "headed by Moncef Marzouki (29 seats), and Ettakatol (the Rally, headed by Mustapha Ben Jaafar) (20 seats)."[29] Essentially, these results indicate a mix of Islamist and secular parties winning the highest numbers and percentages of the Assembly seats. Why is this? Dr. Shakman Hurd explains that

> In the Tunisian election, parties that differentiated themselves successfully from Ennahda but were willing to work with it, and that emphasized the importance of the secular nature of the state while expressing respect or understanding for the religious feelings of many Tunisians, did quite well.

> Among them was CPR, a non-Islamic centrist party led by a physician and dissident human rights activist that did not support an anti-Islamist platform. Part of the reason for CPR's success, as Melani Cammett has argued, was a refusal to buy in to the scare tactics employed by other parties against Ennahda, while also acknowledging the revolutionaries' calls for dignity and respect.[30]

However, this is not without calls for caution, especially when dealing with "Islamists" and Islamism. Renowned sociologist Asef Bayat warns that, "We should attend carefully to the limitations of Islamist organizations' positions and shortcomings in the areas of individual rights, religious pluralism, and democratic practice, just as we would assess our own parties across the spectrum in the United States or elsewhere."[31] While the track record for suppressing rights, pluralism, democracy, and rule of law under secular authoritarian dictators in the MENA region has been horrendous, thus far Islamist political experiments in modern history have been equally disastrous. Therefore, the pressures on Ennahda to prove itself willing and capable of engendering a new Tunisia with a flourishing democracy, pluralism, gender equality, freedoms and rights, and rule of law have been unrelenting.

Now that we have described secularism in the Tunisian context, it is imperative to examine the obvious question, "what is Islamism, or political Islam?" In the context of the era of modern history, the collapse of the Ottoman Empire around the time of World War I plunged global Muslims into an ideological crisis of sorts. The colonial legacy in many Muslim countries continued to influence cultures, societies, women's rights movements, and, in many ways and at many levels, spread Westernization. The Ottoman Empire embodied the remaining symbol and vestige of Islamic civilization. Its downfall signifies the stagnation of Islamic political and religious imperial conquests and sovereign rule over subjects ranging across vast territories that even reached into Europe. Westernization and secularization threatened to eclipse the collapse of the Ottoman Empire, and clearly that is not what many Muslims wanted, while at the same time some like in Turkey and Tunisia envisioned a future path of secularization. In the eyes of the founder of the Turkish republic, Mustafa Kemal Atatürk, and also of Habib Bourguiba in Tunisia, Western-modeled secularism is the only path to progress.

Islamic Studies scholar Muqtedar Khan elaborates on these events and their effects on the Muslim psyche:

> The key moment when the decline of Muslim power was crystallized in the Muslim psyche was when the Ottoman Empire disappeared and the Islamic Caliphate as an institution was abolished in 1924. Many Islamic movements have since emerged with the explicit goal to revive the Muslim *Ummah* (Muslim community at large), reform Muslim societies, and restore them to their past glory.

Professor Khan goes on to explain that the general belief among many Muslims (globally) is that the Islamic imperial decline is due to abandoning the path to and practice of "true shari'a," and that reimplementing this "true Shari'a" will, supposedly, lead to the reemergence of "Islamic glory." In the view of some Muslims, the mechanisms for this reemergence involve the politicization of Islam:

> Clearly there are many groups that are seeking to establish some kind of Islamic polity, which then can become an instrument for global Islamic resurgence and even political unification. Islamic polities, states or caliphates are not the endgame. They are to become means and instruments of global Islamic resurgence. Political Islamic movements can also be divided according to the means that they wish to employ in order to realize their first goal – the Islamic polity. I submit that there are two types, those who seek the Islamic polity through force and violence, even terrorism, and those who seek it through peaceful means including democratic processes. Those who use force are now widely referred to as *Jihadis*, and those who don't use force are identified by academia and media as *Islamists*.[32]

Charles Hirschkind contends that the term "political Islam" is far too complex to even define in the abstract. He resolutely warns us about not only the complexities involved in defining this term, but also the double standards involved in comparing political Islam to secular political systems, structures, and leadership. Hirschkind says:

> Terms such as "political Islam" are inadequate here as they frame our inquiries around a posited distortion or corruption of properly religious practice. In this way, the disruptive intrusions or outright destruction enacted upon society by the modernizing state never even figure in the analysis. In contrast, the various attempts of religious people to respond to that disruption are rendered suspect, with almost no attempt to distinguish those instances where such a critical stance is warranted from those where it is not. It is not surprising, in this light, that militant violence and public intolerance have become the central issues of so many studies of *al-sahwa al-islamiyya*

> (Islamic awakening), while the extensive coercion and torture practiced by governments get relegated to a footnote.[33]

Today, many scholars argue for a more nuanced approach to and understanding of political Islam, notwithstanding the rise of the Islamic State (ISIS/ISIL) and the relentless assaults on humanity at the hands of Al Qaeda and its affiliates, the Taliban, and a vast matrix of militant Islamist organizations worldwide. The Tunisian people have also suffered terribly from Islamic extremism, which continues its violent efforts to undermine the fledgling democracy and its economy, which is heavily dependent on tourism. Yet, in spite of these assaults, Tunisia has managed to preserve its "bizarre concoction" of reconciled political parties that symbolize the ideological spectrum from the secular to the religious end, and with a lot of diversity in between. Maintaining the balance between them without violence, chaos, and counter-revolution remains the ultimate challenge.

Furthermore, it is wholly appropriate to invoke the Revolution Theory and Economic Theory of the eminent fourteenth-century Arab/North African scholar, philosopher, theorist, and historiographer Ibn Khaldun to this study. Born in today's Tunisia, Ibn Khaldun is known as the "Father of Sociology," and although his observations are based on occurrences in the MENA region during the fourteenth century, his theories and elucidations are still pertinent to the modern era. Not only do Ibn Khaldun's assessments and descriptions of social structures, systems, and institutions apply to the present, but also his emphasis on the need for visionary leadership—which has been wholly lacking in the region—is extremely relevant today.

Ibn Khaldun's groundbreaking work, *Al Muqaddimah*, outlines his social and economic theories, which contend that

> reduced government expenditure for mercenary armies [has been heeded] by many developed countries which are in the process of implementing [his] policy prescriptions in order to increase economic surplus by shifting resources to education and human development. [Ibn Khaldun] opposed taxation and tariffs that discouraged trade and production.
>
> Ibn Khaldun opposed state involvement in trade and production activities. He thought that bureaucrats cannot understand commercial activities and they do not have the same motivations as businessmen. He

predicted relative decline of economic surplus and the decline of countries in which state involvement in trade and production exists. He saw a large army as an impediment to the expansion of trade, production and economic surplus.[34]

Moreover, Ibn Khaldun posited theories about the "rise and fall of civilizations," revolution, and the concept of change. His criteria for the rise of nations, presupposing political stability, include the following:

(a) A firm establishment of private property rights and freedom of enterprise,
(b) Rule of law and a reliable judicial system for the establishment of justice,
(c) The security of peace and the security of trade routes,
(d) Low taxation in order to increase employment, production and revenues,
(e) Less bureaucracy and a much smaller efficient army,
(f) No government involvement in trade, production and commercial affairs,
(g) No price fixing by the government,
(h) A rule that does not give monopoly power to anyone in the market,
(i) Stable monetary policy and independent monetary authority that does not play with the value of money,
(j) A larger population and a larger market for greater specialization,
(k) A creative education system for independent thinking and behavior, and
(l) The collective responsibility and internal desire to establish a just system to encourage good deeds and prevent vice.[35]

According to Ibn Khaldun, in Arab societies social transformation and evolutions most often have been based on "vertical" changes and rarely, if at all, based on grassroots multilevel social revolutions. As Muhammad Dhaoaudi observes,

> Arab states and governments were found to be very precarious and fragile. Change in this type of society takes place vertically rather than horizontally. Change is rotated from one head of a tribe to another. Thus, the phenomenon of change does not have a chance to widen its impact and affect the grass roots of the population. In other words, there are only a few individu-

als whose political regimes perish with their own disappearance in this Khaldunian society. Seen this way, the growth and evolution of Arab societies depended very much on political variables.

Furthermore, one can also relate the logic of Ibn Khaldun's sociological thought on Arab society's limited growth and evolution to his own dialectical approach in his socio-historical analysis of social phenomena. For him, dialectics is the clear future of the nature of human societies' dynamics. On the one hand, the starting point in the movement of societies and civilizations toward growth and evolution is bedounity (primitiveness). On the other hand, the end result to this movement is the sedentary phase (*al-hadara*) where materialistic affluence (*al-taraf*) prevails.[36]

Also, as part of his sociological discourse involving Arab society and social structures, Ibn Khaldun founded the concept of *Asabiyyah*, which refers to "social solidarity with an emphasis on group consciousness, cohesiveness, and unity [...]. *Asabiyyah* is neither necessarily nomadic or based on blood relations. In the modern period, the term is analogous to solidarity."[37] Based on this concept, applying it to modern era state and non-state actors in the MENA region, we see a direct correlation to identity and ideological cohesiveness.

In "International Relations" terms, the concept of *Asabiyyah* can be classified as an element of Constructivism, which "focuses on ideas of norms, the development of structures, the relationship between actors and said structures, as well as how identity influences actions and behavior amongst and between actors, as well as how norms themselves shape an actor's character."[38] All of these variables and concepts pertain to the political economy of, and the issue of democratization in, the MENA region, and, again, they are all interconnected, especially given the interdependent nature of the modern globalized world. The preexisting post-colonial structures and "Old Guard" MENA actors have experienced the ultimate demands for political change as protestors took to the streets in solidarity during the 2011 Arab Awakening movements. The results have been the restructuring of some regimes, while others collapsed into bloody civil conflicts, and Egypt, in particular, has suffered the pains of counter-revolution while wholly impeding opportunities for evolution. These events must be viewed within the lens and scope of the theoretical framework.

The 2011 Arab Awakening

Change hardly comes to the MENA region, but when it does, it is usually extremely abrupt and often volatile and tumultuous, if not alarmingly violent. Bearing in mind the theoretical factors described above, the 2011 Arab Awakening uprisings and revolutions attempted the nearly impossible: revolutionary change from *within*, that is, demanding the "downfall of the regime," which became a popular chant for the protestors in the streets. Specifically, the masses have demanded an end to dynastic rule, for example, in the hands of the Hosni Mubarak family in Egypt, Colonel Muammar Qaddafi's family in Libya, and the like.

The people want greater political participation and more equity and openness in political representation. They demand political structures and institutions to embrace democratization. For too long, post-colonial Middle Eastern and North African countries have been under the oppressive and authoritarian grips of autocratic dictators and their families and cronies. This has to end, as the chant demanding the downfall of regimes exclaims.

Along with these fundamental demands for democratization and equitable political systems, there are equal demands for granting greater freedoms and rights. The MENA region has borne the ominous reputation for severe oppression of rights and freedoms throughout the post-colonial era. In fact, political rights and freedoms have been ruthlessly repressed. Coinciding with these injustices, economic inequalities, the rampant use of indefinite detentions, torture, and biased judiciaries and security forces that have supported, protected, and preserved dictators at the expense of the masses have been the daily realities for the average citizen. The 2011 Arab Awakening uprisings have demanded an end to torture and oppression, independence of the judiciary and implementation of unbiased rule of law and real justice, economic equality—which also requires an end to corruption and bribery—and in general to be treated as a human being with dignity and respect. Overall, the uprisings and revolutions have demanded an end to the status quo, which has only led to political, economic, social, educational, and institutional stagnation, as well as the gross repression of the masses.

This has occurred to the advantages and grandiose benefits that the political and economic elites have enjoyed, alongside the leadership hierarchy and its clientele. The economic divisions between the elites and masses have been worsening over the last several decades, and they are reflected in all levels of society and nearly all geographical sub-regions within a given country.

The 2011 Arab Awakening revolutions and uprisings that have reverberated throughout the MENA region have not rendered smooth transitions from repressive autocratic systems to liberal democracies, freedoms, and rights. Each country experiencing the Arab Awakening has suffered some degree of tumult, confusion, anxiety, and, in some cases, complete breakdown of law and order, as in the cases of Yemen, Libya, and Syria. Tunisia has been considered one of the more successful stories, despite suffering terrible growing pains following its revolution.

Secularists are pitted against Islamists; feminists are experiencing anxiety about women's rights; political constituents on all sides are wrangling for power and influence; the military in Egypt has ousted a democratically elected—yet failure in governance—president; and Islamist militants are calling for retaliation and violence in both Tunisia and Egypt, while average citizens are caught in the middle while they worry about the economy and putting food on the table. With this backdrop, Tunisia has still managed to change its politics by non-violently replacing an Islamist political party in power with a more secular coalition.

There is no magic elixir to resolve all the problems in post-revolution Tunisia, but the Tunisian people have proven their determination to keep their country on the path of democracy, to strengthen its economy, to preserve and protect laws and policies pertaining to human rights and women's rights in particular, and to fend off the assault of religious extremists who constantly seek to derail Tunisian democracy. These are all extremely difficult tasks and endeavors, but, nonetheless, the Tunisian people continue to face their daunting political, economic, and security challenges with unwavering resolve.

In addition, Tunisia has received recognition, respect, and pledges of assistance from Western powers, including the United States, especially to strengthen the Tunisian economy. In August 2015, the *Washington Post* published an op-ed entitled, "Why the United States Should Act Quickly to Help Tunisia." The op-ed is written by Frank G. Wisner, international affairs adviser at Squire Patton Boggs law firm and former undersecretary of Defense for Policy and undersecretary of State for International Security Affairs, and W. Bowman Cutter, a senior fellow and director of the Next American Economy Project, Roosevelt Institute, and a former deputy assistant to President Bill Clinton and former director of the National Economic Council. In this op-ed, both authors argue that quick U.S. assistance to Tunisia, especially in the economic domain, is imperative, since "Tunisia has written a modern constitution, seen the flowering of a vibrant civil society, elected a functioning government and created a truly competitive politics. It is a 99 percent Muslim nation committed to a secular society that respects all faiths. It is also the Arab nation that has been most committed to the equality of women."[39]

The authors highlight some of the inherent challenges that Tunisia faces today, including the following: "Its civil society is recovering from years of authoritarian, kleptocratic government, which presided over major human rights abuses and a disastrous economy. The state remains way too large and too entangled in the private sector. Its regulatory processes are complex beyond belief, seriously inhibiting domestic and foreign investment. As a result of all this, Tunisia is struggling to escape a low-growth, low-investment trap that prevents it from meeting the legitimate aspirations of its people, especially its youth."[40] Both authors emphasize that, "To be blunt, we do not believe Tunisia can solve its economic and security problems simultaneously without the United States as a committed partner."[41]

The article outlines the economic needs for Tunisia's development and progress, and this does not encompass US foreign aid. Tunisia does not need to render itself dependent on Western powers for foreign aid. Rather, it needs to be self-sufficient, but with healthy and robust economic and trade relations between Tunisia and the global community, particularly the advanced economies. The authors recommend a US-Tunisian free trade agreement (FTA), which would greatly assist the Tunisian economy, and the United States would benefit both politically and economically from its role in the FTA. The authors also recommend that the United States help facilitate foreign direct investment (FDI) in Tunisia. According to the authors, such initiatives "should be tied to policies that will help produce a competitive, free-market economy" in Tunisia.[42] Both writers conclude that, "if we do not do more, and do it quickly, ten years from now the United States will bitterly regret that it failed to act when it had the chance to help Tunisia build an inclusive, prosperous and lasting democratic society."[43]

Overview of the Contents of the Book

This book analyzes the causal factors of Tunisia's Jasmine Revolution from a political economy lens and its impact on the MENA region. The implications of the developments since January 2011 until now for Tunisia's political economy, religious, and security variables are explained. U.S.-Tunisian and European-Tunisian relations are also analyzed. The ramifications of the civil war and violent chaos in Libya for Tunisia's security and stability are examined. Moreover, the threats and challenges that a variety of militant Islamic groups, such as Al Qaeda's Ansar al-Sharia as well as the Islamic State, pose on Tunisia's security and stability are explained.

Women's rights issues and the tensions between secularism and Islamism in Tunisia are analyzed. The future outlook for Tunisia's political, economic, security, human rights and gender equality, and sociocultural health and status is presented. The implications of Tunisia's post-revolution progress and challenges for the MENA region are also analyzed. Conclusions are presented in the final chapter.

Methodology

The author has conducted field research in Tunisia in November 2003, March 2012, and July 2017. The methodology of this analysis encompasses interviews and observations during these field experiences. Content analyses and political economy data for Tunisia are examined. A brief historical analysis of Tunisia is also presented, and the relevance of Tunisia's modern history to the present is explained.

Contents of this Book

This chapter has provided a detailed introduction to the broader subject matter of the political economy and Islamism in the MENA region, and the specific case of Tunisia, especially as it copes with post-2011 revolution challenges. Below is a descriptive list of the rest of the chapters in this book.

Chapter 2: Tunisia's Jasmine Revolution Demands Dignity
This chapter examines the historical background and political economy causal factors leading up to Tunisia's 2011 revolution that removed from power the dictator Zine al-Abidine Ben Ali. Comparisons are presented between Tunisia's case and those of Libya, Egypt, Yemen, Bahrain, and

Syria (all of which have experienced "Arab Awakening" revolutions or uprisings).

Chapter 3: Women in the Frontlines: Tunisia's Revolution
The role and impact of women's activism in Tunisia's 2011 revolution are examined, and the current status of the women's rights movement in Tunisia is also described. The tensions between the secular feminists and religious hardliners are presented, and implications for Tunisia's future political economy as it pertains to gender relations and issues are articulated. Sen's Social Choice Theory is applied to gender equality in the Tunisian context. Observations about similar women's activism in post–Arab Awakening MENA countries are presented.

Chapter 4: Tunisia's Political Health
This chapter examines the "political" side of the political economy equation. The pre- and post-revolution political variables are presented and brought up-to-date. Observations about the political health of post–Arab Awakening MENA countries are also presented.

Chapter 5: Tunisia's Economic Health
This chapter examines the "economic" side of political economy equation. The pre- and post-revolution economic variables are presented and brought up-to-date. Observations about the economic health of post–Arab Awakening MENA countries are also presented.

Chapter 6: Secularism Versus Political Islam: The Case of Tunisia
The unique dynamics of political negotiations between "secularists" and "Islamists" in Tunisian politics in the post-2011 revolution era are highlighted. A comparative analysis of political Islam in the MENA region is also presented.

Chapter 7: Conclusion
In the conclusion, summaries of the analytical findings and results are presented, along with discussion about the hypothesis. The current situation regarding the political economy of the MENA region and specifically Tunisia is assessed. Tunisia is presented as an ideal model for the region to follow for peaceful political, social, and economic *evolution after revolution*.

While turning the pages that follow, the reader should bear in mind Thomas Friedman's profound words: "The Arab Awakening has been, up to now, a lot about freedom from dictatorial regimes – Syria, Yemen, Libya, Tunisia, Bahrain and Egypt. But once you got freedom *from*, then you need freedom *to*. Freedom from is about destroying things. Freedom to is about constructing things, constructing the rule of law."[44]

Notes

1. Sameer Rahim, "Ibn Khaldun: The Man Who Invented Modern History," *Prospect Magazine*, April 30, 2018: https: //www.prospectmagazine.co.uk/philosophy/ibn-khaldun-the-man-who-invented-modern-history
2. Ibid.
3. See *Arab Human Development Report 2002* (New York: UN Development Program, 2002): http://hdr.undp.org/sites/default/files/rbas_ahdr2002_en.pdf
4. Carl Cavanaugh Hodge, "Imperialism," *Oxford Bibliographies*, September 19, 2014, accessed on June 12, 2018, from http://www.oxfordbibliographies.com/view/document/obo-9780199743292/obo-9780199743292-0010.xml
5. "The State, Policy-Making and Political Economy," School of Oriental and African Studies (SOAS), Political Economy of Public Policy, no date, accessed on June 12, 2018 from https://www.soas.ac.uk/cedep-demos/000_P527_PEPP_K3736-Demo/unit1/page_13.htm
6. Melanie Cammett, Ishac Diwan, Alan Richards, and John Waterbury, *A Political Economy of the Middle East,* 4th edition (Boulder: Westview Press, 2015), p. 2.
7. Ibid.
8. Jonathan Steele, "Food for Thought – The Guardian Profile: Amartya Sen," *The Guardian,* March 30, 2001: http://www.guardian.co.uk/books/2001/mar/31/society.politics
9. Amartya Sen, *Development as Freedom* (New York: Alfred A. Knopf, 1999), p. 189.
10. Ibid., p. 4.
11. Ibid., p. 11.
12. "Economic Theory, Freedom and Human Rights: The Work of Amartya Sen," ODI Briefing Paper, *Overseas Development Institute (ODI),* November 2001, p. 1: http://www.odi.org.uk/resources/docs/2321.pdf
13. Ibid., p. 3.
14. Ibid., p. 4.
15. Ibid., p. 11.
16. Ibid., p. 10.

17. Ibid., p. 32.
18. See Michael Laurence, "Democratic Theory," *Oxford Bibliographies*, February 22, 2018, accessed on June 15, 2018 from http://www.oxford-bibliographies.com/view/document/obo-9780199756223/obo-9780199756223-0162.xml
19. Ibid.
20. Philippe Schmitter, "Democratization and Political Elites or Political Elites and Democratization or The Process of Democratization and the Role of Elites or the Role of Elites in Democratization or Democratization: The Role of Elites," European University Institute, p. 1: https://www.eui.eu/Documents/DepartmentsCentres/SPS/Profiles/Schmitter/DEMOCRATIZATION-AND-POLITICAL-ELITES.REV.pdf
21. See Guillermo O'Donnell, "The Perpetual Crises of Democracy," *Journal of Democracy*, vol. 18, January 2007 (pp. 5–11): https://www.journalofdemocracy.org/article/perpetual-crises-democracy
22. Elizabeth Shakman Hurd, "Tunisia: Democracy after Secularism: The Rise of So-Called Islamist Parties in the Wake of the Arab Spring is a Product of Democracy, Not an Obstacle," *Al Jazeera*, April 11, 2012: http://www.aljazeera.com/indepth/opinion/2012/04/20124795440442662.html
23. Ibid.
24. Ibid.
25. Aidan Lewis, "Profile: Tunisia's Ennahda Party," *BBC News*, October 25, 2011: http://www.bbc.com/news/world-africa-15442859
26. Ibid.
27. Ibid.
28. Ibid.
29. Shakman Hurd, "Tunisia: Democracy after Secularism."
30. Ibid.
31. Ibid.
32. Muqtedar Khan, "What is Political Islam?" *E-International Relations,* March 10, 2014: http://www.e-ir.info/2014/03/10/what-is-political-islam/, quoted in Hayat Alvi, "The Post-Secular Republic: Turkey's Experiments with Islamism," *Air & Space Power Journal (USAF)*, 2nd Quarter, vol. 6, issue 2, Summer 2015 (22–39): http://www.au.af.mil/au/afri/aspj/apjinternational/aspj_f/article.asp?id=151
33. Charles Hirschkind, "What is Political Islam," *Middle East Research and Information Project (MERIP)*, Winter 2015: http://www.merip.org/mer/mer205/what-political-islam
34. Selim Cafer Karatas, "The Economic Theory of Ibn Khaldun and the Rise and Fall of Nations," *Muslim Heritage*, Foundation for Science, Technology and Civilization, April 2006: http://www.muslimheritage.com/article/economic-theory-ibn-khaldun-and-rise-and-fall-nations

35. Ibid.
36. Muhammad Dhaouadi, "The Concept of Change in the Thought of Ibn Khaldun and Western Classical Sociologists," *Ýslâm Araþtýrmalarý Dergisi,* Sayý 16, 2006 (p. 68): http://www.isam.org.tr/documents/_dosyalar/_pdfler/islam_arastirmalari_dergisi/sayi16/043_087.pdf
37. "Asabiyyah," *Oxford Islamic Studies Online*, 2018: http://www.oxfordislamicstudies.com/article/opr/t125/e202
38. "Constructivism in International Relations," InternationalRelations.org, 2018: http://internationalrelations.org/constructivism_in_international_relations/
39. Frank G. Wisner, and W. Bowman Cutter, "Why the United States Should Act Quickly to Help Tunisia," *The Washington Post*, August 6, 2015: https://www.washingtonpost.com/opinions/why-we-should-act-quickly-to-help-tunisia/2015/08/06/f5d27f8c-324e-11e5-8353-1215475949f4_story.html
40. Ibid.
41. Ibid.
42. Ibid.
43. Ibid.
44. Thomas Friedman, "A-Z Quotes" (emphasis added): http://www.azquotes.com/quote/1573822?ref=tunisia

CHAPTER 2

Tunisia's Jasmine Revolution Demands Dignity

Eppur si muove
("Nonetheless, it moves")
—Galileo

Defiance is dangerous in the Middle East and North Africa (MENA) region. Challenging the state, and even the religious establishment, invites threats to one's well-being. That has been the case for many decades following independence from the grip of colonial powers. The threats to one's well-being have not been unlike in Old Europe when no one would dare question the monarchy and the church. In some respects, the MENA region has resembled these harsh realities of absolute rule and tyranny by ruthless authorities who silence and repress anyone challenging the status quo. Hence, the quote attributed (arguably) to Galileo, *Eppur si muove*, or "Nonetheless, it moves," is appropriate to cite in the context of defiance in the face of tyranny.

The legend describes the famed seventeenth-century philosopher, astronomer, mathematician, and physicist Galileo as having uttered "Nonetheless, it moves" in defiant reference to his theory that the Earth moves around the Sun, and not the reverse as the church believed and preached; it is a theory, or belief, for which Galileo was brought before the Roman Inquisition and charged with "heresy" and placed under house

H. Alvi, *The Political Economy and Islam of the Middle East*, Political Economy of Islam,
https://doi.org/10.1007/978-3-030-17050-9_2

arrest for the rest of his life. The MENA region resonates with many parallels to such impediments to defiance, or to simply reasonable questioning of the status quo or demands for improving quality of life.[1] Because defiance has been dangerous, it is all the more astonishing to see the repressed rumblings of pro-democracy movements erupt to the surface and disgorge the dictators and regimes from the state, which happened in the form of the 2011 Arab Awakening uprisings and revolutions. The protest movements of the Arab Awakening "weaponized" defiance with massive non-violent—albeit angry—street protests and demonstrations, illustrating to the world that, for them, the one word symbolizing defiance appearing on placards, signs, graffiti, and shouting through their lips is: *Enough*!

The Jasmine Revolution lifted the curtain of fear. On July 19, 2017, I attended an open-air concert in the Carthage Amphitheatre. The popular Lebanese singer, Ragheb Alaama, made the young ladies in the audience absolutely giddy, screaming and dancing and singing along in the ancient Roman amphitheater's stands.

When he first entered the stage, Ragheb Alaama took the mic and greeted his adoring fans. Then, he expressed gratitude and recognition to the current president of the Republic, Mohamed Beji Caid Essebsi. What happened next is extremely stunning for the MENA region, and wholly unprecedented—many in the audience *booed* upon hearing Essebsi's name. This would have been unheard of prior to the 2011 Arab Awakening.

Tunisia is a small country in terms of geography and population size, comparatively speaking. In 2017, Tunisia's population numbered about 11.4 million, while it reached 11.5 million in 2018.[2] The age structure ratio in Tunisia is important, because it indicates a youth bulge that has constituted the educated youth unemployment crisis. In Tunisia, 43 percent of the population is of age 25–54 years, 25 percent is of age 0–14 years, and 13.9 percent is of age 15–24 years.[3]

Hence, Tunisia possesses a large educated youth demographic, and at the same time very high rates of unemployment. In fact, in 2009 Tunisia's youth unemployment measured 30.99 percent, in 2011 it was 42.48 percent, and in 2012 it stood at about 38.44 percent.[4] According to the World Bank (Table 2.1):

> Unemployment is high, particularly for youth and women, and in the interior regions, given limited progress towards greater job creation, one of the chief demands of the 2011 revolution. Unemployment has declined from its peak of 19 percent in 2011, right after the revolution, to 15.5 percent in 2017, but remains above pre-Revolution levels (13 percent in 2010).[5]

Table 2.1 Tunisia's ethnic and religious demographics

Demographic category	*Data*
Population	11.7 million
Ethnic groups	About 98 percent Arabs 1 percent Berber (residing in the Dahar mountains and island of Djerba)
Religions	Muslim (Sunni) 99 percent, other (includes Shias, Baha'is, Jews, and Christians)

Sources: "Tunisia Population 2018," *World Population Review*, December 7, 2018: http://worldpopulationreview.com/countries/tunisia-population/; and the U.S. Department of State: https://www.state.gov/documents/organization/193121.pdf

It is easy to see why the rumblings for the 2011 revolution have erupted upon Mohammed Bouazizi's act of self-immolation, out of frustration from selling fruits and vegetables and facing incessant harassment from corrupt authorities. Everyone in Tunisia could relate to Bouazizi's anger, frustrations, and desperation in the face of suffocating corruption and brutal repression. The simple act of supporting one's family, then, became an unbearable hardship, a daily humiliation, and a reminder of having no hope and no optimism for one's future. The mere act of living from day to day had been stripped of dignity, honor, and self-respect, and the forces of gross corruption, brutality, and demeaning repression won the battle every day and reaped the rewards of their criminality. This scenario pervaded Tunisian society from top-down and bottom-up. No one was safe from Ben Ali's secret police, and the educated youth, in particular, saw the future in the gloomiest terms. The storm clouds—politically, economically, and demographically—formed the "perfect storm" to enable the Jasmine Revolution to burst.

Certain variables have been ripe for setting the revolution in motion, specifically in Tunisia. In addition to the educated, unemployed youth demographic, it helps Tunisia that the size of the country is small, both in terms of population and physical land mass. These factors allowed for a relatively quick revolution, although many other simultaneous variables also facilitated Ben Ali's ouster. The other important factor is the backdrop of the MENA region's political economy in the years leading up to the 2011 Arab Awakening revolutions and uprisings. The MENA's political economy is characterized by authoritarianism, lack of economic development, progress, and diversification, lack of a "knowledge society," and lack of women's empowerment, as the *2002 Arab Human Development Report (AHDR)* has indicated in its groundbreaking findings.

Moreover, because the entire MENA region (specifically the Arab countries) encompasses the analyses and findings of the *2002 AHDR*, it is logically inferred that the region itself has also been ripe for finding inspiration from Tunisia's 2011 revolution, and then experiencing its own—within respective countries—uprisings and revolutions as a result. The remarkable impact of Tunisia's revolution on its own political economy, as well as on inspiring or triggering similar uprisings and revolutions against authoritarian regimes throughout the MENA region, cannot be underscored enough. Yet, the colonial impact on the MENA region's political and economic development also cannot be emphasized enough. It is imperative to examine Tunisia's colonial legacy under French rule, in order to understand the colonial stage setting for the country's path toward post-colonial governance, secularism, and authoritarianism, followed ultimately by the 2011 Jasmine Revolution and democratization.

French Colonialism and Habib Bourguiba

Near the end of World War I, the Ottoman Empire, once a vast, powerful, formidable Islamic empire, was in a state of stagnation and collapse. It earned the label, "Sick Man of Europe," and the British and French watched closely with increasing interests in anticipating the Ottoman Empire's full collapse and in carving up its territories for their own colonial ambitions and agendas. These ambitions led to the secret agreement between the United Kingdom and France called the "Sykes-Picot Agreement" (May 1916), which redrew the MENA map according to the territories that each country wished to colonize, respectively. However, the Sykes-Picot carving of new borders in the MENA region was problematic, and continues to affect the political, economic, tribal, religious/sectarian, ethnic, and other structures and relationships in the region.

Tarek Osman explains further why the Sykes-Picot Agreement has caused so many problems in the Middle East since its implementation (Map. 2.1):

> First, it was secret without any Arabic knowledge, and it negated the main promise that Britain had made to the Arabs in the 1910s – that if they rebelled against the Ottomans, the fall of that empire would bring them independence.

Map 2.1 Sykes-Picot Map, 1916

When that independence did not materialize after World War One, and as these colonial powers, in the 1920s, 30s and 40s, continued to exert immense influence over the Arab world, the thrust of Arab politics – in North Africa and in the eastern Mediterranean – gradually but decisively shifted from building liberal constitutional governance systems (as Egypt, Syria, and Iraq had witnessed in the early decades of the 20th Century) to assertive nationalism whose main objective was getting rid of the colonialists and the ruling systems that worked with them.

This was a key factor behind the rise of the militarist regimes that had come to dominate many Arab countries from the 1950s until the 2011 Arab uprisings.

> ... But the thinking behind **Sykes-Picot** did not translate into practice. That meant the newly created borders did not correspond to the actual sectarian, tribal, or ethnic distinctions on the ground.
>
> ... The third problem was that the state system that was created after World War One has exacerbated the Arabs' failure to address the crucial dilemma they have faced over the past century and half – the identity struggle between, on one hand nationalism and secularism, and on the other, Islamism (and in some cases Christianism).[6]

France claimed most of the North African territories, including Tunisia, Algeria, and Morocco, as protectorates. France colonized Tunisia from 1881 until independence in 1956. Once the French colonialists stepped in Tunisia, their powers superseded those of the preexisting Turkish *bey*, an Ottoman title for governor or local ruler. "The 1881 Treaty of Bardo (also known as Al Qasr as-Sa'id) guarantees French protection for the bey's territory and dynasty, but it also limits his authority to internal affairs. All other aspects of Tunisian policy are henceforth to be dealt with by the French."[7] By the early 1920s, nationalist stirrings threatened French colonial rule in Tunisia, and the Destour party began to demand complete independence from France. The word "destour" means "constitution."

In 1934, the Destour Party fell into deep internal divisions due to ineffective tactics to gain independence. By then, Habib Bourguiba led the party, and he, along with younger nationalists, demanded a more effective approach and strategy. They argued:

> That France had broken its promise to be Tunisia's partner, to help Tunisians develop their economic and political systems in ways that would improve their lives. Instead, France had become a colonial overlord, controlling the government and the economy to serve French interests while most Tunisians remained poor and powerless. After years of fruitless petitions, articles, and delegations to Paris, the time had come to organize a broad-based movement that would steadily pressure France for reforms leading to full independence. Unable to convince conservative elements in the party to adopt a more confrontational strategy, Bourguiba and his allies concluded that they would have to break with the Destour's leadership and convince the rank and file to follow them.[8]

Bourguiba preached his stance to the Destour nationalists, and he spent months spreading his message: "He explained how a broad-based movement could unify all Tunisians behind a careful strategy that could withstand French repression, gain international support, and win independence in stages."[9] His efforts bore fruit, as he gained a considerable following and in a few months he established the Neo-Destour Party, "the organization that would lead Tunisia to independence and would become, in the words of one of the country's most respected observers, 'possibly the most effective regime in the Afro-Asian world for leading its people toward a modern society'."[10]

President Bourguiba ran under one-party rule and renamed the Neo-Destour Party as the *Parti Socialiste Destourien* (Destour Socialist Party—PSD):

> The first Ten-Year Plan (1962–1971) envisaged an annual growth rate of 6 percent that would increase self-sufficiency, raise living standards, and begin to achieve an equitable distribution of income. Limited structural reforms anticipated state intervention in critical, but previously neglected, sectors of the economy, such as industry; bringing foreign-owned enterprises under Tunisian control (the last stage of decolonization); and the establishment of a network of agricultural cooperatives.[11]

By the 1970s, Tunisia's one-party state was heavily criticized domestically and internationally, and pressures for democratization intensified. Fifty people were killed during riots calling for political change in 1977, but "Bourguiba's rule was generally peaceful."[12] In the early 1980s, he hinted at his willingness to transition to a multiparty political system. President Bourguiba also spearheaded secular reforms, which some might describe as "forced extremist secularization,"[13] much like Turkey's Mustafa Kemal Ataturk. Bourguiba fiercely opposed religious militancy, and he "gave women the vote and scrapped polygamy and the veil. He balanced his pro-Western stance by giving refuge to the Palestine Liberation Organization (PLO) following its expulsion from Lebanon."[14]

Nonetheless, Tunisia under Bourguiba for the most part remained Western leaning, which, some argue, contributed to the most advanced women's rights and social policies in the region. Quoting a former Tunisian minister of culture, Tunisia's models "are the French and the Italians, not the Algerians and Libyans."[15]

However, under Bourguiba domestic problems still surfaced, "including unemployment among the middle class and fears that Western values introduced by tourists might undermine Muslim values."[16] While fierce secularism constituted official domestic policy, many in the populace remained privately faithful to their Islamic identity, which has manifested itself in post-Ben Ali politics after the 2011 revolution, as the Islamist party Ennahda ("Renaissance") won the most seats in parliament. In fact, despite the strict secularism under both Bourguiba and Ben Ali, consider the official preservation of Tunisia's Islamic identity: "*Shari'a* (Islamic Law) courts were abolished in 1956, but the constitution declares Islam the state religion and stipulates that the President of the Republic must be a Muslim."[17]

By the 1980s, Bourguiba faced serious economic problems, "coupled with a long-running dispute with the country's main trades union, [which] paved the way to his eventual downfall."[18] Zine al-Abidine Ben Ali, prime minister at the time, removed Bourguiba from power in November 1987, after the former president was deemed medically unfit to rule. The deposed president went into "internal exile in his hometown of Monastir, 100 miles south of Tunis. The cult of his personality which surrounded him, which included a colossal equestrian statue in the center of Tunis, was dismantled."[19] In reflection of Bourguiba's rule, many contend that his time in office "saw Tunisia take a mighty leap from the Middle Ages into the 20th century."[20]

Ben Ali's Rule

It is President Zine al-Abidine Ben Ali's rule that sealed Tunisia's fate and ultimately led to the Jasmine Revolution. Born in the city of Sousse in 1936, Ben Ali was Western educated, both in France and the United States, and "he rose up the hierarchy in the Tunisian security establishment and served as ambassador to Poland in the early 1980s."[21]

Once in power, Ben Ali changed the name of the PSD to the *Rassemblement Constitutionnel Démocratique* (Democratic Constitutional Rally, RCD).[22] He also made promises about democratization, but in 1999 when a multiparty system was permitted, he continued winning the presidential elections with overwhelming majority votes. In addition, "the constitution was changed twice so he could continue to serve."[23] Consider what Kenneth Perkins writes about the Ben Ali regime, in his book *A History of Modern Tunisia* (2004), on the last page:

> As the weak and fragmented opposition prepared for the autumn 2004 parliamentary and presidential elections, it faced the daunting task of doing what, until this point in Tunisian history, only Neo-Destour and its later

> incarnations have done – galvanize and mobilize a disillusioned population. Taking advantage of the 2002 referendum enabling him to seek an additional term in 2004, Ben Ali seems certain to win, in effect becoming Tunisia's second 'president for life'. If the results of the legislative elections also replicate those of the past, the *prospects for democratizing the political system, at least by non-violent means, might well be more dismal than at any time since independence.*[24]

In an interview, Dr. Radwan Masmoudi, president of the Center for the Study of Islam and Democracy (CSID) with offices in Washington, DC, and Tunis, described the climate under Ben Ali in Tunisia:

> Between 1990 and 2000, the political situation in Tunisia was really bad. In the 1990s it was dangerous to even pray, that's how bad it was; just for praying [it] was a danger.
>
> During the 1990s [my friends] would go to different mosques every Friday so they are not known, because there were police officers looking at who is coming and going … it was a dilemma for most people because if they go to the same mosque a lot of times, they risk being arrested, even just for the Friday prayers.[25]

The Ben Ali regime's political and religious repression coincided with some economic growth and reforms, and Europeans flocked to Tunisia as a tourist destination, bringing in substantial revenues. However, "unemployment among a swelling population of young people remained high, and large sections of the Tunisian interior remained poor."[26] Therefore, while Tunisia may have enjoyed steady economic growth under Ben Ali, deficient income distribution, unemployment, and rising inflation continued to worsen. In fact, the gross corruption attributed to Ben Ali and his wife, Leila Trabelsi, and her clan is blamed for much of the income and wealth disparities in Tunisia. The corruption factor is discussed in more detail below.

Political prisoners swelled Ben Ali's prisons, and human rights organizations criticized the regime for its abuses and heavy-handedness. However, his economic policies brought in much needed foreign investments and strengthened the tourism industry. Ben Ali also kept the Islamists in check, precluding a scenario similar to Tunisia's neighbor, Algeria, and the bloody civil war (1991–2002) that ensued there, by the end of which an estimated 200,000 civilians were killed. Tunisia's economic growth, foreign investments, and secularism repelled any serious criticism of the Ben Ali regime by the global community. In fact, economically, his rule was viewed relatively as a "success story."

In the end, Ben Ali and his one-time hairdresser wife, Leila Trabelsi, and her clan crossed the line with their overt corruption and abuses of power and his inability and unwillingness to meet the basic needs of an increasingly discontented population with a growing educated youth that faced dire unemployment and adversity. The Ben Ali regime failed in the areas of human development, basic human security, and especially equitable economic progress. Along with these failures came an iron hand brutalizing any dissent.

The only area where both Bourguiba and Ben Ali made considerable advancements pertains to women's empowerment. In that regard, Tunisia has remained ahead of the rest in the region. Denying freedoms and rights, restricting the political process, ruling with brutal authoritarianism, and embezzling the masses are all formulas for arresting socioeconomic development. These are attributes of Ben Ali's legacy.

Several months after Ben Ali fled to Saudi Arabia, "he and his wife were found guilty in absentia by a Tunisian court for embezzlement and misuse of public funds and sentenced to 35 years in prison."[27] They remain in Saudi Arabia, where their hosts have refused to extradite them back to Tunisia.

Under the former President Ben Ali, unemployment (especially among the educated youth), poverty, and corruption reached unbearable levels. With high corruption levels, increasing poverty rates, and especially terribly high unemployment among the youth, the situation in Tunisia became bleak. The educated youth had nothing to look forward to, and the political leadership brutally repressed any dissension. In addition, Ben Ali's secret police, or *mukhabarat*, transformed Tunisia into a virtual prison, or police state.

Freedom House, which ranks countries' political rights and civil liberties based on a 1–7 scale (with 1 = more free), ranks Tunisia as follows: for the year 2002, freedom score was 5.5, civil liberties 5, and political rights 6; in 2007, its status was "not free," with a freedom score of 5.5, civil liberties 5, and political rights 6. And, in 2010, Tunisia's freedom status was "not free," with a freedom score of 6.0, civil liberties 5, and political rights 7.[28]

Compare that to Egypt for the same years 2002, 2007, and 2010: respective status and scores: 6.0, 6, and 6; "not free" in 2007, 5.5 freedom score, 5 and 6; and the same scores and status in 2010 (as 2007).[29] Libya scored 7 across the board for the same years and "not free" status as well.[30] These scores do not even include press freedom and other aspects of civil rights.

These factors set the stage for Tunisia's 2011 Jasmine Revolution. The Ben Ali regime suffocated the public, politically, economically, socially, and ideologically.

The 2011 Jasmine Revolution

The first time I visited Tunisia was in the fall of 2003, during the dictator Ben Ali's era. Upon landing at the airport, passengers heading to the passport check area immediately noticed the large poster-sized photographs of Ben Ali plastered everywhere. Big Brother Ben Ali's photos watched over shopkeepers and their customers in the heart of downtown Tunis; from the walls of government offices; in the corners of tourist hubs and winding streets; Ben Ali was everywhere. His ubiquitous photos reminded everyone that he was "The Leader" and he should not be challenged, or else there would be severe consequences. Such has been the method of operation of MENA political leaders, including the likes of Iraq's Saddam Hussein and the Bashar al-Assad regime in Syria, as well as previously his father, Hafez al-Assad. The posters, murals, billboards, and photos came complete with sophisticated multilevel secret police apparatuses, the ideal and effective tools of repression that kept watchful eyes on the public and took note of who was doing what and with whom. Detention and torture were commonplace. The public was stripped of dignity, rights, freedoms, and overall human condition.

In addition, the other highly noticeable attribute of 2003 Tunisia was the countless groups of educated youth idly hanging out in idyllic tourist locales and streets of Tunis. Clusters of youth with seemingly distressed and frustrated facial expressions hung out, like we see in the shopping malls, but the difference is that these youth were mostly graduates from universities, and they were jobless, frustrated, politically and economically repressed, and hopeless. I spoke to groups of young women and men, and individuals expressed to me how life was aimless in Tunisia (although no one dared to utter Ben Ali's name), because despite their education and degrees they cannot find jobs. The economy depended heavily on tourism, but the immense corruption in Ben Ali's Tunisia never allowed the public to benefit from tourism and other sources of revenue. Plus, the economy's stagnation coupled with violent political repression caused the educated youth to feel deep despair, which one could read on their faces. One of the major causal factors of the 2010–2011 Tunisian uprising and Jasmine Revolution has been the despair of the educated jobless youth. When the street vendor Mohamed Bouazizi set himself on fire on December 17, 2010, this was the last straw for Tunisians across the economic and social strata. The rest is history.

"Ash-shaab yureed isqaat an-nizaam!" ("The people want the downfall of the regime!") was the popular Arabic chant throughout the Middle East and North Africa, starting with the January 2011 mass protests on Bourguiba Avenue in Tunis, successfully toppling Tunisian dictator Zine al-Abidine Ben Ali. The masses took to the streets in Tunisia when Bouazizi, frustrated by endless corruption and abuse at the hands of local authorities, doused himself with gasoline and lit a match. The enraged people drew the line in the sand and declared, "no more," and "enough!" This reverberated throughout the MENA region, with enormous protests in Cairo's Tahrir Square, Benghazi, Sanaa, Manama, Dera'a, to name a few. In the case of Libya and Syria, civil wars have raged. In the case of Egypt, the revolution has reversed, reinstalling a military regime and repressive dictatorship.

Habib Bourguiba Avenue in the heart of Tunis is where the catalyst took place in 2010–2011. There is a tall clock tower that casts a shadow over the main street, and its time keeping symbolizes the changing of an era from the decades-long rule of the dictator Ben Ali, to a social revolution that has ushered in democracy.

Here is how *Time Magazine* describes the Bouazizi self-immolating flame in 2011 that sparked the MENA region's Arab Awakening:

> On December 17 [Bouazizi's] livelihood was threatened when a policewoman confiscated his unlicensed vegetable cart and its goods. It wasn't the first time it had happened, but it would be the last. Not satisfied with accepting the 10-dinar fine that Bouazizi tried to pay ($7, the equivalent of a good day's earnings), the policewoman allegedly slapped the scrawny young man, spat in his face and insulted his dead father.
>
> Humiliated and dejected, Bouazizi, the breadwinner for his family of eight, went to the provincial headquarters, hoping to complain to local municipality officials, but they refused to see him. At 11:30 a.m., less than an hour after the confrontation with the policewoman and without telling his family, Bouazizi returned to the elegant double-storey white building with arched azure shutters, poured fuel over himself and set himself on fire. He did not

> die right away but lingered in the hospital till January 4 (2011). There was so much outrage over his ordeal that even President Zine el Abidine Ben Ali, the dictator, visited Bouazizi on December 28 to try to blunt the anger. But the outcry could not be suppressed and, on January 14, just 10 days after Bouazizi died, Ben Ali's 23-year rule of Tunisia was over.[31]

Many Tunisians actually prefer the term "Dignity Revolution" (*al-thawra al-karaamah*), rather than the Jasmine Revolution. This preferred wording is illustrative of the profound meaning in the hearts of the masses in toppling the dictatorship and restoring dignity. Tunisians are also proud of their legacy.

Tunisia has played significant roles in regional politics, and especially its famous fourteenth-century historian, known as the "father of sociology," Ibn Khaldun, is a source of pride. In his groundbreaking work, *Al Muqaddimah* (The Introduction), Ibn Khaldun presents explanations for social structures and political and economic systems in the context of the fourteenth century. His keen observations during his time resemble striking similarities and some differences in the modern Middle East and North Africa. Ibn Khaldun's core concept has been *Asabiyyah*, which describes the bond among humans in a social group forming a community. Asabiyyah is that bond, or glue, that holds the community together. Ibn Khaldun explains that Asabiyyah

> exists at any level of civilization, from nomadic society to states and empires. Asabiyyah is most strong in the nomadic phase, and decreases as civilization advances. As this Asabiyyah declines, another more compelling Asabiyyah may take its place; thus, civilizations rise and fall, and history describes these cycles of Asabiyyah as they play out.[32]

In the colonial and post-colonial context, "Asabiyyah" can refer to nationalism, and Ibn Khaldun contends that every dynasty intrinsically embodies the "seeds of its own downfall" when the rulers' concerns increasingly focus on their own advantages in power rather than the public's well-being. This wisdom foreshadows the events of 2011 and the "Arab Awakening," which began in Tunisia.

Former President Ben Ali's regime and his wife's clan suffocated the people with their brutality, authoritarianism, unemployment and wealth distribution problems, and corruption that earned them the description "mafia-like." Tunisian youth in particular despaired with no hope for change and progress. Ibn Khaldun wrote about Economic Theory and the concept of the "social contract" between leaders and citizens. Leaders' failures to fulfill the social contract of providing opportunities for citizens to utilize their labor and earn a living, and to thrive and progress in society, ultimately only leads to change of leadership. That is what happened in 2011 when the Tunisian populace could take no more of the Ben Ali regime's injustices and failures in fulfilling the social contract.

It is not just Tunisians who are proud of the revolution, but the entire Middle East and North Africa region. The masses in the region have viewed the Jasmine Revolution as an inspirational impetus to remove their own corrupt, authoritarian regimes. The protestors have even used the same chants and slogans from Tunisia. The fundamental reason behind the grievances of the masses is the failure of governments to meet the basic needs of the people. In other words, the desire to democratize respective political systems coincides with the desire to improve quality of life and human rights, and human development statuses in a given country. Rampant corruption, abuses of power, gross brutality, and economic stagnation have exacerbated the grievances of the people. Everyone wants to live with dignity.

Many Tunisia analysts contend that there are three main *economic* causal factors that eventually led to the downfall of Ben Ali's regime, which include: (1) youth unemployment, (2) corruption, and (3) coastal-interior wealth gap.

Unemployment of Educated Youth

For many years, college graduates in Tunisia have discovered that their education and degrees did not translate into jobs. Tunisia has about 80,000 graduates from college every year, and only 40,000 jobs can be created, on average per year.[33] Also, "women constitute the majority of graduates. Yet only 38 percent of women are employed compared with 51 percent of men."[34] In addition, the most vulnerable unemployed demographic "are the illiterate and school dropouts. They represent 34 percent of all unemployed youth."[35]

For about the last ten years, the educated jobless youth rose in numbers, which translates into about 400,000–500,000 college graduates without jobs.[36] They are the ones who started the Jasmine Revolution. As Dr. Masmoudi said, "They had no hope." This sentiment was reflected during this author's first visit to Tunisia in November 2003. Large groups of idle, jobless, educated youth lined the street corners, and they expressed deep frustrations with the lack of economic opportunities and hope for the future. In conversations with some of them, they expressed that they could not marry and settle down, because they had no jobs to support their families, despite their college degrees. This was in 2003, and youth joblessness grew exponentially by 2011. Their frustrations and restlessness, as well as their resentment toward the Ben Ali and Trabelsi-inflicted injustices, contributed to the outbreak of demonstrations, which ultimately led to the 2011 revolution. The collective outrage arising from the Bouazizi episode was an inevitable and natural reaction, given the circumstances, especially for the educated unemployed youth, in Tunisia in 2010 and early 2011:

> With no obvious rivals to Ben Ali, there was speculation that he was looking to pass on power to one of his relatives.
>
> In the final days of 2010, a series of protests began in the center of the country after a young graduate set himself on fire when stopped from selling fruit and vegetables without a license.
>
> The protests, advertised widely through social media networks, gradually spread.
>
> Ben Ali initially blamed the demonstrations on a fringe of 'extremists'. But he changed tack on 13 January, expressing deep regrets for the deaths of protesters, pledging to introduce media freedoms, and promising not to stand in 2014.
>
> But his offer of concessions failed to quell the unrest, and the following day, after huge crowds took to the streets of Tunis and clashed with the security forces once again, he fled the country.[37]

Corruption at the Core and Everywhere

According to the *BBC News*, under the surface,

> There was resentment against the perceived corruption surrounding the ruling elite, some of which was detailed in US diplomatic cables published by Wikileaks at the end of 2010.
>
> Ben Ali was married twice with six children. His second wife, Leila Trabelsi, played a prominent role in Tunisian public life and reportedly helped amass huge economic holdings for her extended family.[38]

In fact, the above BBC excerpt is an understatement. Dr. Masmoudi explained that under Bourguiba corruption was minimal. But, under Ben Ali "corruption grew really, really exponentially."[39] The clan of Leila Trabelsi, in particular, was

> Widely despised as the ultimate symbol of corruption and excess. Leila and her 10 siblings are said to have operated like a mafia, extorting money from shop owners, demanding a stake in businesses large and small and divvying up plum concessions among themselves. Their control over the North African country's economy was vast. The Trabelsi and Ben Ali's own families were said to have a stake in Tunisian banks and airlines, car dealerships, Internet providers, radio and television stations, industry and big retailers.[40]

According to Dr. Masmoudi, the last four to five years of Ben Ali's rule saw an intolerable rise in corruption: "It really became unbelievable. The Trabelsi clan, the family, there was no limit; there was no way to stop them. If they saw something they liked, they took it. In the end, there's not a single family in Tunisia that has not been touched by corruption [at all levels of society]. This family could get away with anything."[41]

Dr. Masmoudi described how there were occasions when customs officers tried to open the packages that Trabelsi family members tried to bring into the country, and when these officers tried to open them, "they were actually beaten in front of other officers by the Trabelsi clan or the people who work for them. [The family] was completely out of control."[42]

A brother of Leila Trabelsi had an office in downtown Tunis, and it served the purpose of taking care of Tunisians' legal problems for a fee. Dr. Masmoudi explained, "You tell them what your problem is, they tell you how much you have to pay, and they'll solve your problem for you. Everybody knew this. You pay maybe 5,000 or 10,000 dinars, depending on the case, and they'll go and bribe the judge to make sure you win the case."[43] Not everyone could afford this. This operation was out in the open; every Tunisian knew about this office run by the first lady's brother. The people did not like corruption; they did not accept it. In fact, they resented it.

"At the end, what really brought down Ben Ali so quickly is that even people in the government were fed up," said Dr. Masmoudi. "People within the ruling party (RCD) were fed up; people within the police were fed up; people within the army were fed up. Everybody was fed up with this corruption. That's why you see [Ben Ali] basically crumbled in 24 hours."[44] Leila Trabelsi, in particular, was reviled in the eyes of average Tunisians: "If Ben Ali was despised by many in Tunisia, Trabelsi, it seems, was truly hated. Wives of overthrown leaders are usually reviled for their love of luxury and designer clothes or shoes – [Imelda] Marcos had 2,700 pairs – but Trabelsi, an elegant 53-year-old, appears to have gone even further, with unsubstantiated reports that she fled Tunisia last week with more than $50m worth of gold bars."[45] How ironic is it that Leila Trabelsi is the daughter of a fruit and nut vendor. Trabelsi

> was brought up with 10 brothers in the heart of the Tunis medina, the daughter of a fruit and nut seller. She was working as a hairdresser when she met her future husband and gave birth to their first daughter while he was married to his first wife.
>
> When Ben Ali took power in 1987 he obtained a divorce and wed Trabelsi, who allegedly set about installing members of her family in positions of power. In the decades that followed the Trabelsi name became synonymous with the corruption that riddled Tunisian society and business, and a byword for shameless greed and excess – a son-in-law reportedly kept pet tigers in his garden, which he fed cuts of prime beef.
>
> 'Whether it's cash, services, land, property, or yes, even your yacht, President Ben Ali's family is rumored to covet it and reportedly gets what it wants,' said a US government cable revealed by Wikileaks recently.
>
> Another stated: 'Often referred to as a quasi-mafia, an oblique mention of 'the Family' is enough to indicate which family you mean. Seemingly half of the Tunisian business community can claim a Ben Ali connection through marriage, and many of these relations are reported to have made the most of their lineage. Ben Ali's wife, Leila Ben Ali, and her extended family – the Trabelsis – provoke the greatest ire from Tunisians.'
>
> Graciet, whose book *La Régente de Carthage*, written with Nicolas Beau, is being quickly reprinted, says Leila Trabelsi's reputation and that of her relatives, is deserved. 'She was extremely powerful in running her family and ensuring they had their hands on very large parts of the economy. She also had political power making decisions about government posts and firing ministers.'
>
> She concludes that Trabelsi was a 'Machiavellian figure ... intelligent, ambitious, calculating, manipulating and utterly without scruples or morals.'[46]

A week before Ben Ali fled the country, "he gave orders to bomb the city of Kasserine with airplanes, and the military said 'no, sorry Mr. President, we cannot do it'."[47] He also gave orders to police officers and the army to shoot civilians, and many of them refused. On January 14, "in addition to the big demonstrations which were on Habib Bourguiba Avenue in downtown Tunis, there were some people who attacked two restaurants owned by the Trabelsi family, and they burned them. And they tried to attack a house belonging to one of Leila Trabelsi's brothers. So, the Trabelsi family was really scared."[48]

The Trabelsi clan called the first lady and asked her what they should do, because they were very frightened and concerned about their safety and security. She advised them to bring all their families and meet her at the airport.

> By 2:30 p.m., there were about 70 or 80 Trabelsi clan members assembled at the airport, waiting in the VIP lounge for an airplane to take them somewhere in Europe, most likely France. Then, the most intriguing aspect of this story occurred:
>
> The head of the Anti-Terrorism Brigade, which is the strongest brigade in the Ministry of Interior, the most armed and the best equipped, heard about this (because his wife works at the airport; she informed him that the Trabelsi clan is trying to flee the country). He became furious, because, here we are trying to manage a big demonstration and people are being killed, and the Trabelsi family, after all the damage that they've done, now they're going to escape to go somewhere else?
>
> He decided to take twelve people from his brigade and went to the airport and stopped them and said, 'You're not going anywhere.' And this is when Ben Ali fled, because he thought this is a *coup d'état* against him. The head of the Anti-Terrorism Brigade is now a hero.[49]

The corruption of the Ben Ali regime and Trabelsi clan penetrated every aspect of Tunisian society, including the security forces, military, police, customs officers, businessmen and women, bureaucrats, street vendors and sellers in the souk, and average citizens. Not only did this entrenched corruption undermine the economy and wealth distribution in Tunisia (and only worsened with each passing year), but it also, in the end, was the nail in the coffin of the Ben Ali regime. Simultaneously, youth unemployment has been the other causal factor in the revolution.

The pervasive corruption and youth unemployment together rendered the prospects for socioeconomic development increasingly dismal. The variable exacerbating these harsh realities for the average Tunisian is the coast-interior wealth gap, which constitutes another major causal factor (simultaneously) for the 2011 revolution.

Intra-Regional Coastal-Interior Wealth Disparities

Dr. Masmoudi explained that there are two Tunisias: the coastal Tunisia, and the interior Tunisia:

> If you spend three weeks visiting only the coastal areas of Tunisia, you will feel like you're in America. These areas are very advanced, very sophisticated, with nice roads, everything is nice. If you go inside, in the rural interior areas, you will feel like you're living in the 16th century, literally. It's black and white. The vast majority live on the coastal areas, maybe around 6 or 7 million out of the ten million population. But, you have about 3 to 4 million who live in the rural areas, and they are devastated, I mean those people have nothing.
>
> The problem is [that] a lot of them come often to the coastal areas, and either they study in universities in big cities, or some of them work, or visit, so they constantly go back and forth, and they see the discrepancies, they see the poverty, and they see how the rich people are living. The discrepancies became huge.
>
> Bourguiba, he was a patriotic dictator. He was not a corrupt dictator. But, Ben Ali was a dictator who didn't care about the nation, he was very corrupt; he had no values at all. Bourguiba was trying to make Tunisia developed. His goal, in an authoritarian way, was to have Tunisia developed. But Ben Ali was the opposite: his goal was to enrich himself and his family, that's all he cared about.[50]

In 2009, the rural population in Tunisia numbered 3,453,000, and the number of rural poor stood at 480,000.[51] As a result, the combination of the rampant corruption, unemployment, and interior rural-coastal wealth disparities all contributed to the discontent and deep frustrations of the masses.

The stage was set by the deteriorating socioeconomic variables over decades, together with the political repression and violations of human rights. Tunisians did not enjoy freedoms, rights, and choices for many years, hence the arrested development. Ben Ali and his family's corruption only reinforced the tightening noose on society, and their collective and individual grievances.

However, some argue that the Bouazizi case was more of a culmination, rather than the actual cause, of the 2011 Jasmine Revolution.

On July 19, 2017, I interviewed Lotfi Hajji, a respected journalist and bureau chief for *Al Jazeera*, who spoke to me (in Arabic, which has been translated here) at an office in Tunis, expressing his personal views. Mr. Hajji emphasized that the path to the 2011 revolution did not begin with Bouazizi's self-immolation in December 2010. In fact, according to him, it can be traced to the 2005 October 18th Movement that encompassed a mass protest and hunger strike against the Ben Ali dictatorship. Mr. Lotfi says, "It was the most important human rights and political activism against Ben Ali. It involved many diverse activists. The October 18th Movement actually planted the seeds for the 2011 Jasmine Revolution."[52] He points out that the source of the October 18th Movement was a scheduled "International Conference on Information," which served as the point of contention between pro- and anti-Ben Ali activists. Those against it argued that under the Ben Ali dictatorship there is no freedom of information, the press, and expression, and, in general, human rights are severely repressed and denied.[53]

The protest slogans served as equally important precedents for the 2011 revolution, since they called for democracy, freedoms, and rights for the people. Plus, they called for amnesty for the countless political prisoners languishing in Ben Ali's prisons. The October 18th Movement signified the first time in Tunisian history that opposing ideological groups—namely Islamists and secularists—united, and the foreign journalists who were going to cover the International Conference on Information instead focused their attention on the hunger strike and protests. The Ben Ali regime censored media coverage of the protests and activism in Tunisia, which, in turn, allowed the activists to emphasize that there is no freedom of the press and expression under Ben Ali.

The October 2005 hunger strike resulted in a unified activism between Islamists and secularists. Mr. Hajji says that they had a common vision, despite their ideological differences, and this was unprecedented.[54]

Then, this all came to a head later in 2010–2011 when the Bouazizi case was plastered throughout the Internet and eventually the news media. The Tunisian people were already boiling with anger, and the Bouazizi case was the catalyst to the eruption of grassroots protests that, to everyone's surprise, swiftly led to Ben Ali's ouster.

In a July 2017 interview, Souad Goussami Hajji, a prominent teacher, civil society activist, and a founding member of the Center for the Study of Islam and Democracy (CSID), underscored the point that "It was a grassroots and spontaneous revolution, with no preparations. It was an outburst of anger by the Tunisian people, mainly due to corruption and economic hardships. The rich exploited and oppressed the poor."[55]

Popular Culture and the 2011 Revolution

In 2011, *Time Magazine* named Hamada Ben Amor, a popular Tunisian rapper known as El Général, as one of the top hundred most influential people in the world. Here is how *Time* describes El Général in his profile:

> TIME 100
> El Général
> Tunisian Rapper
>
> 'When I became a rapper, I wasn't looking for love. I was looking to rap for the good of the people.'
>
> —Hamada Ben Amor, *21, better known as El Général, the Tunisian rap star whose song "Rais Lebled" [President of the Nation] is credited with helping inspire the uprising in his country that overthrew President Zine el Abidine Ben Ali. The song, which includes blunt allegations of government corruption, also became the anthem of protesters in Cairo's Tahrir Square.*[56]

Throughout the Arab Awakening movements in the MENA, musicians, rap artists, poets, singers, and political cartoonists have played a major role in criticizing and at times ridiculing given regimes. These artistic messages, in turn, appeared on social networking sites, like Facebook and Twitter, and YouTube videos as well as cell phone footage of events pertaining to regime oppression and/or artists' performances. All of this went viral on the Internet and had a tremendous impact on the personal emotional and political sentiments of the masses (Fig. 2.1).

Fig. 2.1 Vive La Revolution Graffiti in Tunis. (Photo courtesy of the author, taken in March 2012)

Tunisia's Political Economy and Islamism

Tunisia operates in, and is affected by, the twists and turns of economic globalization. This renders Tunisia vulnerable to the impact of inflation and economic and financial crises on Tunisia's trade partners primarily in Europe (i.e., France, Italy, and Germany). In the years prior to the 2011 Jasmine Revolution, Europe faced rising inflation, high unemployment, and contagious financial crises. Consider the World Bank's report about the rise in food and energy prices in Europe:

> The World Bank food price index has matched its peak of 2008 with the energy price index still below the July 2008 peak. The increase in food prices in 2010–11 represents a generalized increase in the prices of several commodities. These commodity market developments reflect a combination of temporary and permanent factors. Rising incomes around the world, and particularly in emerging and developing countries, have increased demand for food and fuel. In addition, supply factors, related to fuel supply constraints and inventories, have affected prices both in the short and longer runs, while policies supporting bio-fuel production have affected grain prices.[57]

Tunisia has felt the effects of the rising food and energy costs in Europe, which have rippled throughout the world. Other developing economies in the MENA have also borne the brunt of rising inflation, combined with extremely high unemployment especially among the educated youth. That is the case in Egypt, Libya, Algeria, and elsewhere in the MENA. Therefore, Tunisia's unemployed youth along with the destitute residents of the interior region saw no other recourse but to rise up and topple the Ben Ali dictatorship.

According to Tunisia's minister of finance, Jaloul Ayed, "It was not surprising that Tunisia's revolution was the first of the so-called Arab spring because earlier in its history Tunisia had been the first Arab country to abolish slavery and to grant equal rights to women. Tunisia had even adopted a written constitution as far back as 1861." He added, "The corrupt old system was bound to fail – and it did fail."[58]

Specifically, for post-revolution Tunisia, Minister Ayed listed four principal priorities that the transitional government is currently focusing on: "Reducing unemployment; Restoring economic growth; Reducing regional disparities; and Assisting Tunisians in need."[59]

Minister Ayed reported that his ministry "is starting major initiatives on infrastructure projects and financial reform." In addition, the government "has also created a confiscation committee to investigate and recover state assets stolen by the former president and his family."[60]

Dr. Masmoudi further emphasized that, "While religion will continue to be a major force in the country, no one wants a theocratic state – everybody wants a democratic civil state that fully respects human rights and Islamic values and culture."[61] Dr. Masmoudi added that the challenge will be "to find a good balance between Islamic religious values and democratic values. And I think Tunisia is well placed to develop this model of a moderate Islamic state."[62]

It comes as little surprise that Tunisia's Jasmine Revolution has been the source of inspiration for pro-democracy movements rippling throughout the region. Failures in comprehensive human development, the prevalence of economic stagnation, unemployment, wealth disparities, authoritarianism, as well as the restrictions on rights and freedoms remain the fundamental impetuses for the 2011 uprisings and revolutions in Egypt, Libya, Bahrain, Syria, and elsewhere. In some of these cases, the human development variables and repression have been even more severe than in Tunisia. Hence, the mass mobilizations calling for the downfall of repressive and corrupt autocratic regimes, in light of the events in Tunisia, could be seen, in retrospect, as only natural.

The Tunisian people have been proud of the revolution and immensely patriotic, given their achievements since January 2011. "*Ultra Tunsie*," then, is a label each Tunisian would be proud to own and display. It will be the next generation that will carry the political, economic, and socio-cultural torch in each country in the MENA region. With the young, educated, innovative, and tech-savvy demographic in the region, the prospects for development have never been better, presupposing that rights and freedoms would facilitate such progress.

However, competition for power at the domestic level involves the Islamist Ennahda Party, the opposition coalition, the hardline Salafists, and the youth activists consisting of diverse advocates for secularism, feminism, and liberal democracy. Tensions have flared in Tunisian politics, especially with the February 6, 2013, murder of Chokri Belaid, a prominent leftist politician.

Tunisia's future is not without significant challenges, especially as Salafists extremist groups, such as Ansar al-Sharia, increasingly act up and apply pressures on the government to comply with their policy preferences. The Salafist militant threats became all the more acute with the assassination of Chokri Belaid, a human rights advocate who fearlessly and vocally criticized Ennahda. Belaid "publicly challenged [Ennahda's] failure to investigate or prosecute violent acts of intimidation carried out by shadowy gangs of religious extremists."[63] Belaid was shot four times in his car, and as of late February 2013 four Islamist extremist suspects have been in custody, but a fifth gunmen escaped. The murder triggered a political shake-up. Belaid's widow has fingered Ennahda for alleged complicity in her husband's killing. Her unrelenting public condemnation of Ennahda and the ensuing political crisis, which included Ennahda's refusal to build a non-partisan coalition with technocrats, led Prime Minister Hamadi Jebali to resign in late February 2013.

Ali Laarayedh, a former opposition activist during the Ben Ali era, became Tunisia's new prime minister from 2013 until 2014. Laarayedh was an Ennahda political activist and suffered torture and 13 years of solitary confinement under the prior regime. Upon coming to office, he reassured the public and media that "There will be no Islamization of post-revolutionary Tunisia, and the Islamist-led government has no hidden agendas or intention to monopolize power."[64]

Tunisian politics has faced another blow and pitted into another crisis with the July 25, 2013, assassination of a second secular politician, Mohamed Brahmi, who was a critic of the Ennahda administration. This murder provoked more public demonstrators,

> Blaming the ruling Islamist party and its followers for Mr. Brahmi's killing and shouting for the government to go. Scores of relatives, party members and supporters draped in the Tunisian flag arrived at the entrance of the hospital in the southwestern suburb where Mr. Brahmi's body lay.
>
> Tunisian news media accounts said Mr. Brahmi, 58, had been shot outside his home, an attack witnessed by his wife and children, in the middle of the day by two men on a motorcycle who escaped. Although the accounts of the precise version of events differed, the audacity of the assassination amplified the outrage, as many Tunisians feel the government has failed to deliver on law and order and allowed radical Islamists a license to act with impunity.[65]

Opposition secular politicians have received threats, and many continue to blame Ennahda for these developments. Ennahda has never governed Tunisia, much like the Muslim Brotherhood (MB) in Egypt, as it was banned under the dictatorship. Once in power, Ennahda "[leads] a coalition with two smaller secular parties and has struggled to complete the drafting of a new Constitution and prepare elections within the allotted one year."[66] Ennahda's greatest challenge has been "controlling the extremists among its followers."[67] Ennahda "has long been criticized for allowing what the opposition calls a growing Islamization of the country, and a tolerance of extremist groups: Salafis and jihadis who were recruiting young men to fight in Syria, and groups preaching fundamentalist views and threatening women who worked outside the home or went unveiled."[68]

The Ennahda-led Tunisian government took some positive measures since the revolution. For example, under its leadership, an assets-retrieval committee has been set up to reclaim financial and material assets that the Ben Ali and Trabelsi clan have squandered over the decades of the dictatorship. The new revised constitution has been composed with input from diverse sources and constituents. Some steady political and economic reforms have been initiated in order to improve the country's economy and restart the tourism industry.

Foreign direct investment (FDI) endeavors have been actively pursued to build foreign investment interest in Tunisia. Despite all the hurdles and challenges, Tunisia continues to forge ahead, even as heated political debates and ideological differences abound.

Ennahda has been commended for its inclusive politics and a post-revolutionary maturity missing not only in Egypt but also in the other Arab Awakening upheavals in Libya, Syria, and Yemen. Ennahda negotiated a compromise on the Constitution, dropping all mention of Islamic law, for example, and ensuring full freedoms, including equal rights for women and freedom of religion and expression, though not without tense debates and overt pressures from secularist activists.

Following Mr. Brahmi's assassination, Ennahda assigned the military to launch major anti-terror operations, especially in the Tunisian-Algerian border region. In early August 2013, Tunisian forces

> launched air and ground strikes on Islamist militants near the border with Algeria [on Friday] after fierce overnight clashes in the area, which coincided with increased instability and political turmoil in Tunisia. Aircraft bombed caves in the Mount Chaambi area, where the military has been trying to track down a band of 15 to 20 Islamist militants since December, an army spokesman said Friday. The operation was launched in the same area where militants killed eight soldiers [on Monday] in one of the deadliest attacks on Tunisian security forces in decades. Tunisia's Islamist-led government is grappling with instability and a mounting protest movement. The opposition, angered by the assassination of one of its leaders [last week], wants the transitional Constituent Assembly dissolved.[69]

As Egypt's political turmoil, with the military intervening and ousting President Mohamed Morsi from power and placing him under arrest, intensified there, Tunisia has struggled to balance the ideological and national interests of its revolutionaries, secularists, Islamists, and feminists. In late August 2013, Tunisia and Ennahda managed to sustain a degree of stability, despite demonstrations and pressures to step down, and appeared to fare better than Egypt. Then, finally, in January 2014, the Ennahda Party stepped down from its ruling status, which has been lauded as a significant gesture to ensure non-violent political transitions, peace, stability, and security in Tunisia's domestic domain. This gesture has proven unique, in fact, an anomaly, in the MENA region, and hence it underlines Tunisia's worthiness as an ideal model for others to learn from and follow for political dialogue, compromises, and commitment to democratization.

Conclusion

There are numerous causal factors that have contributed to the 2011 Jasmine Revolution. We can go as far back as the beginning of the colonial era in the MENA region, and the collapse of the Ottoman Empire.

The youth demographic existing throughout the MENA region has served as a pivotal factor in embracing the Tunisian revolution as an inspiration to improve their own circumstances in their own countries. Tarek Osman emphasizes this point:

> [The] changing demographics proved to be the trigger. Over the past four decades, the Arab world has doubled its population, to over 330 million people, two-thirds of them are under 35 years old.
>
> This is a generation that has inherited acute socioeconomic and political problems that it did not contribute to, and yet has been living its consequences – from education quality, job availability, economic prospects, to the perception of the future.
>
> At core, the wave of Arab uprisings that commenced in 2011 is this generation's attempt at changing the consequences of the state order that began in the aftermath of World War One.
>
> This currently unfolding transformation entails the promise of a new generation searching for a better future, and the peril of a wave of chaos that could engulf the region for several years.[70]

The *2002 AHDR* specifically mentions the deficiency in women's empowerment throughout the Arab Middle East. The 2011 Arab Awakening uprisings and revolutions provided prime opportunities for women to assert themselves. Thousands of women suffered blows at the hands of security forces in Tunisia, Egypt, Libya, and elsewhere. The next chapter examines Tunisian women and their role in the 2011 Jasmine Revolution.

Notes

1. As of this writing, we are learning about the brutal murder of Saudi journalist Jamal Khashoggi at the hands of a Saudi death squad at the Saudi Consulate in Turkey, October 2018. Countless journalists, bloggers, and dissidents throughout the MENA region remain in detention, and a number have met their tragic demise. Many still have fled into exile.

2. "Tunisia," *US News and World Report*, World Rankings, 2019: https://www.usnews.com/news/best-countries/tunisia
3. "Tunisia Demographics Profile 2018," *Index Mundi*, 2018: https://www.indexmundi.com/tunisia/demographics_profile.html
4. "Tunisia: Youth Unemployment Rate from 2007 to 2017," *Statista*, 2019: https://www.statista.com/statistics/813115/youth-unemployment-rate-in-tunisia/
5. "The World Bank in Tunisia," The World Bank, April 18, 2018: http://www.worldbank.org/en/country/tunisia/overview
6. Tarek Osman, "Why Border Lines Drawn with a Ruler in WWI Still Rock the Middle East," *BBC News*, December 14, 2013: http://www.bbc.com/news/world-middle-east-25299553
7. Bamber Gasciogne, "History of Tunisia," *HistoryWorld*, from 2001 ongoing: http://www.historyworld.net/wrldhis/PlainTextHistories.asp?historyid=ac93
8. Christopher Alexander, *Tunisia: Stability and Reform in the Modern Maghreb* (New York: Routledge, 2010), pp. 10–11.
9. Ibid., p. 11.
10. Ibid.
11. Kenneth J. Perkins, *A History of Modern Tunisia* (New York: Cambridge University Press, 2004), p. 147.
12. "Habib Bourguiba: Father of Tunisia," *BBC News*, April 6, 2000: http://news.bbc.co.uk/2/hi/obituaries/703907.stm
13. Interview with Radwan Masmoudi, Center for the Study of Islam and Democracy (CSID), Tunis, February 29, 2012.
14. "Habib Bourguiba: Father of Tunisia," *BBC News*.
15. Alexander, p. 1.
16. *Oxford Atlas of the World*, 17th edition (New York: Oxford University Press, 2010), p. 62.
17. Cecily Hilleary, "Return of Islamic Leader Worries Some Tunisian Women," *Voice of America (VOA)*, February 4, 2011: http://www.voanews.com/english/news/middle-east/115291829.html
18. "Habib Bourguiba: Father of Tunisia," *BBC News*.
19. Ibid.
20. Ibid.
21. "Profile: Zine el-Abidine Ben Ali," *BBC News*, June 20, 2011: http://www.bbc.co.uk/news/world-africa-12196679
22. Perkins, p. 185.
23. "Profile: Zine el-Abidine Ben Ali," *BBC News*.
24. Perkins, p. 212. Emphasis added.
25. Interview with Radwan Masmoudi.
26. "Profile: Zine el-Abidine Ben Ali," *BBC News*.

27. "Profile: Zine el-Abidine Ben Ali," *BBC News.*
28. "Freedom in the World 2002, 2007, and 2010: Tunisia," *Freedom House*: http://www.freedomhouse.org/report/freedom-world/2002/tunisia
29. "Freedom in the World 2002, 2007, and 2010: Egypt," *Freedom House*: http://www.freedomhouse.org/report/freedom-world/2002/egypt
30. "Freedom in the World 2002, 2007, and 2010: Libya," *Freedom House*: http://www.freedomhouse.org/report/freedom-world/2002/libya
31. Rania Abouzei, "Bouazizi, the Man Who Set Himself and Tunisia on Fire," *Time Magazine*, January 21, 2011: http://content.time.com/time/magazine/article/0,9171,2044723,00.html
32. Tim Worstall, "Paul Krugman on the Inevitable Decline of Apple and Microsoft," *Forbes*, August 25, 2013: http://www.forbes.com/sites/tim-worstall/2013/08/25/paul-krugman-on-the-inevitable-decline-of-apple-and-microsoft/
33. Interview with Radwan Masmoudi.
34. "Tunisia Country Fact Sheet," *International Fund for Agricultural Development (IFAD)*, 2011 Governing Council: http://www.ifad.org/events/gc/34/nen/factsheet/tunisia.pdf
35. Ibid.
36. Interview with Radwan Masmoudi.
37. "Profile: Zine el-Abidine Ben Ali," *BBC News.*
38. "Profile: Zine el-Abidine Ben Ali," *BBC News.*
39. Interview with Radwan Masmoudi.
40. "Biography of Zine al-Abidine Ben Ali," *Africa Success*, January 23, 2011: http://www.africansuccess.org/visuFiche.php?id=964&lang=en
41. Interview with Radwan Masmoudi.
42. Ibid.
43. Ibid.
44. Ibid.
45. Kim Willsher, "Leila Trabelsi: Tunisia's Lady MacBeth: Tunisia's First Lady was Said to be Manipulative and Ruthless," *The Guardian*, January 18, 2011: http://www.guardian.co.uk/world/2011/jan/18/leila-trabelsi-tunisia-lady-macbeth
46. Ibid.
47. Interview with Radwan Masmoudi.
48. Ibid.
49. Ibid.
50. Interview with Radwan Masmoudi.
51. "Tunisia Country Fact Sheet," *IFAD.*
52. Interview with Lotfi Hajji, Tunis, Tunisia, July 19, 2017.
53. Ibid.
54. Ibid.

55. Interview with Souad Goussami Hajji, Tunis, Tunisia, July 17, 2017.
56. "The 2011 Time 100: El Général, Tunisian Rapper," *Time Magazine*, 2011: http://www.time.com/time/specials/packages/article/0,28804,2066367_2066369_2066242,00.html
57. "Rising Food and Energy Prices in Europe and Central Asia," *The World Bank*, 2011: http://www-wds.worldbank.org/external/default/WDSContentServer/WDSP/IB/2011/04/14/000333037_20110414015110/Rendered/PDF/610970WP0P1262171World1Bank1Combine.pdf, "Summary," p. 1.
58. Jaloul Ayed, quoted in Conference Report, "Tunisia's and Egypt's Revolutions and Transitions to Democracy: What is the Impact on the Arab World? What Lessons can We Learn?" Edited by Thomas W. Skladony, Peter Winston Fettner, and Alexandra Tohmé. Center for the Study of Islam and Democracy (CSID) 12th Annual Conference, Washington, DC, April 15, 2011, p. 3.
59. Ibid., p. 4.
60. Ibid.
61. Radwan Masmoudi, quoted in Conference Report, "Tunisia's and Egypt's Revolutions and Transitions to Democracy: What is the Impact on the Arab World? What Lessons can We Learn?" Edited by Thomas W. Skladony, Peter Winston Fettner, and Alexandra Tohmé. Center for the Study of Islam and Democracy (CSID) 12th Annual Conference, Washington, DC, April 15, 2011, p. 5.
62. Ibid.
63. "An Assassination in Tunisia," *The New York Times*, February 8, 2013: http://www.nytimes.com/2013/02/09/opinion/the-assassination-of-chokri-belaid-in-tunisia.html?_r=0
64. Seumas Milne, "Tunisian Government has No Hidden Agendas, Says New Prime Minister," *The Guardian*, April 2, 2013: http://www.guardian.co.uk/world/2013/apr/02/tunisia-government-agenda-prime-minister
65. Carlotta Gall, "Second Opposition Leader Assassinated in Tunisia," *The New York Times*, July 25, 2013: http://www.nytimes.com/2013/07/26/world/middleeast/second-opposition-leader-killed-in-tunisia.html?pagewanted=all&_r=1&
66. Ibid.
67. Ibid.
68. Ibid.
69. "Tunisia: Military Hunts Militants Near Algerian Border," *The New York Times*, August 2, 2013: http://www.nytimes.com/2013/08/03/world/africa/tunisia-military-hunts-militants-near-algerian-border.html
70. Osman, "Why Border Lines Drawn with a Ruler in WWI Still Rock the Middle East," *BBC News*.

CHAPTER 3

Women in the Frontlines: Tunisia's Revolution

As the world watched the events unfold during the 2011 Arab Awakening, many people assumed that with these protests and revolutions an effective feminist revolution would explode on the scene, resulting in policies and laws that would finally acknowledge the plight of females. The Middle East and North Africa (MENA) region is notorious for woeful violations of women's rights and freedoms, as it is a predominantly patriarchal, traditional, and conservative, and often sexist and misogynist, society. Many observers thought that with women so prominently active in the 2011 Arab Awakening, they would be ensured greater political participation and rights and freedoms. The results have been extremely disappointing and dispiriting for the women's rights and empowerment movements in the MENA region, as the patriarchal system continues to win out against feminist activism.

In fact, this author refers to the predominant patriarchal repression of women in the MENA region as "patriarchal despotism." This follows the model of a historical theory entitled "Asiatic," or "Oriental Despotism." The gender-based despotism in the region should not be overlooked.

The original version of this chapter was revised. The School of Law in Tunisia was incorrect in the original publication. Hence, the related text has been edited in this revised version. A correction to this chapter can be found at https://doi.org/10.1007/978-3-030-17050-9_9

H. Alvi, *The Political Economy and Islam of the Middle East*, Political Economy of Islam,
https://doi.org/10.1007/978-3-030-17050-9_3

In particular, the religious institutions tend to keep pressure on governments to comply with their ideological parameters pertaining to women's issues. This is also the case in secular republics, though it is not so overt. Nonetheless, this is one of the main reasons why Islamism, or political Islam, rattles the nerves of feminist activists in the MENA region. History shows that Islamist governments have been hostile to women's rights and feminism, and one of the first items on their agendas once coming to power has been to intensify rules, laws, and policies to exert more control over women's lives and curtail their personal choices and efforts to empower women's agency in life and society. In turn, this is the opposite direction of what Amartya Sen's Social Choice Theory proposes for socioeconomic progress.

In some cases, the regime responses to Arab Awakening protests have specifically targeted women with violence and sexual crimes. This happened in Egypt with the Supreme Council of the Armed Forces (SCAF). Upon the overthrow of Hosni Mubarak, sexual assaults and violence against women increased. Under SCAF's rule, women detainees were subjected to "virginity tests" and sexual humiliation.[1]

Moreover, post-regime-change elections in Egypt and Tunisia failed to open the floodgates of rights, freedoms, and gender equality to women, even though women suffered violent responses from the security forces, sexual assaults, and detention, and, in some cases, even torture and death, during the Arab Awakening protests. However, that is mostly the case in Egypt, Libya, Bahrain, Syria, and Yemen, whereas in Tunisia, due to its long history of secularism and women's rights, there have been notable exceptions. Regarding this perspective, Tunisia is the outlier in the MENA region, but there is always room for improvement when it comes to women's empowerment.

Overall, the MENA region has yet to embrace the idea that women possess "agency" to make personal choices and social change, as exhibited in their huge numbers and fearlessness during the 2011 protests and revolutions. At the most fundamental level, and in daily life, women's agency must be regarded as equal to men, which in turn is fundamental to human rights and socioeconomic development. This is recognized in the *2002 Arab Human Development Report (AHDR)*, where it identifies major deficiencies in women's empowerment throughout the MENA region. This reality still holds true today, despite some hollow cosmetic attempts at improving women's lives, such as the Saudis have attempted mainly for public relations and opening its economy to the West because of declining oil prices. The reality is that at the grassroots level, the plight of women, especially in the two theocracies—Saudi Arabia and Iran—remains precarious and wholly dominated by ultra-conservative patriarchal despotism. These realities exist to the detriment of socioeconomic progress of their own societies.

The world applauded when Saudi Arabia, which has one of the worst global track records for the treatment of girls and women, recently allowed women to drive cars. However, what went practically unnoticed in the news media is the fact that, at the same time while this was happening, Saudi authorities "have arrested the internationally recognized women's rights activist Samar Badawi and an Eastern Province activist, Nassima al-Sadah … the latest victims of an unprecedented government crackdown on the women's rights movement that began on May 15, 2018, and has resulted in the arrest of more than a dozen activists."[2] According to Human Rights Watch (HRW), Badawi is the recipient of the 2012 United States' International Women of Courage Award, and she "is best known for challenging Saudi Arabia's discriminatory male guardianship system. She was one of the first women to petition Saudi authorities to allow women the right to drive as well as the right to vote and run in municipal elections. Al-Sadah, from the coastal city of Qatif, has also long campaigned both for abolishing the guardianship system and lifting the driving ban. She was a candidate in the 2015 local elections, the first time women were allowed to run, but the authorities removed her name from the ballot, ultimately barring her from running."[3]

Thus, looks can be deceiving when it comes to government attempts at granting women's rights, freedoms, and empowerment in the MENA region. The irony is that these governments and patriarchal systems deny women their rights and freedoms at their own peril, in terms of the tremendous costs to the socioeconomic development and progress of their countries.

In addition, non-state actors, particularly violent extremist organizations (VEOs) like Al Qaeda, the Taliban, and the Islamic State (IS) and their affiliates, take misogyny to yet another level in the MENA region. They are known for attempting to render women wholly invisible from society, except when it comes to using them for their own selfish agendas, such as allowing women to serve as suicide attackers. In general, the VEOs strip women of any and all forms of agency.

What is "agency"? Nobel Laureate for Economics Amartya Sen emphasizes women's agency and social change in his book, *Development as Freedom*, in which he underlines the importance of the role of both women and men in serving as active agents of change, referring to them as, "The dynamic promoters of social transformation."[4] Dr. Sen links agency to women's well-being, saying that, "There is [also] an urgent and basic necessity, particularly at this time, to take an agent-oriented approach to the women's agenda."[5] According to Dr. Sen, the variables for women's well-being include: earning an independent income; employment outside of the home; ownership rights; literacy and education; and decision-making authority.[6]

The variables for women's well-being contribute directly to women's agency, which also promote empowerment and gender autonomy. All of these variables require *freedom*. Dr. Sen states a simple fact: "Freedom in one area…seems to help to foster freedom in others," and these factors facilitate what he calls "survival advantages," as opposed to "survival disadvantages."[7]

Lower fertility rates and infant mortality rates constitute examples of survival advantages. It is important to note that Dr. Sen's freedom-based theories of development are predicated on the "*removal of repressive states*," because a person cannot enjoy freedoms in a repressive society, no matter if it is secular or religious. Obviously, if authoritarian and violently repressive governments want their countries to develop socioeconomically in the modern era, then realistically such goals cannot be achieved without individual rights and freedoms, as embodied in personal agency. Therefore, patriarchal despotism persists at its own peril.

Everything pertains to the right to make personal choices, that is, the freedom for individuals to make personal choices in society. Dr. Sen explains the "real conflict" in traditional cultures and societies (as found pervasively in the MENA region), which "can impede freedoms of choice; they revolve around the following core issues and factors: (1) The basic value that the people must be allowed to decide freely what traditions they wish or not wish to follow; and, (2) the insistence that established traditions be followed (no matter what), or, alternatively, people must obey the decisions by religious or secular authorities who enforce traditions—real or imagined."[8] These traditional and conservative impediments to freedoms, gender equality, and rights are prominent in the MENA region, and they pose serious and, at times, even violent backlash against the region's feminist movements. Patriarchal despotism is violent by nature.

When discussing and analyzing feminism in the MENA region, it is important to consider that Islamic feminism exists along with secular feminism. Islamic feminism seeks gender parity strictly in the context of Islam, with the intention of preventing any conflict with, or violation of, Islamic laws and principles. Essentially, Islamic feminism is an attempt to reconcile feminism with the religion of Islam. Moreover, the inherent ideological competition between secular and Islamic feminists underlies the general feminist activism and struggles in the region.

Scholar Margot Badran describes Islamic feminism as deriving "its understanding and mandate from the Quran, seeks rights and justice for women, and for men, in the totality of their existence."[9] Hence, Islamic feminism is a *global* phenomenon, and it is even active in cyberspace: "Islamic feminism is being produced at diverse sites around the world by women inside their own countries, whether they be from countries with Muslim majorities or from old established minority communities. Islamic feminism is also growing in Muslim Diaspora and convert communities in the West. Islamic feminism is circulating with increasing frequency in cyberspace [...]."[10]

Islamic feminism is based on a *feminist hermeneutics*, that is, interpretation of scripture, which "renders compelling confirmation of gender equality in the Quran that was lost sight of as male interpreters constructed a corpus of *tafsir* (exegesis, or interpretation) promoting a doctrine of male superiority reflecting the mindset of the prevailing patriarchal cultures."[11]

However, Islamic feminism does not eliminate patriarchal despotism completely, and, in some cases, even reinforces it by insisting on including women in the role of exegesis but not challenging the preexisting male-dominated religious structures that remain in place. In addition, the male biases embedded in exegesis since the seventh century AD have persisted to the present. Uprooting these biases would be nearly impossible, especially since the object of discourse is linked to "Divine" attributes. Attempts at doing so would dilute the "Islamic" essence of Islamic feminism and also would promptly invite violent threats against the activists.

Secular feminist ideologies in the MENA region, for the most part, are inspired mainly by Western feminism. But, usually feminist ideals are applied to their own regional and cultural contexts outside of religious frameworks.

Finally, it is imperative to understand that feminism is a congruent ideology and principle of human rights. Gender equality does not seek the domination of one gender over another, but it demands that basic human rights be equally applied to both genders justly and judiciously. Patriarchal societies misconstrue feminism and gender equality as demands for female domination over men, which is not the case, and these misperceptions trigger insecurities within the patriarchies from the familial level all the way to the national level. Feminism and gender equality do not demand or seek domination over men. However, the empowerment of female agency allows women entry into jobs, educational institutions, and other domains that are likely to provoke male insecurities, especially in traditional and conservative patriarchal societies. Given these realities, pursuing women's empowerment in the MENA region is an extremely difficult and dangerous endeavor, but an indispensably vital one. Although observers thought that the 2011 Arab Awakening would be the gateway for women's empowerment, the results have been far from encouraging.

That said, Tunisia once again has served as a positive example of accommodating both secular and religious feminism as part of its sociopolitical national dialogue in the post-revolution period. Tunisian feminists have sustained their proactive and unrelenting activism during the political transitions following Ben Ali's ouster. Secular feminists have been particularly apprehensive due to Ennahda's entry into the political scene. However, Islamic feminists have also been highly active in Tunisia's social and political dialogues and discourses. These Tunisian feminist actors and institutions make an extremely interesting test case for analyzing and understanding the stakes, dynamics, agendas, methods, and determination of a significant segment of society that has embraced Tunisia's legacy of women's rights and has remained steadfastly committed to the preservation of its values, principles, and laws.

Tunisian Feminists: The Arab Awakening and Women's Rights

National Public Radio's (NPR's) correspondent Eleanor Beardsley reported on the ground in Tunis while the revolution was unfolding in late January 2011. According to Beardsley, "In Tunis, old ladies, young girls and women in black judges' robes marched down the streets demanding that the dictator leave. Hardly anyone wears the Muslim headscarf in the capital, and women seem to be everywhere, taking part in everything, alongside men."[12] She adds,

> Irgui Najet, 36, argues with a group of men on the sidewalk, defending the country's provisional leaders. She does more than hold her own. The men are so impressed with her knowledge, they tell her she should run for president. No one seems to think being a woman is a hindrance.

Najet, a criminal lawyer, explains the difference between Tunisian women and their sisters in the rest of the Arab world.

> 'We feel more free and more civilized than other Arab women,' she says. 'And especially since our revolution, we pity the women in neighboring countries. Look at Libya where they have to wear headscarves and can't even talk with men. This is a catastrophe.'[13]

Moreover, Tunisian women "have the same rights to divorce as men, and polygamy is illegal. Women [in Tunisia] have had access to birth control since 1962 and have had access to abortion since 1965—eight years before *Roe v. Wade* gave American women the same right. Tunisian women credit a 1956 civil rights code for their many freedoms and equality, as well as an excellent education system that is open to all."[14] Tunisian feminists give complete credit to Bourguiba, for, as Beardsley points out, "no one gives an ounce of credit to Ben Ali"[15] for women's rights and freedoms in Tunisia.

Tunisia has reserved 27.6 percent of the parliamentary seats for women, which is 58 women out of 217 seats, a considerably progressive percentage compared to other Arab countries.[16] Still, women in Tunisia have continued to protest and remain vigilant against potential policy changes that would infringe on women's rights. The Islamist Ennahda party has faced pressure from the Salafists calling for implementation of Islamic law on the one hand and from the secularists who demand secular liberal democracy ensuring rights and freedoms to all on the other hand. Tunisian activists were "not happy with a stipulation in a draft of the constitution that considers women to be 'complementary to men' and want a pioneering 1956 law that grant women full equality with men to remain in place."[17]

Thousands of protestors mobilized in Tunis when possible constitutional changes that would threaten gender equality seemed likely to pass during Ennahda's rule. One of the protesters said, "Normally, more important issues ought to be tackled like unemployment, regional development. Ennahda seems bent on making steps backwards but we are here to say that Tunisian women will not accept that. I fear for the future of my daughters who may grow up in a totally different Tunisia."[18] Ennahda representatives denied that the draft constitutional amendment would lead to misogynist and regressive policies for women. The chair of the assembly's human rights and public freedoms panel, Farida al-Obeidi, explains that the draft stipulates "sharing of roles and does not mean that women are worth less than men."[19] However, many Tunisians worried that passing the amendment would result in forthcoming policies and laws threatening gender equality and women's rights, which would be a significant reversal for human rights and feminism in Tunisia.[20] Activists have feared an agenda of greater Islamization on the horizon, especially when Ennahda was in power. The activists are determined not to give up or let up pressure to maintain women's rights and gender equality in Tunisia, which has been rooted in Tunisian society since the post-colonial era.

While Ennahda has claimed to be "moderate" in its Islamism, Tunisian politics still has powerful religious and secular constituencies, mainly the Salafists and secular activists on opposite ends of the ideological spectrum, who are locked in an ideological tug-of-war. Ennahda has been in the unenviable position of trying to balance between the two forces pulling it in diverse directions. In general, Tunisians are not extremists, nor can they be portrayed as wholly Salafist or ultra-orthodox in their religious ideology. In fact, in its own Islamic history, Tunisia has a legacy of Sufism, or Islamic mysticism, which has the reputation for great tolerance, openness, inclusiveness, and non-violent principles and values.

Tunisia's Islamic history and legacy, due to these ideological foundations, have embraced a tradition of reform, or reformism, especially in the education sector. Furthermore, this part of Tunisian history shows more openness to the West, particularly Europe, and Tunisia embraced constitutionalism at a very early stage in its political evolution.[21]

Tunisia's first president, Habib Bourguiba, "put reforms related to women and family law at the center of his agenda, although women's organizations did not play a real autonomous role in this discourse."[22] Bourguiba's reforms pertaining to women's rights is often referred to as "state feminism," or "institutional feminism," which "has been employed as a governmental tool for use in promoting gender equality and women's rights, with the objective of excluding alternative politics experienced by independent feminist activists. This has meant that those who advocated gender rights and women's empowerment in contrast with the government view had to pay a heavy price and were subjected to vigorous oppression."[23] According to scholar Giulia Daniele,

The feminist tradition in Tunisia is very deep-rooted.

Whilst on the one hand, such a kind of institutionalized feminism has been promoted, on the other hand, women activists had to struggle strongly against the dictatorship where any form of freedom was prohibited. These words demonstrate the way in which the Tunisian government made use of the advancement of women's rights merely as a strategy which could be deployed in order to become internationally accepted by Western countries. However, the relatively successful results obtained by independent women's and feminist movements must be kept in mind, starting with the earliest contributions made at the end of the 1980s when the Tahar Haddad Club was founded. This organization embraced critical debates on women's perspectives, with these ranging from topics such as the effect of Tunisian statutory legislation on women to the contribution of women in the labor force. Among their most significant initiatives, the launch of the women's feminist magazine *Nissa* in 1985 (although it was not published for long, and folded two years later in 1987) helped to enable women to confront diverse internal views and examine their desire for autonomy from institutions and parties, and, in a parallel way, from other forms of subjugation such as the cultural influences originating from within Western feminist thought.

From that time, two of the foremost women's organizations began to emerge. The *Association Tunisiennes des Femmes Démocrates* (ATFD) and the *Association des Femmes Tunisiennes pour la Recherche et le Développement* (AFTURD) were formed in 1982 and in 1986 respectively, although they did not become fully institutionalized until after President Bourguiba's departure. These groups worked together whilst retaining their individual focus, with the former pursuing an activist political agenda, and the latter being directed towards a more research-oriented perspective (Labidi 2007: 15–18). Referring to what the interviewees have stated whilst describing their political engageme nt, the majority of ATFD activists recognized themselves as feminists, by reflecting on the political methods they have used to pursue women's issues and to make these struggles effective. Among them, Souha Ben Othman, one of the leading ATFD activists, stressed her feminist identity thus: I am a feminist and I cannot deny it in my everyday political activism. I cannot take out my feminist identity since it is part of me. For me 'feminism' means women should occupy the same position in society in comparison with men. Women should have same rights as well as same obligations, without any kind of discriminations. Feminism means protecting women regardless of their social background, political identity, position. Women and men are equal in all sectors.[24]

Politics shamelessly exploits women's issues globally, but that especially rings true in the MENA region, and Tunisia is not the exception, though it has yielded more lasting impacts on women's rights and freedoms than in other places in the Arab and Muslim world. Daniele, quoting feminist Ilham Marzouki, warns that "The current women's associations, set up on such a difficult ground, have not realized that what is at stake could represent the re-establishment of a just balance since their elite formations have turned more towards a political partnership, rather than a social mobilization."[25]

> Despite their strong cohesion during the earliest phases of the uprising, just a few months after Ben Ali's downfall some divergences based on the differences listed in the previous sentence have progressively emerged. Contrasting such internal divisions can be crucial to overcoming the misleading dichotomy between modernity, Islam and tradition in order to understand in depth the transitional process in which all Tunisian women are involved. Women's rights have become the core issue at the center of the agenda for an egalitarian society both at grassroots and institutional level, but it is also necessary to take account of the emerging political role of Islamic women's organizations.[26]

These political conundrums are not unprecedented, since even historically Tunisians have endured the pressures of choosing between secularism—albeit that has been enforced under Bourguiba and Ben Ali—and Islam, *shari'a* (Islamic law) versus secular laws and civil codes, and the overall regional traditional culture of being more receptive to political legitimacy through ties with religious establishments.[27] Even within the body of Islamic scholars, the *'ulama*, they have been torn between the schools of law and interpretative methodologies encompassing *taqlid* (described as "blind imitation") and *ijtihad* (reinterpretation with more flexibility).[28] Although those espousing ijtihad have been in the minority, they have tended to wield more influence because of close ties to the political elites. Hence, Tunisia's Islamism has moderate, if not more flexible, origins in interpretative methodologies. These variables are likely to account for modern Tunisia's accommodations of feminism, secularism, and "moderate" Islamism, and especially the ideological and activist competition between secular and Islamic feminists.

> Resulting from experiences of violence, discriminations and arrests, an example of this kind of Islamic activism is embodied by the Tunisian Women

Association, which is based in Tunis and was established just after the revolution in April 2011 with the purpose of improving women's knowledge (especially those women who live in situations of socio-economic adversity such as poverty, illness, divorce and prison) by making them aware of their effective roles in the development of their society.

As the president of this association, Ibtihal Abdellatif, and the general secretary, Mounira Ben Kaddour, explained: 'We are Tunisian women, we define ourselves as Tunisian activists. At the same time, we are Muslim. We do not like the term 'Islamist', since it has been used in disparaging ways and often linked to the 'terrorist' one. We are struggling for all Tunisians, women and men. We are dealing in particular with women ex-prisoners who were oppressed by the previous regime and who suffered both mental and physical tortures. Today we are working on more than 400 political prisoners' dossiers [...] In many cases, other women's and feminist organizations did not want to know the reality of what Tunisian Muslim women had to suffer during their struggles against the regimes of Bourguiba and Ben Ali.[29]

Islamist women have been successful in post-2011 revolution politics in Tunisia, wherein "women Islamists played a leading role in the country's democratic transition: 42 out of the 49 women elected to the 2011 National Constituent Assembly that later drafted Tunisia's post-revolution constitution were from the Islamist Ennahda party."[30] In addition, these Islamic feminists "reached across the aisle to secular and leftist feminists to pass a bill requiring gender parity in national elections, mandating that half of parties' candidates be women. In 2016, they teamed up again to pass a second bill requiring an equal number of men and women on the ballot in municipal elections."[31] One of the most prominent Islamic feminists in Tunisian politics is Meherzia Labidi, who leads the committee on women and family in parliament. In 2014, she "played a key role in drafting Article 46, a constitutional article guaranteeing gender equality, equal rights, protection against gender-based violence, and gender parity in all elected bodies. It was a watershed for Arab women's rights."[32] According to Ms. Labidi,

'Men and women have equal rights in Islam, it is the men's interpretation of the religion that has led us astray,' (Ms. Labidi told *The Christian Science Monitor* in an interview from her office in Tunis). The revolution was a chance, she and others say, to prove that women's rights are not exclusive to secular Western feminism.

'Why am I obliged to only seek empowerment from outside my religion?' Labidi asked. 'Instead, I want to re-appropriate my religion and re-empower myself and other women who are empowered by Islam.'[33]

In July 2017, I met with Ennahda's Meherzia Labidi, the first woman vice president of Tunisia's Constituent Assembly, and she is considered the Arab world's highest-ranking elected female official in modern history. She is proud of placing women's issues on the political agendas following the 2011 revolution. Ms. Labidi has suggested "creating a united working group between Islamic and secular women, [as] such an idea has never been applied to the current reality."[34]

Ms. Labidi began the interview, sitting in the noisy lobby of the Tunisian parliament, by pointing out that Tunisia, like Turkey, has the most advanced status of women among Muslim countries. Since independence, Tunisia's Personal Status Code forbids polygamy, forbids forced marriages, establishes the minimum age for marriage at 18, and allows adoption; hence, it is really very advanced compared to most other Muslim countries. She adds, "Yet, we still have some issues to solve, for example, all Tunisian women do not have access to the same laws, they need to know their rights and claim them; they lag due to social, economic, or educational factors"[35] (Fig. 3.1).

Ms. Labidi explains, "Some in the rural areas never heard about their rights. So, we have to guarantee more rights for women [everywhere]."[36] During the revolution, "women stood shoulder-to-shoulder with men; and after the revolution, we promoted laws for new visibility of women in politics."[37] The new activism did not come without risks. "With this explosion of liberties, there is a great deal of fear for women. For example, the religiosity linked to Salafism, the wearing of black gowns, and you have [the terrorist group] Ansar al-Sharia, so many Tunisian women feared for their lives."[38] However, Ms. Labidi ended on a positive note, saying, "But there is a lot of hope to go further in Tunisian women's rights."[39]

Both secular and Islamic feminists' efforts have borne fruit. President Beji Caid Essebsi helped pass laws granting gender equality in inheritance rights, and he also "lifted a ban on Muslim women in Tunisia marrying men outside their faith. In most Muslim-majority countries, Muslim men can marry Jewish or Christian women, but Muslim women can marry only Muslim men."[40]

These measures have rankled the Islamic establishment and Islamists in society throughout the MENA region, even provoking Al Azhar

Fig. 3.1 Photo of Meherzia Labidi. (Source: Author)

University's scholars to chime in, saying that "equitable distribution of inheritance was 'undebatable,' 'contradicted Islamic edicts,' and that regulation of inheritance in Islam was determined by Shari'a, with 'no space for independent reasoning or uncertainty.' Those same scholars warned that allowing women to marry outside of their faith would 'obstruct the stability of marriage'."[41] Al Azhar University in Cairo, Egypt, is the highest Sunni global clerical authority in Islam. Therefore, in the political sphere, it seems that embracing women's empowerment and agency, or denying them, result in social controversies in the MENA region, and also internally within respective countries' domestic arenas. As Mona Eltahawy eloquently explains,

> Some have criticized the Tunisian president's progressive stance as 'state-imposed feminism.' Opponents have accused Essebsi of using women's rights as a 'political football' to distract from other issues (namely a controversial law granting amnesty to corrupt former officials under previous regimes). Others say he is just trying to secure women's votes for upcoming local elections in March. Is that a bad thing—to court women's votes by removing obstacles to their equality?

In the same way that it sparked revolutions against dictators in other countries, Tunisia is leading the way for women's rights in the region. Post-revolution, it made gender parity on electoral lists mandatory and now has the most progressive constitution among countries in its neighborhood.

Whenever opponents of women's equality use the 'state-imposed feminism' or 'distraction' card against gains for women's rights, they fail to see that Tunisia's parliament, where women make up a third of lawmakers—higher than in the United States, Canada and Britain—passed a sweeping domestic violence law last year that serves to protect women from sexual harassment and economic discrimination. The law also ended a loophole in the penal code that allowed rapists to escape punishment if they agreed to marry their victims. Soon after, Jordan and Lebanon also closed similar loopholes. Morocco ended its 'marry your rapist law' in 2014 following the suicide of a 16-year-old girl and the attempted suicide of a 15-year-old, both of whom were forced to marry their rapists. In all three countries, women's rights activists had long campaigned to abolish 'marry your rapist' laws.

Tunisia's moves to give women equal marriage and inheritance rights are revolutionary not just for women in that country but also for Muslim women *everywhere*. This is how a revolution that began against the dictator in the presidential palace can evolve into revolutions against the dictators women face in the street and the dictators women face at home. Tunisia's moves to afford women equality in marriage and inheritance are important steps in dismantling the trifecta of misogyny across our region.[42]

In Egypt, Libya, Syria, Iraq, Iran, and the Gulf Arab states, women's empowerment is still extremely lagging. For example, in Egypt, the custom of female genital mutilation (FGM), which is not an exclusively Muslim practice and dates back to the Pharaonic era, is still prevalent, despite government and non-governmental organizations' efforts to eliminate it. The UN Children's Fund conducted a survey in 2016, which found that "87 percent of women and girls aged 15–49 in Egypt have undergone the 'procedure'. According to the World Health Organization, more than 200 million girls and women have been cut in 30 countries in Africa, the Middle East, and Asia."[43] In addition, women continue to suffer from domestic violence, the so-called honor killings, sexual crimes, lack of due process in courts, and harassment and discrimination in employment, education, and other domains in the MENA region. Patriarchal despotism continues to thrive in the region.

Conclusion

Tunisia continues to lead the way in bottom-up and top-down secular and Islamic feminist activism, and it should also be considered the regional trailblazer as a proponent for women's rights, freedoms, agency, and empowerment. The secular and Islamic feminists in Tunisia have engaged in crucial national and local negotiations and agreements to find common objectives and collectively act on achieving them. Theirs has been a fairly successful endeavor, and because they have embraced dialogue and negotiations, they represent an important thread and cross-section within the national political system of post-revolution Tunisia, which has strived to maintain non-violent dialogue between diverse political parties.

The MENA region has a lot to learn from Tunisia's example, but patriarchal despotism and misogynist systems prevailing throughout the countries persist in repressing feminism. They have help in this endeavor from the various violent extremist organizations (VEOs) proliferating throughout the region. The good news is that, despite these formidable obstacles and ominous threats, the feminist activists in the MENA region are not deterred.

In my 2015 article about "Women's Rights Movements in the 'Arab Spring'," in the *Journal of International Women's Studies (IJWS)*, I close with these words, which still profoundly resonate in the MENA region today:

> The marginalization of the women's rights movement does not mean it is dead or it has surrendered to the forces that be, but it does require women's rights activists to maintain pressures on the newly formed governments. The resounding message to these governments is that women who participated in the Arab Awakening are not exploitable, nor are they forgettable. Their sacrifices and activism that helped empower these new governments serve as the mirror in the politicians' faces. The latter ignore this mirror at their own risk, and at the same time jeopardize the socioeconomic progress of their respective country.[44]

Tunisia's commitment to women's rights and empowerment is a testament to its political wisdom and health, and bodes well for the future, presupposing that those in power do not waver from its shining example and path of national dialogue and non-violent transitions. The next chapter examines Tunisia's political health, as part of the political-economy equation.

Notes

1. See “Egypt: A Year after ‘Virginity Tests’, Women Victims of Army Violence Still Seek Justice,” *Amnesty International*, March 9, 2012: https://www.amnesty.org/en/latest/news/2012/03/egypt-year-after-virginity-tests-women-victims-army-violence-still-seek-justice/
2. “Prominent Saudi Women Activists Arrested,” *Human Rights Watch (HRW)*, August 1, 2018: https://www.hrw.org/news/2018/08/01/prominent-saudi-women-activists-arrested
3. Ibid.
4. Hayat Alvi, “Women’s Rights Movements in the ‘Arab Spring’: Major Victories or Failures for Human Rights?” *Journal of International Women’s Studies (JIWS)*, volume 16, issue 3, July 2015: https://vc.bridgew.edu/cgi/viewcontent.cgi?referer=https://www.google.com/&httpsredir=1&article=1828&context=jiws, p. 298.
5. Ibid.
6. Ibid.
7. Ibid.
8. Ibid.
9. Margot Badran, “Islamic Feminism: What’s in a Name?” *Al-Ahram Weekly*, 17–23 January 2002: http://weekly.ahram.org.eg/2002/569/cu1.htm
10. Ibid.
11. Ibid.
12. Eleanor Beardsley, “In Tunisia, Women Play Equal Role in Revolution,” *National Public Radio (NPR)*, January 27, 2011: https://www.npr.org/2011/01/27/133248219/in-tunisia-women-play-equal-role-in-revolution
13. Ibid.
14. Ibid.
15. Ibid.
16. “Women in National Parliaments,” June 30, 2012: http://www.ipu.org/wmn-e/classif.htm
17. Tarek Amara, “Thousands Rally in Tunisia for Women’s Rights,” *Reuters*, August 14, 2012: http://af.reuters.com/article/worldNews/idAFBRE87C16320120814
18. Ibid.
19. Ibid.
20. Ibid.
21. For more details about Tunisia’s Islamic history, see Anne Wolf, *Political Islam in Tunisia: The History of Ennahda* (London: Hurst and Company, 2017).

22. Giulia Daniele, "Tunisian Women's Activism after the January 14 Revolution: Looking within and towards the Other Side of the Mediterranean," *Journal of International Women's Studies (JIWS)*, volume 15, issue 2, July 2014: https://vc.bridgew.edu/cgi/viewcontent.cgi?referer=https://www.google.com/&httpsredir=1&article=1750&context=jiws, p. 18.
23. Ibid., pp. 18–19.
24. Ibid., pp. 19–20.
25. Ibid., p. 20.
26. Ibid., p. 29.
27. See Anne Wolf, *Political Islam in Tunisia: The History of Ennahda* (London: Hurst and Company, 2017), pp. 15–16.
28. Wolf, pp. 15–16.
29. Daniele, p. 25.
30. Taylor Luck, "Islamist and Feminist: A New Generation Stakes Its Claim," *The Christian Science Monitor (CSM)*, June 18, 2018: https://www.csmonitor.com/World/Middle-East/2018/0618/Islamist-and-feminist-A-new-generation-stakes-its-claim
31. Ibid.
32. Ibid.
33. Ibid.
34. Daniele, p. 29.
35. Interview with Meherzia Labidi, Tunisian Parliament, Bardo, Tunis, July 18, 2017.
36. Ibid.
37. Ibid.
38. Ibid.
39. Ibid.
40. Mona Eltahawy, "Seven Years after the 'Arab Spring,' Tunisia is Leading in Another Revolution – on Women's Rights," *The Washington Post*, January 31, 2018: https://www.washingtonpost.com/news/global-opinions/wp/2018/01/31/seven-years-after-the-arab-spring-tunisia-is-leading-another-revolution-on-womens-rights/?noredirect=on&utm_term=.7062213b5ccf
41. Ibid.
42. Ibid. Emphasis added.
43. Hayam Adel, "Egypt Struggles to End Female Genital Mutilation," *Reuters*, March 8, 2018: https://www.reuters.com/article/us-womens-day-egypt/egypt-struggles-to-end-female-genital-mutilation-idUSKCN1GK1ZL
44. Alvi, "Women's Rights Movements in the 'Arab Spring': Major Victories or Failures for Human Rights?" p. 315.

CHAPTER 4

Tunisia's Political Health

In political economy, politics and economics are interdependent. This chapter examines the political side of the political economy–interdependence equation. The main focus is on Tunisia's political health and processes following the 2011 Jasmine Revolution. Some aspects of the other regional actors' politics are brought into the analysis where relevant for comparative purposes.

The essence of Tunisia's post-revolution political process is democratic evolution; to describe it more aptly, ***evolution after revolution***. After the 2011 revolution expelled Ben Ali, the political processes for the evolving democracy have involved difficult negotiations among disputing parties, groups, and civil society; the challenging process of preparing the country for the *first ever* democratic elections; the seemingly impossible task of organizing a committee to revise the constitution; and all the while maintaining stability and security in the country during the most fragile and vulnerable stages of its post-revolution reformation, transitions, and political development.

Tunisians Demand Dignity

When it comes to the demands for dignity, Tunisia has seen some glitches in applying the rule of law, human rights, and in providing jobs, especially for the educated youth, who served as the primary actors in the Jasmine

H. Alvi, *The Political Economy and Islam of the Middle East*, Political Economy of Islam,
https://doi.org/10.1007/978-3-030-17050-9_4

Revolution. The previous regime's elements lingering in the country's political orbit continue to threaten setting up roadblocks in democratic and political development, in the guise of staving off the Islamists' political empowerment. In terms of the economy, checks on corruption, which has been a rampant, overwhelming problem during the Ben Ali dictatorship, have hit some bumps in the road as well. However, overall, Tunisia's political economy, sustainability of the revolution's progress, and its multisector *post-revolution evolution* have fared better than in Libya, Egypt, Yemen, Bahrain, and Syria.

Under Ben Ali's rule, indefinite detention and torture were common practices. In post-2011 revolution Tunisia, the horror stories of people who suffered the Ben Ali regime's torture and brutality have been reported to the Truth and Dignity Commission, which was set up "by the country's constitution-drafting body in 2013, [and] has already compiled more than 62,000 complaints and testimonies from victims of the regime of autocrat Zine al-Abidine Ben Ali."[1] Though the commission may be far from perfect, it signifies the first and only one of its kind in the MENA region, addressing some of the worst human rights abuses under autocratic rule. That in and of itself is a milestone for the entire Arab world. No other country in the MENA has set up such a commission.

In the end, Ben Ali and his wife, Leila Trabelsi, and practically her entire clan crossed the line with their overt corruption, abuses of power, and his inability and unwillingness to meet the basic needs of an increasingly discontented population (i.e., fulfilling the social contract), with a growing educated youth that faced dire unemployment and adversity. The Ben Ali regime failed miserably in the areas of human development, and especially equitable economic progress and wealth distribution, due to the regime's incessant greed.

Denying freedoms and rights, restricting the political process, ruling with violent authoritarianism, and embezzling the masses are all formulas for arresting socioeconomic development. These are descriptions of Ben Ali's legacy, which remain in Tunisians' collective memories.

Tunisia's post-revolution political transitions can be summarized with these chronological descriptive phrases:

- From dictatorship to democracy
- First democratic elections held, with Ennahda coming to power
- National dialogue—that involves civil society and unions
- Constitutional reforms

- Democratic gradualism
- Ennahda steps down
- Renegotiations among political groups
- Secular and religious coalition established

Despite the daunting challenges that Tunisia has faced in its post-revolution transitional period, the results have been impressive and admirable, especially when compared to the other countries in the Middle East and North Africa that have experienced similar Arab Awakening uprisings and revolutions. For Tunisia, its top national priority has been to prevent the country's collapse into violent chaos and conflict. Tunisians witnessed the bloody chaos gripping its neighbor, Libya, and violent turmoil in Egypt, and they became resolutely determined not to allow these dangerous pitfalls to take down Tunisia, the birthplace of the 2011 Arab Awakening. Tunisia's "success story" could not have happened without the prominent role that Ennahda and the civil society have played following the 2011 revolution.

Evolution after Tunisia's revolution has involved individuals, institutions, and organizations that overcame significant challenges to stabilize the country and secure it on a path toward liberal democracy. The collective goals of all the actors focused on the country's political, economic, and physical stability and security. Notwithstanding the internal differences and disagreements among them, the new political actors on the revolutionary stage hammered out deals and agreements and built consensus. They had to identify and agree on common goals and the ways and means to achieve them. Specifically, all of them could agree on one thing: Tunisia's post-revolution evolution in political economy terms must be successful for the country's future. At the same time, each actor has been compelled to ask, "what does the revolution mean for us/me?"

Evolution and Transitions in Post-2011 Revolution Tunisia

The 2011 Jasmine Revolution took everyone by surprise. For the political actors, both new and old, this meant that institutions, organizations, and individuals had to scramble to make sense of what was happening upon Ben Ali's departure. Simultaneously, these actors had to build consensus within their own groups and organizations, as well as negotiate with each other, that is, a diverse array of secular and religious civil society and non-governmental organizations vying for political empowerment in a new climate of pluralism.

The public sentiments toward newfound freedoms, rights, and political liberalization spanned ideologies across the spectrum. Therefore, previously repressed interest groups had to make significant adjustments to meet public demands for sustainable dignity, rule of law, freedoms, and rights. These groups also had to ensure the public that the ideologies they represent will embrace and fulfill these demands. Some organizations actually had to redefine and reinvent themselves. This was especially true for Ennahda due to its "Islamist" character.

Ennahda's Darwinism

Ennahda was one of many organizations caught in the fog and whirlwind of post-revolution political scrambling. Within Ennahda the senior leadership often found itself at odds with the youth in terms of missions, goals, visions, strategies, and methods for the way ahead. Even among high-ranking Ennahda members the question about the organization's essence took center stage. Many disagreements led to some members quitting, but given the organization's decentralized structure, it was able to maintain its operations particularly at the grassroots level.

The main problems that Ennahda has faced concern the consistency of its Islamic nature while openly pursuing political participation in an arena in which secularism has been predominant. Ennahda's leadership found itself at a crossroads, which imposed pressures for reconciling these internal tensions. Ennahda's insider critics opposed its new focus on "politicization," as they viewed it as a departure from its real purpose of *da'wa* (preaching) in order to eventually "Islamize" society. Not only was Ennahda contending with these inner rumblings, but it also had to avoid the woeful errors and pitfalls of the MENA region's Islamist organizations, like the Egyptian Muslim Brotherhood, as Tunisia's political system rebuilt itself. Even semantics and identity politics came into play at this critical juncture immediately following the Jasmine Revolution. Instead of calling Ennahda an "Islamist" organization, Rachid al-Ghannouchi eventually proposed the idea that it should instead be considered an organization of "Muslim democrats." Suddenly, Ennahda was competing against a long list of political parties and entities, and given the country's secular legacy, and the fact that Ennahda had to operate underground during the dictatorship, its new post-revolution decisions and strategies were to take place in a delicate transitional context. For decades, the public had been persuaded to harbor deep suspicion of religious entities trying to enter politics. Ennahda had to shatter the negative myths and overcome these suspicions, and, at the same time, internally the organization had to reconcile differences of opinion and ideological views and maintain stability.

Despite these overwhelming challenges, Ennahda has emerged bruised but not broken. Rory McCarthy describes Ennahda's abilities to adapt to the drastically changing environment in post-revolution Tunisia: "The case of Ennahda demonstrates how an Islamist organization makes strategic and intellectual adaptations as its surrounding political and social environment changes. These adaptations show flexibility, but they are limited by dense networks of belonging and they incur costs, particularly to the stability of the organization and the coherence of its vision."[2] The change in semantics and reinvention of Ennahda's identity as "Muslim democrats" have allowed for a degree of ambiguity in the metamorphized organization in an attempt to sanitize its stigma as a tool of political Islam. The ambiguity has, in turn, allowed for flexibility within the organization to adapt itself from a violently repressed underground preaching network, to a rebranded post-revolution sophisticated pro-democracy organization participating in politics and claiming to embrace freedoms, rights, and the rule of law.

Furthermore, this ambiguity "resisted those efforts to categorize Islamist movements by their attitude to the state, in which statists are seen as having ambitions to acquire state power, while non-statists either avoid politics or have a vision of a community not bound to the modern nation state."[3] McCarthy emphasizes that "the logic behind the organization's structural ambiguity would be to consider the movement of the 1980s as reflecting not some transnational Muslim Brotherhood organizational model, but rather the mirror image of the structure of Tunisia's own ruling party."[4] According to McCarthy, this is referred to as "unconscious imitation," as the Islamists "built a movement with branch organizations across the country, centralized around a president, and reaching into social sectors that in many ways mimicked the ruling party of Bourguiba and Ben Ali."[5]

Perhaps, this would be the only way for Ennahda to enter post-revolution Tunisian politics and empower itself institutionally. This venture has required Ennahda to dilute its "Islamicity" as a "political Islam," or "Islamist" organization. This dilution has been particularly required in Tunisia because of its secular legacy since the end of colonialism.

Moreover, as part of Ennahda's public relations strategy, "an evolving vocabulary accompanied the conceptual shift."[6] Following the 2011 Jasmine Revolution, Ghannouchi

> described Ennahda as no longer as Islamist but rather 'civil party with an Islamic reference'. Others talked of a 'national party that is the heir to a movement of religious, political, and social reform'. By 2016, Ghannouchi and others were using the broad term 'Muslim democrats'. They positioned themselves as the antithesis of violent Islamic groups who threatened Tunisian security, a framing that recalled how movement leaders had previously tried to offer themselves as a bulwark against violent Salafists in the late 2000s. The movement insisted its intellectual shift did not mean the 'secularization' of Ennahda, though that was precisely what some Nahdawis feared. The Islamic reference would remain in the political project, but it was now defined through Ennahda's '*maqasidi* understanding of the Islamic reference', referring to the idea of the broader objectives of the shari'a (*maqasid al-shari'a*). Ennahda defined the Islamic reference in the most general terms. It was a 'program of reform' (*manhaj li-l-islah*) and a 'guiding force' (*quwwa tawjihiyya*), but one that was still linked to the holy texts through a revivalist reading (*qira'a tajdidiyya wa ijtihadiyya*) of the Quran and Sunna.[7]

This reconceptualization has come to be known as "post-Islamism," which entails recasting "the role of Islam and [asserting] a cultural Islamic identity in its discourse."[8] Sociologist Asef Bayat "notes that the post-Islamist turn remains largely untested in relation to minority rights, gender rights, and freedom of thought, religion, and lifestyle."[9] Following Ben Ali's ouster in 2011, Ennahda has engaged in "rethinking, testing, and refining."[10] However, Ennahda "had yet to convince the rest of the Tunisian political elite and electorate of the sincerity of its strategic adaptation."[11] As a result, Ennahda's leadership decided that the best way forward was to separate its political ambitions from its preaching mission. The organizational separation "of the political and preaching projects in 2016 was the culmination of many years of internal debate and disagreements, dating back to well before the democratic transition. It was the latest effort at adaptation: a structural decision to allay the criticisms of political rivals and to reimagine what it meant to draw on an Islamic reference for a political project."[12]

Ennahda has performed a remarkable political act by making dramatic structural and ideological adjustments to the changing realities on the ground. Ennahda has been refining the clarity of its course of action and strategy as adjustments have been made. In redefining "Islamism" within Ennahda's Tunisian contexts, it has incorporated concepts of democracy, statism, pluralism, and collective identity. Additionally, Ennahda, unlike its numerous Islamist counterparts throughout the region, has had to forego the ideal of establishing a post-revolution Islamic "utopia" in the country complete with the implementation of the shari'a.

Yet, Ennahda's greatest move was its decision in early 2014 to step down from political power in order to prevent a breakdown of stability and security as had transpired in Egypt. The Ennahda Prime Minister Ali Larayedh resigned "to make way for a caretaker government in an agreement with secular opponents to complete the country's transition to democracy."[13] This has been seen as an act of selflessness, which is extraordinary for an Islamist movement in the modern era. This gesture is unprecedented, especially in the MENA region. In addition, Ennahda illustrated integrity by negotiating with its secular counterparts, including the civil society. Tunisia's civil society has played a significant role in this transitional process, and its importance cannot be emphasized enough.

Tunisia's Civil Society and Institutions

The role of civil society has always been important in Tunisia. If it had not been for the civil society, the 2010–2011 protest movements would not have emerged and succeeded. Wafa Ben-Hassine reports in *The Atlantic Council* that Tunisia has seen more than 11,000 civil society organizations (CSO) sprout following the 2011 revolution.[14] These organizations

> work on everything from governance and accountability in the public sector, such as Al Bawsala, to protecting minority rights, such as Mnemty. Luckily, and unlike the government, these organizations exist all over the country too. I-Watch, another CSO, works to combat corruption in all four corners of Tunisia, and has several offices throughout the country. As protests break out to address economic woes, it's important to remember that the development and evolution of CSOs in Tunisia since the 2011 revolution continues to play a vital role in the democratization of the state and represents a foundational pillar in Tunisian society.

The impact of civil society is hard-hitting as it is effective, too. The government listens—most of the time. For instance, when the government of the United Arab Emirates issued a blanket entry ban on all female Tunisian nationals in early January, civil society groups did not hold back. The government came under severe pressure and ultimately responded by banning Emirates Airlines from landing on Tunisian territory. Another example is human rights groups publicly calling out forced rectal examinations that prosecute the homosexual community. The government formally accepted a recommendation at the UN Human Rights Council last September to ban the abusive practice in Tunisia.

The most important example is the Tunisian National Dialogue Quartet, a group of four civil society groups that were instrumental in pulling the country through the political crisis of 2013 by building consensus across political groups. The quartet effectively paved the way for a peaceful transition by bringing groups together to draft a new constitution and start planning reforms. The group received the 2015 Nobel Peace Prize in recognition of its efforts.[15]

Safwan Masri extols the virtues of Tunisia's civil society. He says, "Well educated and exposed to values of human rights and democracy, Tunisians proved predisposed to change and adept at bringing it about. The involvement of civil society, most notably UGTT (Tunisian General Labor Union, *Union Générale Tunisienne du Travail)*, took the anger behind the early protests and channeled it into organized action, helping the protests spread throughout the country and across all strata of society, in a way that was sure to generate mass participation that could not be ignored."[16] Robin Wright in her book *Rock the Casbah*, along with Safwan Masri, add that the arts, including songs by rap artists, and social media also served as "powerful tools that gave substantive, symbolic, and organizational force to the revolution."[17] In addition, Masri emphasizes that, "the Tunisian labor union movement has always been intricately intertwined with the country's intellectual development."[18] However, by late 2017, the Tunisian government claimed that it found "financial irregularities" in hundreds of organizations and even accused some of funding terrorism; hence, "the government dissolved over 198 organizations and delivered 947 notices to others."[19] This is precarious for the country because

[…] Tunisia would not be where it is today had it not been for civil society work and vigilance. It is thanks to a strong and vibrant civil society of associations, labor unions, political parties, and other non-profit organizations that the country emerged out of the 2010–11 revolution in stable condition.

> These groups reconnected the relationship between citizens, the state, and society in a transitional period, supporting political settlements and reducing the potential for renewed conflict. As such, the *role of civil society in Tunisia cannot be understated*. Stifling its expression by arresting and detaining demonstrators only works to hinder—if not arrest—the country's democratic transition.[20]

In particular, the UGTT has a long history dating back to the 1940s. The UGTT along with the Tunisian Confederation of Industry, the Tunisian Human Rights League, and the Tunisian Order of Lawyers (i.e., "The National Dialogue Quartet"), facilitated the post-2011 political dialogue between parties and politicians. Tunisia's Trade and Handicrafts industry also played a significant role in this process. For its role in keeping the peace, the National Dialogue Quartet received the 2015 Nobel Peace Prize. The UGTT and its cohorts are recognized as the key arbiters for contributing to formulating Tunisia's democracy, and doing so peacefully.

According to *The Economist*, "The UGTT has played an outsize role in Tunisian politics since it was established in 1946. It participated in the struggle for independence in the 1950s. (French colonialists killed its founder) The autocrats who ruled Tunisia for the next 54 years occasionally persecuted trade unionists, but the UGTT remained influential, using strikes to win better working conditions."[21] But, some contend that the UGTT is also at the heart of Tunisia's economic problems.

> One of the biggest drags on growth is the bloated bureaucracy. Under pressure from the UGTT, the state went on a hiring spree after the revolution, adding tens of thousands of pen-pushers. Around 800,000 Tunisians now work for the government, out of a workforce of 4 million. Public wages eat up almost 14% of GDP, among the highest percentages in the world.
>
> The UGTT has fought against attempts to cut government spending. It calls privatization a 'red line'. And it often cripples the country with strikes and protests. Indeed, it called for the anti-government demonstrations in 2013. In 2016 it closed the postal service for days to protest against the treatment of a single worker. Threats of a walkout last December forced the government to drop plans for a public-sector pay freeze in 2017.
>
> The unions are particularly strong in Tunisia's interior. That has harmed the region. [...] After the revolution, unions called strikes and demanded more jobs. So the plant hired 2,500 new workers over the next three years, increasing the workforce by 51%. But the strikes continued and production fell from 8m tons in 2010 to just 3.3m in 2013. The industry has yet to recover.[22]

The government is accused of neglecting the more impoverished interior of the country, which has led to desperation. Noureddine Taboubi of the UGTT is quoted as saying, "We've become an exporter of terrorism."[23] According to the *Economist*, approximately 6000 Tunisians "joined the Islamic State, more than from any other country. Many of them come from the same poor areas that rose up against Mr. Ben Ali."[24] (Map. 4.1)

If the country's sub-regional economic disparities remain pervasive, they will be detrimental to its future. Tunisia's political leaders must make employment and economic equality domestic priorities, which are topics analyzed in Chap. 5. Overall, Tunisia's political economy in the post–Arab Awakening era is still evolving, albeit gradually. The economic gradualism often affects political stability because the Tunisian people desperately need improvements in employment and wealth distribution. If the politicians fail to deliver on these economic priorities, then the country is likely to experience domestic turmoil. No one wants that to happen, which makes all of the stakeholders determined to engage in negotiations and peaceful transitions in politics, rather than precipitating the country into violent chaos. Clearly, Tunisia's civil society has played one of the most important roles in securing the country's political stability. This has been recognized and praised globally.

The Current Evolutionary Stages and Status

I visited the Tunisian Parliament in July 2017. It is buzzing with activity, as members of different parties run up and down the corridors preparing to cast votes when in session. Some meet with members of the public to hear their grievances, cases, and issues. The scene almost resembles a courthouse with attorneys meeting with clients; people bring deeds to their homes, or police records, or photographs and other materials to show individual members of Parliament (MPs). While all this takes place inside, occasionally groups of protestors shout slogans for their causes at the Parliament gates outside. This would have been unheard of during the dictator Zine al-Abidine Ben Ali's era (Fig. 4.1).

The tolerance shown to public protesting is evidence of Tunisia opening up, liberalizing its social and political policies to embrace a post-revolution spirit of freedoms, rights, and dignity. The political process that takes place behind closed doors also exhibits tolerance and a spirit of discussion and negotiation. The process is not without challenges and has

Map 4.1 Map of Tunisia. (Source: University of Texas Library produced by the US Central Intelligence Agency)

Fig. 4.1 Photo of Tunisia's Parliament. (Source: Photo taken by author)

plenty of imperfections. But, the push toward dialogue and negotiations is a collective, pluralist, and holistic effort, because the alternative is unthinkable for Tunisia. Tunisians cannot afford to suffer a counter-revolution like the one in Egypt; nor can they bear the thought of a bloody civil conflict like in Libya, Syria, and Yemen. Hence, Tunisians have opted for a pragmatic approach to politics, one that encompasses political dialogue and negotiations, and commitments to preserving the country's overall political health, despite painful deliberations, gradualism, and difficulties in overcoming stalemates. Democracy is also the pragmatic means for achieving political goals. Both secularists and Islamists have taken the democratic electoral route toward promoting their respective platforms and agendas. Tunisia has always stood out as unique in the Arab world.

Upon independence, Tunisia took a historic path toward secularism, women's rights, and openness toward the West that has been unusual for the modern history of the Arab states in the Middle East and North Africa (MENA) region. The political leadership's decision to take this path is one of the reasons why Tunisia has stood out as "unique" compared to the rest, and it has appeared to follow the Mustafa Kemal Ataturk model in postwar Turkey. It has been a path toward modernization that embodies secularism, women's empowerment, and nationalism.

In fact, something quite remarkable has happened in Tunis. In early July 2018, the public selected its first woman mayor of Tunis, and Souad Abderrahim actually represents the Islamist Ennahda party, although she ran as an independent. Not only is this a paradox of sorts, but it is the only example of its kind in the Middle East and North Africa (MENA) region, where, with the exception of Turkey and Israel, no country has had a female head of state, nor has any country voted for a female mayor, and that too of the country's capital, no less. Ms. Abderrahim won against a former Ben Ali official, and she is described as follows: "The 53-year-old manager of a pharmaceutical firm, known for her pant suits and blow-drys, has risen to the fore as one of the new faces of veteran Islamist party Ennahda as it seeks to modernize its image."[25] Her victory comes from a second referendum of voting which the centrist and left-wing parties boycotted, because they did not want to support anyone representing either of the two main political parties.[26] Ms. Abderrahim defeated Kamel Idir, who represents the Nidaa Tounes party.[27]

The example of the mayoral election in Tunis illustrates the internal complexities of Tunisian politics in the post-revolution era. Despite the spirit of dialogue and negotiations, there remain internal disputes, disagreements, and even occasional boycotts. However, these complexities and disputes have not translated into successful attempts at undermining Tunisian democracy all together. They actually indicate that the democratic processes, warts and all, are indeed working. Democracy evolves slowly, especially in places where it has never taken root in the post-colonial era. It is important to understand the intrinsic gradualism in the evolution of democracy. As the *2002 Arab Human Development Report* (AHDR) has emphasized, the MENA countries typically have formed authoritarian political systems in the post-colonial era. Democracy is *atypical* in the region. Thus, Tunisia's post-revolution democratization process must be viewed in light of these historical realities and democratic gradualism.

Entering the twenty-first century, the MENA region has been characterized by not only authoritarian systems, but highly parasitic political elites that have taken advantage—mainly by means of corruption—of economic growth and development in a given country. Another point to bear in mind is that when we utter the word "democracy," usually it is in the context of Western democracy, or the Western democratic model. In the MENA region, democracy at any stage and in any form should be subject to specific contexts within a given country. Each regional actor has colonial and post-colonial experiences that have led to transformations and political structures conducive to respective cultures, ideologies, leaders, political elites, and demographics. Moreover, the impact of colonialism has rendered context specific outcomes.

Therefore, in the MENA region, democracy and the process of democratization cannot be identical to the Western models of democracy. There may be some similarities and parallels to identify with both Western and non-Western models, but in essence, the MENA actors' notions of democracy pertain to how they are specifically and contextually applied within each country, if at all. Some political parties and movements reject democracy outright, but since the 2011 Arab Awakening, the regional movements calling for democratization, pluralism, and liberalism in terms of rights, freedoms, and choices have been unprecedented and extremely vocal, including in social media. People have died during the protest movements of the 2011 Arab Awakening, and, clearly, they made the ultimate sacrifice in the struggle for democracy within their own country. As a result, it is unequivocally clear that the masses of especially the youth are signaling their demands and readiness for democracy to grow and flourish in the region. What a given democratic model looks like within the context of each respective country is a whole other complex process that encompasses the evolution of democracy.

The philosophy of democracy is also contextual and is subject to the factors of specific contexts outlined above. In the MENA region, the philosophy of any political theory and system is important, because often religion influences politics, and vice versa. Where secularism is rife, as in the case of Tunisia, the philosophy of democracy might conflict more against the Islamist philosophy of democracy. As Safwan Masri eloquently states in his book, *Tunisia: An Arab Anomaly*, "a country where certain liberal conditions existed – women's rights, modern education, and religious moderation – might just have a better chance than most to transition to democracy."[28]

One thing has been evident in the outcome of the 2011 Arab Awakening: the Islamists throughout the region realized that the uprisings and revolutions have provided an ideal opportunity for their own empowerment and agendas. We see how this unfolded in Egypt, Tunisia, and what transpired into violent civil conflicts in Libya, Yemen, and Syria, and to some extent in Bahrain and Saudi Arabia's Eastern Province, which is predominantly Shia.

In Tunisia, the Islamists formed the *Ennahda* Party, meaning "The Renaissance" Party (in Arabic, *hizbu- harakat-un en-nahda*). Rached al-Ghannouchi (b. 1941) remains its "intellectual leader" and president. Like many Islamists, Ghannouchi spent long years in exile during the Ben Ali era. He returned to Tunisia following the 2011 Arab Awakening, and his Ennahda Party has performed well in Tunisia's political transitions and elections.

Safwan Masri quotes the late Edward Said who said this about Tunisia: "It's the gentlest country in Africa. Even the Islamists are highly civilized."[29] I witnessed this dynamic when I visited Tunisia in March 2012 and attended a public talk that Rachid al-Ghannouchi gave at the Center for the Study of Islam and Democracy (CSID) in Tunis. The room filled to the brim with news media crews, cameras, and photographers, and an incredible mix of scholars, analysts, students, businesspeople, and political delegations, including foreign observers from embassies, occupying the seats. Ghannouchi spoke at the podium in the front of the room. His presentation exuded firm conviction, but, at the same time, there was a degree of diplomacy in his tone and delivery. During the Q&A session, the room took on the atmosphere of a tense debate, but no one lost it completely. One by one, those who wished to make statements from the audience were invited to come to the microphone and express their views. I saw feminists pound on the dais fervently insisting that no one—especially the Islamists—will be allowed to undermine women's rights in Tunisia. Secularists affirmed similar messages to the audience and particularly to Ghannouchi and his acolytes. I was impressed with the civility in the room, because as a MENA scholar, I have seen it all when it comes to tense political debates. In fact, the theme of the talk that night was the "Compatibility of Islam and Democracy." That in and of itself is a loaded topic.

However, it is very clear from this experience and the observations from that night that Tunisia's secularists and feminists feel deep anxiety about having Islamists come to power. They fear the reversal at the Islamists' hands of the long-held legacy of secularism and women's rights since Habib Bourguiba, Tunisia's first post-colonial president. The secularists and feminists do not trust the Islamists, especially empowered Islamists, and that has been the true test of Tunisia's democracy—allowing for competing forces, agendas, and party loyalists to engage in dialogue and negotiations with each other without letting things get out of hand. Thus far, Tunisia has managed to balance these internal disputes through national dialogue. The balancing act began immediately after the revolution:

> Soon after the departure of Ben Ali from Tunisia in January 2011, the transitional government, headed by Beji Caid Essebsi, appointed a political reform commission to draw up electoral rules for the elections to the Constituent Assembly, with initial membership gradually expanded to include a wide array of representatives of political and civil society groups. Elections for the Constituent Assembly were held on October 23, 2011, when the Islamist Ennahda secured a resounding victory (41.5 percent of the votes cast), with 51 percent of eligible voters casting ballots. The party won 89 of 217 seats in the Assembly, which translated into a slightly higher proportion than its percentage of votes received given the nature of electoral rules. Three parties, including the secular Congress for the Republic (CPR) and Ettakatol, formed a coalition with the Ennahda Party.[30]

Tunisia's Constitution has been revised, and the Constituent Assembly approved the latest version in January 2014. Tunisia's legal system is based on the French civil code and some elements of Islamic law. The citizens have engaged in the electoral process since the Ben Ali regime fell. Popular votes determine the president for a term of five years, and two terms are permitted. Beji Caid Essebsi won the presidential election in December 2014, marking the first free and democratic elections since Ben Ali's ouster. Essebsi "was a long-serving speaker of parliament under Mr. Ben Ali's rule, and critics believe his rise to power marks the return of the ousted political establishment."[31]

As of this writing, President Essebsi just announced that he will not be seeking a second term. This is highly unusual for the MENA region's reputation for having "presidents for life." Present-day Tunisia still "has some way to go in human rights," admits Prime Minister Chahed.[32] Despite the revised constitution's stipulations to uphold freedoms and rights, Tunisia has yet to enforce laws effectively and install "other constitutional bodies such as the High Authority for Human Rights."[33] According to Human Rights Watch:

> Tunisian lawmakers have made important steps for the consolidation of women's and detainees' rights but have failed to establish key institutions mandated by the constitution for human rights protection, such as the Constitutional Court. They have also adopted laws that threaten the democratic transition, such as the administrative reconciliation law, which grants amnesty for state officials accused of corruption.
>
> Authorities arbitrarily imposed travel restrictions on hundreds under a state of emergency declared in November 2015. Civilians continued to face prosecution in military courts for certain offenses. Laws criminalizing sodomy continued to send men accused of consensual homosexual conduct to prison, often after compulsory anal testing to prove their sexual conduct, although Tunisia committed to taking steps to end the use of forced anal exams. There was no progress on accountability for torture, as most complaints, filed years ago, including for ill-treatment and torture during the dictatorship, remained stalled at the prosecution phase.[34]

Regarding the anti-corruption efforts, Prime Minister Chahed recently announced that "two regulatory decrees related to the 2017 Law n.10 on the reporting of corruption and the protection of whistleblowers will be promulgated shortly."[35] As part of the initiative of the National Anti-Corruption Authority (INLUCC), Prime Minister Chahed "asserted the government's commitment to forge ahead on the path of countering corruption and establish governance. He assured that the various stakeholders, government, civil society, media and international organizations will continue to exert efforts to this end in a spirit of co-operation and partnership."[36] The rule of law cannot be enforced without the successful fight against corruption, and in turn, this effort facilitates the democratic process.[37] The INLUCC president, Chawki Tabib, stated that, "Tunisia is making 'firm' steps on the path of governance and fight against corruption, adding that many achievements have been made in this regard at both the institutional and legislative levels. During the opening session of the meeting, partnership agreements were signed between the INLUCC and municipalities."[38]

Moreover, for post-revolution Tunisia, Minister of Finance Jaloul Ayed listed four principal priorities that the government is currently focusing on:

- Restoring economic growth
- Reducing regional disparities
- Reducing unemployment
- Assisting Tunisians in need[39]

Minister Ayed reported that his ministry "is starting major initiatives on infrastructure projects and financial reform."[40] In addition, the government "has also created a confiscation committee to investigate and recover state assets stolen by the former president and his family."[41]

These are significant steps that the Tunisian government has been taking to fight against corruption. Regarding the ideological contentions, Dr. Radwan Masmoudi of the CSID has emphasized that, "While religion will continue to be a major force in the country, no one wants a theocratic state – everybody wants a democratic civil state that fully respects human rights and Islamic values and culture."[42] Dr. Masmoudi added that the challenge will be "to find a good balance between Islamic religious values and democratic values. And I think Tunisia is well placed to develop this model of a moderate Islamic state."[43] Bouazizi's self-immolation was the spark that charged the masses to take to the streets. The angry masses have been driven by pro-democracy (encompassing political change, freedoms, rights, and social justice), anti-authoritarianism, anti-corruption, and socioeconomic development-focused sentiments. In the post-revolution era, Tunisia continues to face overwhelming challenges in its political development. Primarily, the masses eagerly await implementation of the 2014 Constitution. For example,

> independent bodies conceived in the wake of the 2010–2011 uprising as checks on poor public administration (including the Independent High Authority for Audiovisual Communication, the Authority for Human Rights, the Authority for Sustainable Development and the Rights of Future Generations, the Authority for Good Governance and the Authority for the Fight against Corruption) still do not exist. Nominally independent administrative bodies that are in place lack autonomy from the government and political parties. For example, pressure from Tunisia's ruling coalition on the Independent High Authority for the Elections has already led to postponement of municipal elections. More generally, government officials and political leaders have blocked the process of decentralization mandated by the constitution from starting in earnest.

> The gap between constitutional principle and political reality is widening. But a renewed debate on the revision of the constitution, a step that President Essebsi and several political figures have suggested, would be a mistake. Amid the country's political and economic turmoil, such a debate would be akin to reopening hostilities between the parties over core political and social issues.[44]

By 2016, public opinion pertaining to confidence in Tunisia's institutions has declined, but informal networks have persisted in their activism and efforts to sustain the democratization process. In addition, post-revolution Tunisia has suffered from terrorist attacks and assassinations of high-profile politicians. These security challenges have caused traumatic shocks in the early stages of Tunisia's transitional process. However, Tunisia's counterterrorism efforts have achieved success in recent times. Nonetheless, it is imperative to analyze the political assassinations and terrorist attacks that threatened to derail Tunisia's democratization.

Assassinations and Security Challenges

The Tunisian people are proud and immensely patriotic, given their achievements since January 2011. "*Ultra Tunsie*," then, is a label each Tunisian would be proud to own and display. It will be the next generation that will carry the political, economic, and sociocultural torch in each country in the MENA region. With the young, educated, innovative, and tech-savvy demographic in the region, the prospects for development have never been better, presupposing that rights and freedoms would facilitate such progress.

Competition for power has involved the Islamist Ennahda Party, the opposition coalition, the hardline Salafists, and the youth activists consisting of diverse advocates for secularism, feminism, and liberal democracy. Tensions have flared in Tunisian politics, especially with the February 6, 2013, murder of Chokri Belaid, a prominent leftist politician.

In addition, Salafist extremist groups, such as Ansar al-Sharia, increasingly act up and apply pressures on the government to comply with their policy preferences. The Salafist militant threats became all the more acute with the assassination of Chokri Belaid, a human rights advocate who fearlessly and vocally criticized Ennahda. Belaid "publicly challenged [En-Nahda's] failure to investigate or prosecute violent acts of intimidation carried out by shadowy gangs of religious extremists."[45] Belaid was shot four times in his car, and as of late February 2013 four Islamist extremist suspects have been in custody, but a fifth gunmen escaped. The murder triggered a political shake-up. Belaid's widow has fingered Ennahda for alleged complicity in her husband's killing. Her unrelenting public condemnation of Ennahda and the ensuing political crisis, which included Ennahda's refusal to build a non-partisan coalition with technocrats, led Prime Minister Hamadi Jebali to resign in late February 2013.

Ali Laarayedh, a former opposition activist during the Ben Ali era, served as Tunisia's new prime minister from 2013 until 2014. Laarayedh was an Ennahda political activist and suffered torture and 13 years of solitary confinement under the prior regime. Upon coming to office, he reassured the public and media that "There will be no Islamization of post-revolutionary Tunisia, and the Islamist-led government has no hidden agendas or intention to monopolize power."[46]

Tunisian politics has faced another blow and pitted into another crisis with the July 25, 2013 assassination of a second secular politician, Mohamed Brahmi, who was a critic of the Ennahda administration. This murder provoked more public demonstrators "blaming the ruling Islamist party and its followers for Mr. Brahmi's killing and shouting for the government to go. Scores of relatives, party members and supporters draped in the Tunisian flag arrived at the entrance of the hospital in the southwestern suburb where Mr. Brahmi's body lay."[47]

Tunisian news media accounts said Mr. Brahmi, 58, had been shot outside his home, an attack witnessed by his wife and children, in the middle of the day by two men on a motorcycle who escaped. Although the accounts of the precise version of events differed, the audacity of the assassination amplified the outrage, as many Tunisians feel the government has failed to deliver on law and order and allowed radical Islamists a license to act with impunity.[48]

Opposition secular politicians have received threats, and many continue to blame Ennahda for these developments. Ennahda has never governed Tunisia, much like the Muslim Brotherhood (MB) in Egypt, as it was banned under the dictatorship. Ennahda "leads a coalition with two smaller secular parties and has struggled to complete the drafting of a new Constitution and prepare elections within the allotted one year."[49] Ennahda's greatest challenge has been "controlling the extremists among its followers."[50]

Ennahda has long been criticized for allowing what the opposition calls a growing Islamization of the country, and a tolerance of extremist groups: Salafis and jihadis who were recruiting young men to fight in Syria, and groups preaching fundamentalist views and threatening women who worked outside the home or went unveiled.[51]

The Ennahda-led Tunisian government took some positive measures since the revolution. For example, under its leadership, an assets retrieval committee has been set up to reclaim financial and material assets that the Ben Ali and Trabelsi clan have squandered over the decades of the dictatorship. The new constitution has been revised with input from diverse sources and constituents. Some steady political and economic reforms have been initiated in order to improve the country's economy and restart the tourism industry. Foreign direct investment (FDI) endeavors have been actively pursued to build foreign investment interest in Tunisia. Despite all the hurdles and challenges, Tunisia continues to forge ahead, even as heated political debates and ideological differences abound.

The party has nevertheless been commended for its inclusive politics and a post-revolutionary maturity missing not only in Egypt but also in the other Arab Awakening upheavals in Libya, Syria, and Yemen. Ennahda negotiated a compromise on the Constitution, dropping all mention of Islamic law, for example, and ensuring full freedoms, including equal rights for women and freedom of religion and expression.

Following Mr. Brahmi's assassination, Ennahda directed the military to launch major counterterrorism operations, particularly in the Tunisian-Algerian border region. In early August 2013, Tunisian forces

> launched air and ground strikes on Islamist militants near the border with Algeria [on Friday] after fierce overnight clashes in the area, which coincided with increased instability and political turmoil in Tunisia. Aircraft bombed caves in the Mount Chaambi area, where the military has been trying to track down a band of 15 to 20 Islamist militants since December, an army spokesman said Friday. The operation was launched in the same area where militants killed eight soldiers [on Monday] in one of the deadliest attacks on Tunisian security forces in decades. Tunisia's Islamist-led government is grappling with instability and a mounting protest movement. The opposition, angered by the assassination of one of its leaders last week, wants the transitional Constituent Assembly dissolved.[52]

Under intense pressure, in January 2014 Ennahda ultimately stepped down, signifying a peaceful transition of power. As an outcome of negotiations with the Tunisian General Labor Union, Ali Larayedh, Tunisian prime minister at the time, resigned, and Mehdi Jomaa replaced him as interim prime minister.[53] The Constituent Assembly called for new elections following major protests against Islamists and particularly Salafists since Ennahda came to power in July 2013 in Tunisia's first ever democratic elections. According to the Wilson Center:

> Following the assassination of opposition leader Mohamed Brahmi, thousands of Tunisians demonstrated against the Islamist-led government on July 26. Protesters from diverse secular parties shouted *'Down with the rule of the Muslim Brotherhood,'* referring to Ennahda, the Islamist ruling party in Tunisia. The protests forced the closure of banks and stores, while all flights from the capital were canceled.
>
> The killing of Brahmi was aimed at *'halting Tunisia's democratic process and killing the only successful model in the region, especially after the violence in Egypt, Syria and Libya,'* Ennahda party leader Rachid Ghannouhchi told Reuters. *'Tunisia will not follow the Egyptian scenario. We will hold on.'*[54]

During Ennahda's rule in Tunisia, "tensions ratcheted up to great heights between Islamist and liberal forces, leading to increasing instability, violence, and a seemingly intractable political deadlock."[55] The situation "reduced the credibility of the government, and the overthrow of the ruling Islamists in Egypt created an opening for the opposition National Salvation Front coalition to demand that Ennahda step down in favor of a nonpartisan government of technocrats."[56] Mass demonstrations ensued, upon which a reconciliation deal "was brokered between Rachid Ghannouchi, the head of Ennahda, and Essebsi, who spearheaded an opposition coalition, with the two sides agreeing to a road map for power transfer in October 2013 and settling on a compromise caretaker prime minister by late December."[57]

Indeed, Tunisia has managed to hold on and held parliamentary elections on October 26, 2014, resulting in the main opposition party, the secular Nidaa Tounes party, "emerge victorious … with initial results showing it winning approximately 80 seats, while the moderate Islamist Ennahda party was seen as garnering about 60 seats. Turnout hovered around 60 percent."[58] Then, the presidential election took place on November 23, 2014; "this vote was closely watched and marks a crucial step in Tunisia's democratic transition. Tunisians voted for their first directly elected president since the 2011 revolution."[59] According to GlobalSecurity.org, the vote marked the long-awaited completion of a transition to democracy after Tunisians sparked protests across the region by overthrowing dictator Zine El Abidine Ben Ali three years earlier. Among the more than two dozen candidates, 87-year-old Beji Caid Essebsi, a political veteran from the Nidaa Tounes (Call of Tunisia) party, emerged as the front-runner, followed by [current] President Moncef Marzouki. Essebsi got 39.46 percent of the vote, ahead of Marzouki, who got 33.4 percent.

A runoff was held 21 December as no one secured an absolute majority. The campaign has been marked by negative campaigning. Marzouki has accused Essebsi of wanting to restore the old guard ousted in the revolution. For his part, Essebsi has described Marzouki as an "extremist" whose three-year tenure as president has been disastrous. Essebsi refused to hold a debate with Marzouki ahead of the runoff.

Tunisians cast their ballots in the second and final round of a landmark presidential vote that marked the culmination of a rocky transition to democracy. The vote was split in ideology – pro- versus anti-Islamists – and geographically. The northern, coastal areas tended to vote for Essebsi, while the south went for Marzouki.

Candidate Beji Caid Essebsi's anti-Islamist party quickly claimed victory over his rival, interim president Moncef Marzouki. Essebsi's campaign manager said initial indications showed a victory for the 88-year-old former minister. Marzouki's campaign manager dismissed the claims, saying the election was too close to call. Official results gave 88-year-old Beji Caid Essebsi nearly 56 percent of the vote in Sunday's runoff election – compared to 44 percent for incumbent interim President Moncef Marzouki.

As president, Essebsi is responsible for security, defense and foreign affairs. But his party will also command parliament, although it must first seek political alliances to do so.[60]

President Essebsi is not viewed through completely positive lenses, as he has been accused of attempts at nepotism, a sensitive issue given the Ben Ali and Trabelsi clan's legacy, and this launched a party crisis. However, the coalition has managed to retain itself. Economic and national security problems have continued to plague the Essebsi administration, forcing Prime Minister Habib Essid to be removed in July 2016 following a parliamentary vote of no confidence.[61] In August 2016, Youssef Chahed became prime minister; he is the "40-year-old minister for local affairs with ties to the president's family."[62]

As the years since the 2011 revolution pass, other noticeable trends are emerging in Tunisia's political landscape and dynamics. One of these trends is the decline of the youth's political participation: "Tunisian youth are politically engaged, yet they are increasingly eschewing formal politics (voting, joining political parties, and running for office) in favor of informal politics (starting or joining a civil society organization, protesting, or signing a petition)."[63] According to Sarah Yerkes's study of the topic, the main reason is disillusionment of the youth, as "[they] are disappointed by the trajectory of politics over the past six years and have grown apathetic."[64] However, Tunisia's active civil society consists of high numbers of youths; hence, "evidence shows they are in fact far from apathetic."[65]

Overall, Tunisia's political health can be described as a case of gradual democratization while facing formidable challenges from both the domestic and regional arenas. The Tunisian people and political elite so far have shown tremendous resolve to keep the country's political health from declining to the point of violent and irreversible conflict. Hope is not lost for Tunisia's ability to revive the transitional process on a more progressive path.

Tunisia's Regional and Foreign Policy Priorities

In terms of regional politics, due to the Gulf Cooperation Council's (GCC) internal rifts pertaining to the mainly Saudi and Emirati dispute with Qatar, attempts to bring Tunisia into their respective folds have been apparent in recent months. Also, the GCC monarchies for the most part have expressed contempt at the Arab Awakening uprisings and revolutions, and they have even tried to discredit the Tunisian revolution by spreading conspiracy theories about Mohamed Bouazizi. The primary reason for this is Qatar's support for Egypt's Muslim Brotherhood (MB) and Mohamed Morsi following the Tahrir Square Revolution. Saudi Arabia and the United Arab Emirates (UAE) became enraged with the toppling of the Hosni Mubarak regime in Egypt, and particularly furious with Qatar for its support of the MB. The GCC monarchies feel threatened by democracy and democratization efforts in any part of the Arab Middle East and North Africa. Therefore, they conspire to undermine democracy from taking root and spreading in Arab states. In addition, because of their respective interests and agendas, they are fiercely opposed to the MB, except for Qatar; and since Tunisia's Ennahda party has evolved from its MB chapter there, by default, then, the post-revolution Ennahda victory in Tunisia's democratic election has been wholly unacceptable for the likes of Saudi Arabia and the UAE.

In the same vein, Qatar's opposition in the GCC has vilified the country's news media network Al Jazeera. The latter has broadcast and printed reports that have criticized GCC regimes, and it is accused of facilitating the MB's agendas in the post–Arab Awakening revolution countries, like Egypt. The GCC monarchies, except for Qatar, detest Al Jazeera, and any tolerance for the network is now equated to support for the MB and "terrorists."

These disputes put Tunisia in difficult situations when it comes to regional relations and financial support from oil-rich Gulf countries. Consider the depth of these rifts and the balancing act that Tunisia has had to play in regional relations, according to Youssef Cherif's January 2017 report for the Carnegie Endowment for International Peace:

> Qatari Emir Sheikh Tamim bin Hamad Al Thani, the only foreign head of state attending [Tunisia's investment conference, "Tunisia 2020"], announced a financial package of $1.25 billion, and the Qatari ambassador to Tunisia signed an additional $2.2 million check to cover the costs of the conference. Overall, Tunisia 2020 looked like Qatar's response to the UAE-organized Egypt Economic and Development Conference (EEDC) in March 2015, which had allowed the UAE to expand its influence in that country.
>
> … Once Ennahda resigned from government in January 2014 following a protracted domestic impasse and growing tension, Qatar's standing in Tunisia became less certain. However, Qatar could still claim Tunisia as a foreign policy success—it had supported a country whose democratic transition seemed to work. Qatar has kept backing Tunisia through loans and donations, and continues to provide positive media coverage through influential state-supported outlets such as *Al Jazeera* and *Al-Araby Al-Jadid*. In contrast, the UAE, which had been Tunisia's second-largest trading partner in the Arab world (after Libya), saw its bilateral ties grow tense after 2011.
>
> … The Emirati leadership was looking to move Tunisia into its own camp and away from Qatar's. They had calculated that their support for Nidaa Tounes would exclude Islamists from the political scene and lead Tunisia to recognize Libya's eastern government and Khalifa Haftar, its military strongman and Abu Dhabi's ally. Neither outcome materialized. Furthermore, the government formed by Nidaa Tounes kept excellent ties with Qatar.

> … As tensions continue, *Emirati media and research outlets remain critical of Tunisia's ongoing transition*, also encouraging a number of Tunisian journalists, prominent figures, and intellectuals to share these criticisms… Meanwhile stalled economic cooperation is costing Tunisia billions of dollars in frozen investments, and visas remain an issue. As evidenced by the UAE's small showing at Tunisia 2020, there are no signs of improvement.
>
> The Emiratis have so far favored a zero-sum game: either the Tunisian government accepts their conditions of keeping Islamists out of government and building stronger ties with the pro-Haftar government in eastern Libya, or it gets nothing. But Saudi Arabia, the UAE's main ally, might be able to influence the UAE's approach to Tunisia. Riyadh already pledged $850 million during Tunisia 2020 after years of cold relations between the two countries.
>
> … Even if the Saudis have lost their political leverage over the UAE, they could still assume their former place as one of Tunisia's largest Arab trading partners—at least so long as Saudi Arabia's ongoing financial strains allow it to invest significant amounts abroad.[66]

Given these difficulties in regional relations, Tunisia has had to tread carefully. Political sensitivities tend to drive the MENA powerbrokers especially since the 2011 Arab Awakening. Tunisia has fervently sought to protect itself from regional conflicts and disputes. In fact, the Essebsi government seeks to "consolidate a 'zero-enemy' policy," and it "will likely seek to limit any political adventures, choosing instead to focus on economic and security cooperation."[67] Tunisia is in a tough neighborhood, with Algeria and its bloody civil war legacy and Libya's violent chaos on its borders. According to Youssef Cherif's article in the *Atlantic Council*:

> Libya remains the main foreign policy challenge for Tunisia. As Tunisia's second largest economic partner, Libya remains the primary source of informal cross-border trade, which amounts to roughly 40 percent of Tunisia's gross domestic product. Despite the occasional closure of border crossings, hundreds of thousands of Libyans have taken refuge in Tunisia to escape the ongoing conflict and thousands of Tunisians continue to work in Libya.
>
> The Algerian regime, wary of Islamist forces in power given Algeria's historical baggage and of a potentially successful democracy on its border, disapproved of the 2012–2013 governments. As Tunisia's wealthiest immediate neighbor, Caid Essebsi made it a point to first visit Algeria after his election to the presidency. Algeria-Tunisia security cooperation has grown in importance since the increase of terrorist activity on the borders of the two countries—particularly in the Mount Chaambi region.[68]

While Tunisia has not suffered sectarian violence in the post–Arab Awakening period in the same way as other MENA countries have, Sunni-Shia violence has entered the continent of Africa following the rise of ISIS, with deadly extremist attacks against Shias in Nigeria and Egypt. However, the worst sectarian violence in the MENA region has taken place in Iraq, Saudi Arabia's eastern province, and most notably Bahrain. The Kingdom of Bahrain (meaning, "two seas") is small with a population of only 1.5 million, nearly half of which are foreign workers. The Sunni monarchy's Al-Khalifa family has ruled Bahrain since the eighteenth century. The Sunni minority has ruled over the majority Shia population, presently constituting nearly 70 percent of the population. The rest of the 30 percent consist of Sunnis and other diverse religious identities mainly represented in the foreign workers' demographics.

The 2011 Arab Awakening motivated Bahraini Shias to protest against socioeconomic and political marginalization and discrimination. The Sunni monarchy responded with violent repression and even requested the Saudis and Emiratis to deploy their militaries to brutally crush the demonstrations. Security forces killed, arrested, and tortured many protest leaders and activists and bulldozed the protest camps, which followed the Tahrir Square protest camp model in Egypt, that were set up in the area of the Pearl Roundabout. The "giant white monument in the middle of Pearl Roundabout was brought down … and the mound of grass that had been home for … thousands of demonstrators is now a pile of brown dirt."[69]

While Bahrain's Sunni-Shia problems do not directly relate to Tunisia, there is indirect linkage between them. The Shia uprising in Bahrain has been inspired by Tunisia's Jasmine Revolution and its domino effect in the Arab Awakening throughout the MENA region. Bahraini Shias, like many in the region, saw this as an opportunity to peacefully assert themselves to protest centuries of anti-Shia discrimination and repression at the hands of the minority Sunni monarchy. The Bahrain situation also involves the kingdom's allies Saudi Arabia and the UAE, which came to the Sunni monarchy's rescue. This episode also symbolizes unity among the Arab states in the Persian Gulf region in opposing the Arab Awakening all together, plus it underscores their collective contempt for democracy and all the values and principles for which it stands.

Still, Tunisia cannot afford to isolate itself, especially during the extremely vulnerable transition period. With the Gulf Arab states cutting off their support for Tunisia, the republic has reached out to Western powers for help. Tunisia's economic challenges compel the country to remain beholden to the generosity of these powerful and wealthy stakeholders. That is one of the reasons why Tunisia has broadened its appeals for support and investments to Europe and the United States.

When it comes to Tunisia's European relations, it is natural to preserve French-Tunisian relations in the post-colonial era. France has provided political, financial, and security support to Tunisia following the 2011 revolution. Cherif addresses Europe's interests relative to Tunisia, and vice versa:

> Europe provides economic, security, and geopolitical protection for Tunisia—a relationship the new government will not jeopardize. Nearly 80 percent of all trade in Tunisia occurs with European countries, making the group of Western countries its largest economic partner. Given the proximity, roughly 10 percent of all Tunisians live and work in Europe. Europeans can also provide political disincentives should Algeria start suffocating Tunisia. Essebsi's government will do its utmost to maintain the 'Privileged Partnership' status gained by Tunisia in 2011, marketing its improvements in human rights, its efforts to fight corruption, and the central role his country plays in stopping illegal migration.
>
> Tunisia, traditionally seen as France's *chasse gardée*, has tried to diversify its European partners. France's previous history supporting the Ben Ali regime, its hesitations towards the rise of Islamism, and its own economic difficulties has prompted Tunisia to reach out to countries such as Italy, Germany, and the United Kingdom. While France will remain Tunisia's top partner, others will compete for that rank. Italy may assume a greater role, particularly after the loss of its main North African partner, Libya. Tunisia will look to Italy to upgrade its navy, control illegal maritime immigration, and coordinate on strategies regarding the Libyan crisis. Germany is also keen to support democracy while expanding economic partnerships. The UK has provided security trainings and material, also using Tunisia as a platform for its Libya-related activities.[70]

In the United States, President Barack Obama expressed unwavering support for Tunisia and for investing in its political and economic development. In fact, President Obama co-wrote an op-ed with President Essebsi in *The Washington Post* in May 2015, in which both heads of state express that

> Tunisia's democratic journey has not been easy. During the transition, brave political leaders were gunned down. The old regime's legacy of mismanagement and corruption continues to stifle economic growth. The terrorist

> attack on the National Bardo Museum in March killed Tunisians and foreign tourists alike. Tunisia, a country of 11 million people, has absorbed waves of people fleeing the fighting in neighboring Libya. Despite these extraordinary challenges, Tunisians have remained united and determined to protect their young democracy.
>
> Our two nations now have an unprecedented opportunity to forge an enduring partnership based on shared interests and values. Indeed, since the revolution, the United States has committed more than $570 million, and supported two major loan guarantees, to help Tunisians pursue critical political, economic and security reforms. Over the past year alone, the United States has worked to double its assistance to Tunisia, with $134 million proposed for next year. This is not charity; it's a smart investment in our shared future, and our meetings Thursday will focus on three priorities.
>
> First, we can do more together to help Tunisians consolidate their democratic gains.
>
> … Second, we can partner to ensure that Tunisia's political revolution is followed by an economic revolution that reduces poverty and delivers tangible improvements to the daily lives of the Tunisian people.
>
> … Finally, we aim to deepen the security cooperation that protects our citizens. Working together, we have helped the Tunisian armed forces build their capacity to undertake counterterrorism missions.
>
> … As Tunisians seek to build the Arab world's newest democracy, they will continue to have a strong friend and partner in the world's oldest democracy, the United States of America.[71]

A number of US government delegations has visited Tunisia, the first of which included the late US Senator John McCain and other congressmen who met with Tunisian political leaders, including Ghannouchi. The United States and Tunisia are committed to engaging in "strategic dialogue."[72] The first major US-Tunisian event in 2015 consisted of "an investment and entrepreneurship conference, [which] was attended by Secretary of State for Commerce Penny Pritzker, Assistant-Secretary of State for Economic and Business Affairs Charles H. Rivkin, and former Secretary of State Madeleine Albright."[73]

The story is very different with the current Donald Trump administration. President Trump has "proposed a substantial cut in US assistance to Tunisia, the sole democratizing country in the Middle East and North Africa."[74] The Trump administration seems to have no interest in Tunisia.

> Slashing aid by more than half, from $185.4 million to about $80 million, would send a clear message: Trump could care less about Tunisia. To be fair, in the past year Secretary of State Rex Tillerson called Tunisia 'an important partner' and Deputy Secretary of State John Sullivan said the United States is 'proud to support [Tunisia's] efforts to improve security, develop democratic institutions and practices and foster economic growth.' But, rhetorical flourishes aside, money talks in Washington, even more so since Trump became president.
>
> It's not entirely a surprise that Trump dismisses Tunisia's importance. Tunisia lacks many of the qualities that tend to appeal to Trump: domestic political salience (Israel), vast wealth (Saudi Arabia) and alleged counterterrorism cooperation (Egypt). The Obama administration's hailing of Tunisia as the only Arab Spring success story may be a detriment in the eyes of Trump, who has openly declared his affinity for dictators.[75]

Youssef Chahed earned the title of prime minister in 2016, and his unity government "includes a broad coalition of secular, Islamist and leftist parties, independents and trade union allies. He warned of tough economic reforms, including a possible program of austerity, to satisfy international lenders and boost economic growth and boost job creation. But as the former French colony's youngest ever prime minister, many of Mr. Chahed's critics have questioned whether he has the political clout to overcome the trade union opposition, strikes and party infighting that have dogged past governments."[76] Tunisia will hold its next parliamentary elections in October, and presidential elections in November, 2019.

However, Tunisia's government is already facing political and economic crises as 2018 has turned the corner to 2019. Tunisia's parliament has 217 seats including eight "blocs," and "Ennahda has been at the top with 69 seats, surpassing the governing Nidaa Tunis. Composed at the start of 33 deputies, the new parliamentary bloc now includes 43 deputies. However, more members of parliament are expected to join their bloc, which may cause a shift in power in the parliament."[77]

The political turmoil in Tunisia's government has continued to stir suspense. In September 2018, the Nidaa Tounes Party announced that it had "frozen the prime minister's membership in the latest escalation in a row between the prime minister and the president's son."[78] Tunisia "fell into political crisis after Essebsi's son called for the prime minister's dismissal."[79]

Prime Minister Youssef Chahed said that "the president's son, Hafedh Caid Essebsi, had destroyed the governing Nidaa Tounes party and that the crisis in the party has affected state institutions. The president's son, who is a leader of the Nidaa Tounes, had called for the prime minister's dismissal because of his government's failure to revive the economy. His call was supported by the powerful UGTT union, which has rejected economic reforms proposed by the prime minister."[80] Many analysts blame the UGTT's impediments to economic reforms for the country's ongoing economic stagnation. In addition, Nidaa Tounes has seen eight members resign "to join a new coalition called the National Coalition, which supports Chahed's government."[81] The new parliamentary blocs will be the scene for ongoing shifting alliances.

President Essebsi has supposedly ended his relations with Ennahda, this despite attempts throughout the year 2018 to build consensus between the parties. The labor and employers' unions have also been involved in the talks and even "agreed to start a new economic program."[82] Unfortunately, "talks broke off very quick after the parties failed to hammer out details."[83]

Prime Minister Chahed initiated structural reforms and austerity measures, "such as fuel subsidies that have helped to underpin a $2.8 billion loan from the International Monetary Fund (IMF) and other financial support."[84] However, the problem of educated youth unemployment continues to plague Tunisia. The youth demographic still feels hopeless. In fact,

> It is becoming increasingly clear that political freedom is not enough to bolster Tunisia's fledgling democracy. And should the transition fail, the consequences could be devastating for both the country's progress and the region's stability.
>
> Some early warning signs are already evident. Tunisia recently overtook Eritrea as the country with the largest number of migrants entering Italy by sea. And since 2011, close to 100,000 highly educated and skilled workers have left the country. Equally concerning, Tunisia remains one of the largest contributors of foreign fighters to the self-proclaimed Islamic State, and its suicide rate has nearly doubled. On October 29, 2018, a 30-year-old, unemployed graduate blew herself up in central Tunis, marking the city's first terror attack in several years.[85]

The persisting problems of poverty and socioeconomic deficiencies in Tunisia's interior region, education reforms "to produce graduates with skills that match employers' demands, creating incentives to encourage the large number of informal workers to enter the formal economy, and lifting currency control to improve access to international markets and help entrepreneurs get off the ground," all demand immediate attention.[86]

Also, recent data indicate that many educated Tunisians are leaving the country. The lack of social justice has led to "brain drain, irregular migration, protest, suicide, and violent extremism. Thirteen percent of university graduates left Tunisia in 2014… And Tunisians now make up the largest contingent of irregular migrants by sea to Italy. Most of them are young men, seeking to improve their economic situation in Europe."[87] Furthermore, suicide rates and self-immolation incidents "increased by 1.8 and 3 times, respectively, between 2011 and 2016. And while Tunisia is no longer the top contributor of foreign fighters to the Islamic State in Iraq and Syria, it is still one of the largest."[88]

Tunisia's political development has been focused heavily on politics, elections, and negotiations within and between political parties and constituents in unions, syndicates, institutions, and industries. However, the most difficult decisions for improving the economy and implementing these decisions have yet to come to full fruition, and the core constituents who carried out the revolution—the educated youth—remain marginalized and feeling hopeless.

This is a dire situation in Tunisia, and if the government fails to fulfill the promises made to the revolutionaries, the outlook for the country will be bleak. Despite these realities, Tunisia still remains a positive example in the MENA region, because the Tunisian people have been committed to non-violent dialogues and negotiations. They know that the alternative would be a catastrophe for the country.

Conclusion

The youth demographic existing throughout the MENA region has served as a pivotal factor in embracing the Tunisian revolution as an inspiration to improve their own circumstances in their own countries. Tarek Osman emphasizes this point:

> … [The] changing demographics proved to be the trigger. Over the past four decades, the Arab world has doubled its population, to over 330 million people, two-thirds of them are under 35 years old.
>
> This is a generation that has inherited acute socio-economic and political problems that it did not contribute to, and yet has been living its consequences – from education quality, job availability, economic prospects, to the perception of the future.

> At core, the wave of Arab uprisings that commenced in 2011 is this generation's attempt at changing the consequences of the state order that began in the aftermath of World War One.
>
> This currently unfolding transformation entails the promise of a new generation searching for a better future, and the peril of a wave of chaos that could engulf the region for several years.[89]

Political leaders in the MENA region may not have learned the potent lessons from these developments since the 2011 Arab Awakening. In fact, some regimes have contempt toward democracy, and especially toward Tunisia's democratic successes. Tunisia has shed its dictatorship and is set on a path to remove the characteristics of the Ben Ali regime, including corruption, violent repression, and economic stagnation. Politics do not proceed as usual, because in both domestic and foreign policies Tunisia has to strike a delicate balance.

> Caught in a tumultuous region and suffering its worst terrorist violence in recent memory, Tunisia's government needs to address its economic and security problems while consolidating its nascent democracy. Such tasks require international support, especially from strong and rich democracies, but also fewer enemies. The recent Bardo tragedy and the 'War on Terror' discourse prevailing in Tunisia are a reminder of the country's fragility; foreign policy will play a key role in mitigating these obstacles.[90]

The good news is that Tunisia's "old guard" from the Ben Ali era does not have the power to derail the democratic transition process. According to Thomas Carothers, "Tunisia does not have a charismatic, mobilizing figure who is clearly anti-democratic. There is an old guard in Tunisia that is active in politics and closely connected to the internal security forces and the business sector under ousted dictator Zine al-Abidine Ben Ali. But this old guard is less coherent than the Egyptian military and less capable of stepping back into power. Tunisia does not as of yet have a powerful force outside of the political scene that is poised to come back in and wreck things."[91]

Overall, Tunisia's post-revolution experiment with negotiations and compromise has blazed a trail of democratization unknown in the region. Tunisians have achieved a delicate balance between the secular and Islamist entities, which is not an easy endeavor. In Tunisia, "the Islamist–secular divide is a source of tension, a force in politics that threatens to go off the rails all the time. Tunisians are aware of their country as the only one in the Arab world trying to make the Islamist–non-Islamist divide work in a genuinely democratic way. But Tunisia's coalition government is fairly distinctive beyond the region, as well. Tunisia's effort at political compromise and political balance has gone better than in many other countries."[92] Moreover, despite the competition that Ennahda has faced from secularists and Salafists, it has survived and continues to thrive at the grassroots level and upward. Ennahda remains active in Tunisian politics, and it continues its efforts to influence the transitional democratic process.

Tunisia's political institutions still need strengthening,[93] especially to meet the socioeconomic needs of the people. The situation in the marginalized interior region has been dire for a long time, and the evolving institutions must address the desperate conditions of the poor. Otherwise, individuals will find themselves more susceptible to extremism, as happened during the rise of ISIS in 2014.

The political evolution of Tunisia's democracy must never be deterred, regardless of the challenges ahead. The profound words of Confucius are pertinent to Tunisia's political development: "It does not matter how slowly you go as long as you do not stop."

Tunisia's political health is intrinsically intertwined and interdependent with its economic health. Chapter 5 analyzes Tunisia's economic health, as part of the political economy equation.

Tunisia's Civil Society Organizations[94]

Association of Ennahda Women
Arrhma Association des Femmes Nahdaouis

*** Association of Tunisian Judges**
Association des magistrats tunisiens (AMT)

Association of Tunisian Women
Nissa Tounsyat

*** Association of Tunisian Women for Research on Development**
Association des femmes tunisiennes pour la recherche sur le développement (AFTURD)

Center for Research, Documentation and Information on Women
Centre de recherches, d'études, de documentation et d'information sur la femme (CREDIF)

Health Workers' Union
La fédération générale de la santé

* **International Association for Support of Political Prisoners**
Association internationale de soutien aux prisonniers politiques (AISPP)

* **Liberty and Justice Association**
Association liberté et justice

* **Modernization Movement of the Tunisian Union of Industry, Trades and Crafts**
Mouvement de modernisation de l'Union tunisienne de l'industrie, du commerce et de l'artisanat

* **National Council for Liberties in Tunisia**
Conseil national pour les libertés en Tunisie (CNLT)

National Council for the Protection of the Revolution
Conseil national pour la protection de la révolution (CNPR)

* **National Order of Doctors**
Ordre national des médecin

* **National Order of Lawyers**
Ordre national des avocats (ONAT)

* **National Union of Specialist Doctors and Free Practice**
Syndicat national des médecins spécialistes de libre pratique

* **National Union of Tunisian Journalists**
Syndicat national des journalistes tunisiens (SNJT)

National Union of Tunisian Women
Union National de la Femme Tunisienne (UNFT)

* **Organizations of Emigrants**
Les organisations d'émigrés

Postal Workers' Union
Les travailleurs de la Poste tunisienne

Primary School Teachers' Union
Syndicat National des Enseignements de l'école primaire

Secondary School Teachers' Union
Syndicat National des Enseignements (SNES)

*** Tunisian Association of Chambers of Notaries**
Association tunisienne des chambres de notaires

*** Tunisian Association of Democratic Women**
Association tunisienne des femmes démocrates (ATFD)

*** Tunisian General Labor Union**
Union générale tunisienne du travail (UGTT)

*** Tunisian League for the Defense of Human Rights**
Ligue tunisienne pour la défense des droits de l'Homme (LTDH)

Tunisian Union of Industry, Trades and Crafts
Union Tunisienne de l'Industrie, du Commerce et de l'Artisanat (UTICA)

Union of Independent Tunisians for Freedom
Union des Tunisiens Indépendants pour la Liberté (UTIL)

* "Member of the Higher Authority for the Realization of the Objectives of the Revolution, Political Reform, and Democratic Transition, the body of associations that 'determined the direction of the constitutional process, the interim government, and its authorities',"—as quoted in Veronica Baker, "The Role of Civil Society in the Tunisian Democratic Transition," 2015, p. 6.

Notes

1. Jared Malsin, "Why Tunisians are Testifying about Horrific Tortures by the State," *Time*, January 13, 2017: http://time.com/4634622/tunisia-truth-dignity-commission-zine-al-abidine-ben-ali/
2. Rory McCarthy, *Inside Tunisia's Al-Nahda: Between Politics and Preaching* (UK: Cambridge University Press, 2018), p. 171.
3. Ibid.
4. Ibid.
5. Ibid., p. 172.
6. Ibid., p. 173.
7. Ibid.
8. Ibid.
9. Ibid.
10. Ibid.
11. Ibid., p. 174.
12. Ibid.

13. Patrick Markey, and Aziz El Yaakoubi, "Tunisian Premier Resigns for Caretaker Government, Protests Hit South," *Reuters*, January 9, 2014: https://www.reuters.com/article/us-tunisias-pm-idUS-BREA080MY20140109
14. Wafa Ben-Hassine, "Tunisian Civil Society's Unmistakable Role in Keeping the Peace," *The Atlantic Council*, January 19, 2018: http://www.atlantic-council.org/blogs/menasource/tunisian-civil-society-s-unmistakable-role-in-keeping-the-peace
15. Ibid., emphasis added.
16. Masri, pp. 50–51.
17. Ibid., p. 51; also see Robin Wright, *Rock the Casbah: Rage and Rebellion across the Islamic World* (New York: Simon and Schuster, 2012).
18. Masri, p. 294.
19. Ben-Hassine, "Tunisian Civil Society's Unmistakable Role in Keeping the Peace."
20. Ibid., emphasis added.
21. "Tunisia's Nobel Prize-Winning Trade Unions are Holding the Country Back," *The Economist*, December 14, 2017: https://www.economist.com/middle-east-and-africa/2017/12/14/tunisias-nobel-prize-winning-trade-unions-are-holding-the-country-back
22. Ibid.
23. Ibid.
24. Ibid.
25. "Islamist-backed Candidate becomes First Woman Mayor of Tunis," *France24*, July 3, 2018: http://www.france24.com/en/20180703-islamist-backed-candidate-abderrahim-first-woman-mayor-tunis-tunisia
26. Ibid.
27. Ibid.
28. Safwan M. Masri, *Tunisia: An Arab Anomaly* (New York: Columbia University Press, 2017), p. xix.
29. Ibid., p. xxiii.
30. *A Political Economy of the Middle East*, fourth edition. Edited by Melani Cammett, Ishac Diwan, Alan Richards, and John Waterbury (Boulder: Westview Press, 2015), p. 103.
31. "Tunisia Country Profile," *BBC News*, January 14, 2018: https://www.bbc.com/news/world-africa-14107241
32. "Tunisia Still Has Some Way to go in Human Rights (Youssef Chahed)," Republic of Tunisia, Presidency of the Government Portal, December 12, 2018: http://www.pm.gov.tn/pm/actualites/actualite.php?lang=en&id=11421
33. Ibid.
34. Kenneth Roth, "Tunisia: Events of 2017," *Human Rights Watch*, 2018: https://www.hrw.org/world-report/2018/country-chapters/tunisia#

35. "Two Regulatory Decrees Related to Anti-Corruption Law to be Promulgated Shortly (Youssef Chahed)," Republic of Tunisia, Presidency of the Government Portal, December 8, 2018: http://www.pm.gov.tn/pm/actualites/actualite.php?lang=en&id=11419
36. Ibid.
37. Ibid.
38. Ibid.
39. Jaloul Ayed, "Tunisia and Egypt's Revolutions and Transitions to Democracy: What is the Impact on the Arab World? What Lessons Can We Learn?" In Thomas W. Skladony, Peter Winston Fettner, and Alexandra Tohme (eds.), *Conference Report*, Center for the Study of Islam and Democracy (CSID) 12th Annual Conference, Washington, DC, April 15, 2011, p. 4.
40. Ibid.
41. Ibid.
42. Radwan Masmoudi, quoted in Conference Report, "Tunisia's and Egypt's Revolutions and Transitions to Democracy: What is the Impact on the Arab World? What Lessons can We Learn?" Edited by Thomas W. Skladony, Peter Winston Fettner, and Alexandra Tohmé. Center for the Study of Islam and Democracy (CSID) 12th Annual Conference, Washington, DC, April 15, 2011, p. 5.
43. Ibid.
44. "Strengthening Institutions in Tunisia," *International Crisis Group*, January 31, 2018: https://www.crisisgroup.org/middle-east-north-africa/north-africa/tunisia/strengthening-institutions-tunisia
45. "An Assassination in Tunisia," *The New York Times*, February 8, 2013: http://www.nytimes.com/2013/02/09/opinion/the-assassination-of-chokri-belaid-in-tunisia.html?_r=0
46. Seumas Milne, "Tunisian Government has No Hidden Agendas, Says New Prime Minister," *The Guardian*, April 2, 2013: http://www.guardian.co.uk/world/2013/apr/02/tunisia-government-agenda-prime-minister
47. Carlotta Gall, "Second Opposition Leader Assassinated in Tunisia," *The New York Times*, July 25, 2013: http://www.nytimes.com/2013/07/26/world/middleeast/second-opposition-leader-killed-in-tunisia.html?pagewanted=all&_r=1&
48. Ibid.
49. Ibid.
50. Ibid.
51. Ibid.
52. "Tunisia: Military Hunts Militants Near Algerian Border," *The New York Times*, August 2, 2013: http://www.nytimes.com/2013/08/03/world/africa/tunisia-military-hunts-militants-near-algerian-border.html

53. "Tunisia: Islamist-Led Government Steps Down," *Wilson Center*, January 9, 2014: https://www.wilsoncenter.org/article/tunisia-islamist-led-government-steps-down
54. Ibid.
55. *A Political Economy of the Middle East*, p. 103.
56. Ibid.
57. Ibid.
58. "Tunisia – Politics," GlobalSecurity.org, 2018: https://www.globalsecurity.org/military/world/tunisia/politics.htm
59. Ibid.
60. Ibid.
61. Ibid.
62. Ibid.
63. Sarah Yerkes, "Young People are Staying Away from Tunisian Politics – Here's Why," *Brookings*, March 20, 2017: https://www.brookings.edu/blog/markaz/2017/03/20/young-people-are-staying-away-from-tunisian-politics-heres-why/
64. Ibid.
65. Ibid.
66. Youssef Cherif, "Tunisia's Fledgling Gulf Relations," *Carnegie Endowment for International Peace*, January 17, 2017: http://carnegieendowment.org/sada/67703
67. Youssef Cherif, "Tunisia's Foreign Policy: A Delicate Balance," *Atlantic Council*, March 23, 2015: http://www.atlanticcouncil.org/blogs/menasource/tunisia-s-foreign-policy-a-delicate-balance
68. Ibid.
69. Marin Chulov, "Bahrain Destroys Pearl Roundabout," *The Guardian*, March 18, 2011: https://www.theguardian.com/world/2011/mar/18/bahrain-destroys-pearl-roundabout
70. Cherif, "Tunisia's Fledgling Gulf Relations."
71. Barack Obama and Beji Caid Essebsi, "Helping Tunisia Realize Its Democratic Promise," *The Washington Post*, May 15, 2015: https://www.washingtonpost.com/opinions/us-helping-tunisia-to-make-sure-democracy-delivers/2015/05/20/05b029e4-fe75-11e4-833c-a2de05b6b2a4_story.html?noredirect=on&utm_term=.54b0e439037f
72. Cherif, "Tunisia's Foreign Policy: A Delicate Balance."
73. Ibid.
74. Andrew Miller, "Tunisia is One of the Arab World's Biggest Success Stories. The Trump Administration Doesn't Seem to Care," *The Washington Post*, March 15, 2018: https://www.washingtonpost.com/news/democracy-post/wp/2018/03/15/tunisia-is-one-of-the-arab-worlds-biggest-success-stories-the-trump-administration-doesnt-seem-to-care/?utm_term=.b7093a8b7040

75. Ibid.
76. Ibid.
77. "Political Tensions Rise in Tunisia ahead of 2019 Presidential Elections," *TRT World*, September 28, 2018: https://www.trtworld.com/middle-east/political-tensions-rise-in-tunisia-ahead-of-2019-presidential-elections-20454
78. Ibid.
79. Ibid.
80. Ibid.
81. Ibid.
82. Ibid.
83. Ibid.
84. Ibid.
85. Sarah Yerkes, and Zeineb Ben Yahmed, "Tunisians' Revolutionary Goals Remain Unfulfilled," *Carnegie Endowment for International Peace*, December 6, 2018: https://carnegieendowment.org/publications/77894
86. Ibid.
87. Ibid.
88. Ibid.
89. Osman, "Why Border Lines Drawn with a Ruler in WWI Still Rock the Middle East," *BBC News*.
90. Cherif, "Tunisia's Foreign Policy: A Delicate Balance."
91. Thomas Carothers, "Tunisia in Transition: A Comparative View," *Carnegie Endowment for International Peace*, May 30, 2018: https://carnegieendowment.org/2018/05/30/tunisia-in-transition-comparative-view-pub-76501
92. Ibid.
93. A list of Tunisia's civil society organizations is provided at the end of this chapter.
94. Veronica Baker, "The Role of Civil Society in the Tunisian Democratic Transition," *Undergraduate Honors Thesis*, University of Colorado – Boulder, 2015 (pp. 5–6): https://scholar.colorado.edu/cgi/viewcontent.cgi?article=2212&context=honr_theses

CHAPTER 5

Tunisia's Economic Health

Life is hard in Tunisia these days. The economy is not growing as fast as people expected it to after the 2011 Jasmine Revolution. The economic hardships are straining people, especially the lower economic classes which mainly reside in the interior region. The outlying coastal areas are more upscale and cater most to the tourism industry with soft sandy beaches merging with the lapping waves of the sparkling Mediterranean Sea. Endless grand resorts line the coast stretching across 1148 km. The south consists of mostly desert terrain and climate, and thus is less populated compared to the north, which enjoys a more temperate and accommodating climate.

This is the backdrop to the analysis of Tunisia's economic health. This chapter focuses on the economy side of the political economy equation. Several years following the 2011 Arab Awakening revolution, Tunisia's economy desperately needs improvements, as the educated youth unemployment crisis continues to plague the country, and the coastal-interior wealth gap and intolerable poverty in the interior and south pose serious problems for economic development, growth, and progress.

First, it is important to understand Tunisia's basic economic variables, examining its agricultural, trade, and service sectors and analyzing its financial strengths and weaknesses.

From 2011 to 2015, the agricultural land in Tunisia has been mostly constant at 64 percent, which means that "the share of land area that is arable, under permanent crops, and under permanent pastures."[1] The

H. Alvi, *The Political Economy and Islam of the Middle East*, Political Economy of Islam,
https://doi.org/10.1007/978-3-030-17050-9_5

agriculture sector represents 12.6 percent of gross domestic product (GDP) with nearly 25 percent of the country's total labor force employed in it. Tunisia produces barley and wheat, dates, olives, meat, potatoes, and tomatoes, and its main export product is olive oil. Tunisia's primary trade partner is the European Union (EU).[2]

Trade with the EU has constituted 64 percent of Tunisia's trade in 2017; "78.5% of Tunisia's exports went to the EU, and 54.3% of Tunisia's imports came from the EU."[3] In 2017, total trade between the EU and Tunisia has "amounted to €20.5 billion. The EU's imports from Tunisia are mostly made up of machinery and transport equipment (€3.8 billion, 41.3%), textiles and clothing (€2.2 billion, 23.7%) and agricultural products (€0.5 billion, 6.1%)."[4] Trade in services between the EU and Tunisia have amounted to €3.3 billion (2016), and foreign direct investment (FDI) flows to Tunisia "are concentrated on the development of the infrastructure network as well as of the textiles and clothing sectors."[5] Tunisia's top export partners have been France, Italy, and Germany, with some trade involving Spain, Libya,[6] and, more recently, China. Tunisia's export products include "clothing, semi-finished goods and textiles, agricultural products, mechanical goods, phosphates and chemicals, hydrocarbons, and electrical equipment to export partners."[7]

Tunisia's top import partners are France, Italy, Germany, China, and Turkey, and in 2016 Tunisia's imports were worth $19.5 billion, "resulting in a negative trade balance of $4.22 billion."[8] Tunisia's primary import products are cars, petroleum, wheat, and low-voltage protection equipment.[9]

Tunisia's GDP in 2016 was $42.1 billion.[10] Between 1961 and 2017, Tunisia's GDP averaged $17.28 billion, "reaching an all-time high of $47.59 billion in 2014 and a record low of $0.90 billion in 1962."[11] Tunisia's detailed economic data for 2017 is provided below[12] (Table 5.1):

Table 5.1 Tunisia's Economic Data (2017)

Population (million)	11.5
GDP per capita (USD)	3483
GDP (USD billion)	40.1
GDP growth (annual variation in %)	1.9
Industrial Production (annual variation in %)	−1.0
Unemployment Rate	15.4
Fiscal balance (% of GDP)	−6.1
Public debt (% of GDP)	69.9
Money (annual variation in %)	16.9

(*continued*)

Table 5.1 (continued)

Inflation rate (CPI, annual variation in %)	5.3
Policy interest Rate (%)	5.00
Exchange rate (vs. USD)	2.46
Current account (% of GDP)	−10.4
Current account balance (USD, billion)	−4.2
Trade Balance (USD, billion)	−6.4
Exports (USD, billion)	14.2
Imports (USD, billion)	20.6
International reserves (USD)	5.7
External debt (% of GDP)	N/A

Source: "Tunisia," *Focus Economics*, Economic Forecasts from the World's Leading Economists, November 27, 2018: https://www.focus-economics.com/countries/tunisia

One of the most important data points from the economic data above is the unemployment rate (15.4 percent), which continues to afflict the economy. It is particularly harsh for the educated youth who triggered the 2011 revolution that removed the Ben Ali dictatorship. The issue of youth unemployment is addressed in detail later. Tunisia's GDP growth is modest, and, as always, the GDP does not indicate wealth distribution within the country. However, it is the *negative* data points that are cause for alarm. The fiscal (−6.1 percent), current account (−10.4 percent), and trade balance (−$6.4 billion) statistics illustrate weaknesses in the Tunisian economy. A negative fiscal balance means that the government suffers from a fiscal deficit, as opposed to a surplus. The fiscal balance represents revenue that the government receives from taxes and assets sold, and those values minus government spending equals the fiscal balance. The negative current account balance indicates that the government's payments outweigh the amount of interest and dividends it takes in. The current account balance consists of the trade balance along with direct payments and income and capital transfers. Trade balance represents exports and imports of goods and services, which means that a negative balance of trade translates into a trade deficit for the country's economy. The negative trade balance specifically means that Tunisia's imports exceed exports of goods and services.

Thus, Tunisia has a negative balance of trade, or a trade deficit. This is something that the Tunisian government has been trying to rectify. But when a country has limited resources to diversify its economy in order to restore the balance of trade, it has to innovate the education and vocational sectors and update skills and training to match the demands for goods and services in the modern global economy and enjoy a competitive edge.

Table 5.2 Comparative R&D Data for MENA

	% of GDP
Algeria and Bahrain	0.1
Oman	0.2
Iran	0.3
Jordan and Kuwait	0.4
Palestine and Qatar	0.5
Egypt	0.6
Tunisia, Morocco, and UAE	0.7
Saudi Arabia	0.8
Turkey	0.9
Israel	4.2

Source: "R&D Spending by Country," UNESCO, 2018: http://uis.unesco.org/apps/visualisations/research-anddevelopment-spending/

For innovation to match cutting-edge technology, skills, and training that the developed economies employ, countries like Tunisia must invest in research and development (R&D), but usually MENA countries do not invest heavily in R&D. They typically rely on technology transfers from the West, yet they claim to be engaged in diversifying their economies. In 2015, Tunisia spent 0.63 percent of GDP on research and development[13] and 0.7 percent in 2018.[14] For comparison, the United States spends 2.7 percent of GDP on R&D; Norway spends 2 percent of its GDP (2018)[15] on R&D; and in the United Kingdom the R&D expenditure has been 1.67 percent of GDP (2015 and 2016).[16] In the MENA region the R&D expenditures (as percentage of GDP)[17] are quite low, with the exception of Israel, which has one of the highest percentages of GDP for R&D expenditures in the world (Table 5.2).

Tunisia's tourism and agricultural sectors have rebounded in recent years, but "investment remains weak, unemployment is high especially among the youth and women, and the Tunisians' purchasing power is eroding."[18] Energy subsidy reforms are needed, as well as "strict controls on public sector hiring and remuneration, long-due progress with pension reform, further monetary tightening to contain inflation and high central bank refinancing, and steadfast implementation of the competitive FX auctions will be essential to protect the ongoing recovery"[19] in Tunisia's economy.

Undoubtedly, Tunisia operates in, and is affected by, the twists and turns of economic globalization. This renders Tunisia vulnerable to the impact of inflation and economic and financial crises on Tunisia's trade partners primarily in Europe (i.e., France, Italy, and Germany). In the years prior to the 2011 Jasmine Revolution, Europe faced rising inflation, high unemployment, and contagious financial crises. Agricultural output suffered significant blows too as a result of droughts. Consider the World Bank's report about the rise in food and energy prices in Europe:

> The World Bank food price index has matched its peak of 2008 with the energy price index still below the July 2008 peak. The increase in food prices in 2010–11 represents a generalized increase in the prices of several commodities. These commodity market developments reflect a combination of temporary and permanent factors. Rising incomes around the world, and particularly in emerging and developing countries, have increased demand for food and fuel. In addition, supply factors, related to fuel supply constraints and inventories, have affected prices both in the short and longer runs, while policies supporting bio-fuel production have affected grain prices.[20]

In the *Boston Globe*, Thanassis Cambanis wrote about the "Revolution of the Hungry," wherein he explains that, "The Arab Spring was a revolution of the hungry. The Arab world can't feed itself, and that's how the region's dictators like it."[21] He cites the statistics that the Arab states are "the world's largest net importers of grains, depending on exports from water-rich North America, Europe, and Central Asia,"[22] although centuries ago the MENA region was a fertile breadbasket. Egypt alone supplied grains to the rest of the world at one time. In the post-colonial era, government subsidies for bread and petroleum, as well as land reform programs that reduced agricultural lands, have led to the downfall of the region's status as a fertile heartland. Add to that the impacts of climate change, wars and conflicts, water scarcity, and the stresses on the environment and natural resources stemming from high population growth rates, and the MENA region has the perfect storm.

However, at the end of the day, it is the Arab leaders and political elite who are at fault. In fact, "most scholars now accept the idea first proposed by the economist Amartya Sen, that food shortages and famines are usually caused by political mismanagement, not by an actual lack of food."[23] According to Eckart Woertz of the Barcelona Center for International Affairs, who is quoted in Cambanis's article, "we can explain the crisis in terms of political economy: corruption, crony networks favored over rural populations. Droughts don't cause civil war in Los Angeles."[24]

Cambanis's conclusion is a gloomy assessment of the region: "People in the Arab world have been kept poorer than they should be by corrupt repressive governments that hog national wealth for a tiny elite. Until that changes, hunger and food insecurity will remain yet another symptom of the region's terrible governance."[25] Tunisia is well aware of these stark realities and strives to change the status quo of pre-revolution days.

Tunisia has not been immune to the effects of the rising food and energy costs in Europe, which have rippled throughout the world. Other developing economies in the MENA have also borne the brunt of rising inflation, combined with extremely high unemployment especially among the educated youth. That is the case in Egypt, Libya, Algeria, and elsewhere in the MENA. Therefore, Tunisia's unemployed youth along with the destitute residents of the interior region saw no other recourse but to rise up and topple the Ben Ali dictatorship.

The interdependent economic causal factors of corruption, youth unemployment, and coastal-interior wealth gap in Tunisia, in particular, further exacerbated the situation. Ben Ali and his wife's family, the Leila Trabelsi clan, employed abusive and corrupt practices that directly affected these economic factors.

Under the former President Ben Ali, unemployment (especially among the educated youth), poverty, and corruption reached unbearable levels (see Table 5.3 for data about corruption, unemployment, and poverty in Tunisia during the Ben Ali era).

According to Table 5.3, the educated youth in the age bracket 15–24 have suffered from 30.7 percent unemployment. Also, by early 2011, several hundred thousand have lived in poverty as well as suffered from unemployment. The total poverty rate comes to 24 percent in 2011.

With high corruption levels, increasing poverty rates, and especially terribly high unemployment among the educated youth, the situation in Tunisia became bleak. The educated youth had nothing to look forward to, and the political leadership brutally repressed any dissension. In addition, Ben Ali's secret police, or *mukhabarat*, transformed Tunisia into a virtual prison, or police state.

In addition to the above data, these countries' "freedom rankings" are also available. Freedom House, which ranks countries' political rights and civil liberties based on a 1–7 scale (with 1 = more free), ranks Tunisia as follows: for the year 2002, freedom score 5.5; civil liberties 5; and political rights 6; in 2007 its status was "not free," with a freedom score of 5.5; civil liberties 5; and political rights 6. And, in 2010, Tunisia's freedom status was "not free," with a freedom score of 6.0, civil liberties 5, and political rights 7.[26]

Table 5.3 Corruption, unemployment, and poverty—Tunisia

Human development variable	*Data*
Corruption Index (2007): scale of 1–10, with 1 as "most corrupt" (Transparency International)	4.2
Population	11.1 million
15–24 years: (male 840,907/female 834,320)	15.05%
25–54 years: (male 2,402,272/female 2,554,362)	44.52%
55–64 years: (male 520,305/female 505,612)	9.21%
65 years and over: (male 448,870/female 464,227) (2016 est.)	8.2%
Unemployment (ages 15–24)	37.6% Total Male 35.7% Female 41.8% (2012 est.)
Unemployment Rate (Overall)	15.2% (2015 est.) 15% (2014 est.)
Poverty Rate (living on $2 a day):	24% (May 2011) 15.5% (2010 est.)
Unemployed in Poverty	700,000

Sources: Transparency International; CIA World Fact Book; and Ministry of Social Affairs, Tunisia

Hence, under Ben Ali, Tunisia experienced repression of freedoms and rights, and this counters Amartya Sen's Development Theory that correlates freedoms and rights with economic progress and development. Without freedoms and rights, Tunisia's socioeconomic health remained stagnant. This has been one of the primary reasons for the 2011 Jasmine Revolution, and because other MENA countries have similar repression at the hands of autocratic leaders, the domino effect of the 2011 Arab Awakening should not be surprising.

Specifically, Tunisia's causal factors pertaining to the 2011 revolution have to do with economic variables and policies that perpetuated the educated youth unemployment, the intra-regional wealth gap between the country's wealthier coastal communities and those of the poorer interior, and the stifling corruption that penetrated all levels of society.

Casual Factors

The Youth Unemployment Crisis

As mentioned, Tunisia has about 80,000 graduates from college every year, and only 40,000 jobs can be created, on average per year.[27] Also, "women constitute the majority of graduates. Yet only 38 percent of women are employed compared with 51 percent of men."[28] In addition, the most vulnerable unemployed demographic "are the illiterate and school dropouts. They represent 34 percent of all unemployed youth."[29]

Their frustrations and restlessness, as well as their resentment toward the Ben Ali and Trabelsi–inflicted injustices, contributed to the outbreak of demonstrations, which ultimately led to the 2011 revolution. The collective outrage arising from the Mohamed Bouazizi self-immolation episode was an inevitable and natural reaction, given the circumstances, especially for the educated unemployed youth, in Tunisia in 2010 and early 2011:

> With no obvious rivals to Ben Ali, there was speculation that he was looking to pass on power to one of his relatives. In the final days of 2010, a series of protests began in the center of the country after a young graduate set himself on fire when stopped from selling fruit and vegetables without a license. The protests, advertised widely through social media networks, gradually spread.
>
> Ben Ali initially blamed the demonstrations on a fringe of 'extremists'. But he changed tack on 13 January, expressing deep regrets for the deaths of protesters, pledging to introduce media freedoms, and promising not to stand in 2014. But his offer of concessions failed to quell the unrest, and the following day, after huge crowds took to the streets of Tunis and clashed with the security forces once again, he fled the country.[30]

In his book, *Tunisia: An Arab Anomaly*, Safwan Masri describes the youth unemployment problem in detail:

> One-third of the unemployed were university graduates. At the time of the revolution, unemployment rates reached 50 percent for holders of technical and master's degrees, 68 percent for those with a master's degree in legal studies, 31 percent for engineers, and 70 percent for technicians.
>
> The youth felt cheated. They had been told to go to school, work hard, and that they would be guaranteed a future. Armed with degrees, university graduates were ill equipped for the labor force and mismatched with the needs of the marketplace.[31]

The Ben Ali regime initiated economic reforms, but they were mostly cosmetic with little positive impact on the lower economic classes and jobless youth.[32] Yet, the Western powers applauded Ben Ali's superficial reforms, thinking that they were genuine and effective. In truth, the status quo remained intact.

Upon the ouster of the Ben Ali regime, Tunisia has made noticeable progress in revising its constitution and rebuilding political institutions based on a new democracy. "The model of consensus-driven politics based on the '*Pact de Carthage*' (2016), has created a greater degree of political stability and has allowed for gradual progress on implementation of the 2014 Constitution."[33] However, youth unemployment has continued to plague the Tunisian economy. Although the labor force operates at mid-range levels, men outnumber women (69 percent to 27 percent, respectively) in employment. The World Bank reports that, "This poor performance is driven by weak job creation in the post-revolution period. Following net job destruction in 2015 mostly stemming from the impact on tourism of the two terrorist attacks (-11,700 jobs), job creation picked up in 2016 and 2017 with a modest net job creation of 34,700 and 45,500 jobs respectively, while in comparison the working-age population (and the active population) increased by 80,000 individuals yearly on average (48,000) in 2016–17."[34]

Since the 2011 revolution, Tunisia has taken significant steps to try to alleviate the crisis of unemployment among the educated youth. Along with numerous workshops on entrepreneurship, innovation, job creation, and employment strategies, the post-revolution government has initiated various social service programs to offset the economic hardships that countless Tunisians experience from high inflation, unemployment, low currency value, and waning tourism. According to the World Bank,

> Tunisia has in place an unconditional cash transfer program providing a social safety net (SSN) for vulnerable households which represent approximately eight percent of the population. 28 percent of the population also receives health care insurance cards through this program for subsidized services. Eligibility is based on a combination of categorical criteria and a variation of community-based targeting, determined by social worker interviews and local committees. However, targeting, information and monitoring of these programs is considered relatively weak. In addition, a large share of the working age population is either idle, unemployed, or working in low-quality jobs. In 2014, around one third of the youth population were categorized as Not in Employment, Education or Training (NEET).[35]

Oddly enough, Tunisia is "one of the few countries where a higher level of education decreases employability, in particular for women. Youth and women, in inland areas, are affected to the greatest degree, and the resulting growing outward migration of youth from these regions poses a growing threat to Tunisia's long-term economic competitiveness."[36] Evidently, the inland areas are hit with dual economic pressures and deficiencies: unemployment among the youth demographic, and poverty, especially compared to the wealthier coastal areas of the country.

The Coastal-Interior Wealth Disparities

Economically speaking, we can say that there are "two Tunisias": the wealthier coastal Tunisia, and the poorer interior hinterland of Tunisia. The economic status gap between the two regions is stark, as Dr. Masmoudi explains:

> If you spend three weeks visiting only the coastal areas of Tunisia, you will feel like you're in America. These areas are very advanced, very sophisticated, with nice roads, everything is nice. If you go inside, in the rural interior areas, you will feel like you're living in the 16th century, literally. It's black and white. The vast majority live on the coastal areas, maybe around 6 or 7 million out of the ten million population. But, you have about 3 to 4 million who live in the rural areas, and they are devastated, I mean those people have nothing.
>
> The problem is [that] a lot of them come often to the coastal areas, and either they study in universities in big cities, or some of them work, or visit, so they constantly go back and forth, and they see the discrepancies, they see the poverty, and they see how the rich people are living. The discrepancies became huge.
>
> Bourguiba, he was a patriotic dictator. He was not a corrupt dictator. But, Ben Ali was a dictator who didn't care about the nation, he was very corrupt; he had no values at all. Bourguiba was trying to make Tunisia developed. His goal, in an authoritarian way, was to have Tunisia developed. But Ben Ali was the opposite: his goal was to enrich himself and his family, that's all he cared about.[37]

In 2009, the rural population in Tunisia numbered about 3,453,000, and the number of rural poor stood at 480,000.[38] As a result, the combination of the rampant corruption, unemployment, and interior rural-coastal wealth disparities all contributed to the discontent and deep frustrations of the masses. In fact, the interior hinterland of Tunisia was "the crucible of the 2011 uprising, when protests demanding jobs and reform started in the town of Sidi Bouzid and spread across the country, eventually forcing Ben Ali into exile."[39] Even in the post-revolution era, despite codifying intra-regional economic parity into the 2014 constitution, the disparities remain stark and grim, as the central region continues to suffer from poverty rates as high as four times more than the coastal areas; in some central areas poverty is "as much as 30% in some regions."[40] According to a 2014 World Bank report, "Tunisia needs to create a level playing field by opening up the economy and removing… the dichotomy between the coast and the interior."[41]

President Essebsi and his government have promised to initiate economic reforms to improve the economic health and reduce poverty in the central region, but the center's populace dismisses this as "empty words."[42] The interior region lacks quality infrastructure, turning off investors, and Tunisia's "sorely needed economic stimulus was being held up by cumbersome Tunisian bureaucracy," according to a government official.[43]

The failures of government-sponsored economic reforms to close the wealth gap between the interior and coastal communities are causing discontent and desperation among the masses residing in poverty-stricken areas. Analysts warn that the region has the potential to explode into further protests and instability. In early 2016, "fresh demonstrations and clashes erupted [in January] in nearby Kasserine after an unemployed man died while protesting the removal of his name from a list of hires for public sector jobs."[44] The wealth gap "between its impoverished interior and coastal cities is sparking fresh unrest,"[45] and there are fears that history will repeat itself in Tunisia if this economic disparity is not closed while at the same time the other variables of youth unemployment and corruption are not tackled simultaneously. Under Ben Ali, corruption inflicted rot not just in the core of Tunisia's government, but also pulsated through all levels of society, which, at the same time, exacerbated the youth unemployment and other staggering economic deficiencies.

Corruption at the Core and Everywhere Else

Tunisians did not enjoy freedoms, rights, and choices for many years, hence the arrested development. Ben Ali and his family's corruption only reinforced the tightening noose on society, and their collective and individual grievances. This all came to a head when the Bouazizi self-immolation case was posted throughout the Internet and eventually the news media. The Tunisian people were already boiling with anger, and the Bouazizi case was the catalyst to the eruption of grassroots protests that, to everyone's surprise, swiftly led to Ben Ali's ouster. The Bouazizi case touched everyone in Tunisia, because Tunisians have long felt the sting of economic degradation coupled with violent repression at the hands of the Ben Ali regime, causing hatred and resentment throughout the country.

Safwan Masri adds: "Twenty-one years younger than Ben Ali, [Trabelsi] was nicknamed La *Régente de Carthage* as her influence over the regime grew. Her brother Belhassen Trabelsi helped himself to an airline company, a number of hotels, a private radio station, car assembly plants, a Ford distribution center, and a real estate development company."[46] Citing a 2014 World Bank report, Dr. Masri quotes that Ben Ali and the Trabelsi clan embezzled an estimated $13 billion worth of assets, "equivalent to more than 25 percent of Tunisia's GDP in 2011."[47]

According to *Al Jazeera*, of the 220 Trabelsi family-owned companies that the Tunisian authorities seized after the 2011 revolution, "the World Bank determined that while the firms accounted for only three percent of economic output, they controlled 21 percent of net private sector profits. By tailoring regulations to meet only their companies' needs, the Ben Ali family structured Tunisia's economy to benefit themselves and their closest allies."[48]

Even the media industry has not been immune to the Ben Ali and Trabelsi families' corrupt practices, using restrictions on the press for their advantage and for promoting their own financial interests.[49] State-run TV and radio stations, magazines, and printed press "were at least part-owned by a member of the family … Popular radio station Mosaique FM was also confiscated as a Ben Ali asset."[50]

The overwhelming, multifaceted corruption of the Ben Ali regime and Trabelsi clan penetrated every aspect of Tunisian society, including the security forces, military, police, customs officers, businessmen and women, bureaucrats, street vendors and sellers in the *souk* (market), and the citizens. Not only did this entrenched corruption undermine the economy and wealth distribution in Tunisia (and only worsened with each passing year), but it also, in the end, was the nail in the coffin of the Ben Ali regime.

The National Dialogue Quartet and Fighting Corruption in Tunisia

The role of the General Union of Tunisian Workers (*l'Union générale tunisienne du travail*, or UGTT) proved critical in the 2011 revolution and post-revolution political development, including anti-corruption efforts, in Tunisia. Sarah Chayes of the Carnegie Endowment for International Peace describes the UGTT as "perhaps the only organization whose power and legitimacy rival the Islamists'," crediting the UGTT for Tunisia's "remarkable political settlement."[51]

> Now counting more than half a million dues-paying members (about 5 percent of Tunisia's total population), a [UGTT] branch in every province as well as nineteen organized by activity, it penetrates society down to the grass roots. Its economic clout, together with extensive mediating and negotiating experience acquired through collective bargaining, were critical to the role it played in 2013. So was the determination, talent, and sheer stamina of General Secretary Houcine Abbassi, who personally ran hundreds of hours of negotiations.
>
> The union joined forces with three other respected institutions to drive the settlement process: the employers' union (UTICA), whose participation side-by-side with the normally hostile labor union added to the Quartet's moral as well as economic clout; the Tunisian Bar Association, founded in 1887, whose leadership also helped pilot the fight for independence; and the Human Rights League (LTDH), which has the distinction of being the first independent human rights association in the Arab world.[52]

The coalition of the labor unions, civil society organizations, and activists, referred to as the "National Dialogue Quartet," won the 2015 Nobel Peace Prize for its efforts to build consensus and reconciliation between disputing political groups in Tunisia with a strong commitment to non-violent conflict resolution. The UGTT, the Tunisian Confederation of Industry, Trade and Handicrafts, the LTDH, and the Tunisian Order of Lawyers comprise the National Dialogue Quartet. They are viewed as a civil society model for the Arab world to follow for national consensus-building and non-violent political discourse. A number of lawyers have participated in the national efforts to facilitate reconciliation and pave a way forward for the new democracy. Part of this process involves an unwavering fight against corruption, which continues to coat the fledgling democracy with its rusty criminal endeavors.

In May 2017, the Carnegie Endowment for International Peace interviewed Tunisia's head of the Anti-Corruption Authority, lawyer Chawki Tabib. Segments of the interview provide insight into why the fight against corruption is so difficult even after the Ben Ali era lies in the dustbin of history. According to Mr. Tabib, fighting corruption has become one of the priorities of the current national unity government, and when presenting his platform Prime Minister Youssef Chahed said, 'My government is an anti-corruption government, and I am declaring a war on corruption.' This is a positive development we had been trying to achieve. It is a good thing corruption has become a major issue in Tunisia. Everyone is talking about it, especially within political circles and civil society, but even everyday Tunisians. This plays into our strategy at the National Anti-Corruption Authority to make corruption a national issue. We need political will, which will not happen without the public standing up. The authority has done well in civil society and the media, and Tunisia has moved from denying corruption's existence to admitting it, particularly in the government's official stance. In the past, the government said that we were making a big deal out of nothing, but the situation has changed now.

In 2016, Tunisia passed laws like the Law on Access to Information and the Law on Reporting Corruption Cases and Protecting Whistleblowers, which was groundbreaking for the entire world, not just the Middle East. There is now a draft law in the Assembly of Representatives that requires public disclosure of income and assets and criminalizes illicit gains and conflicts of interest, which is also major progress for the legislative arsenal. All of these gains allowed Tunisia to improve in Transparency International's Corruption Perceptions Index in 2016 for the first time in four years. Tunisia now ranks 75 out of 176, tied with Turkey, Kuwait, and Bulgaria. Our goal is to be one of the 50 most transparent countries in the world within the next three to five years, and this is possible because there is more public awareness, national (public) will, and a consolidation of political will.

Why has corruption been difficult to stamp out?

One of the top goals of the Tunisian revolution was to overthrow the corrupt system headed by Zine al-Abidine Ben Ali. He had put in place a system of laws and administrative practices to protect his own interests and those of his family members and cronies. Unfortunately, after the revolution, we did not dismantle this corrupt system, even as we expelled the most corrupt figures. Ben Ali fled, some of his family members were tried and found guilty, and others had property confiscated. Less than a year after the revolution, his system of corruption was up and running again with new people in charge. Graft was democratized after the revolution—before, it benefited a handful of prominent figures, but it spread to dozens, hundreds, and then thousands of people who knew how to play the system for their own gain. On top of that, state institutions—including security, judicial, and administrative agencies—were badly weakened because Tunisians naturally saw them as pillars of the Ben Ali regime. Many of the people who ruled post-revolution Tunisia were also in unfamiliar roles and preoccupied with other priorities, such as fighting terrorism. Others were fine with using corruption for their own means, like financing their political parties and buying off journalists or bureaucrats. All of these factors together helped spread corruption and do greater damage to Tunisia.

What is the most important requirement to move the fight against corruption forward?

Political will is necessary to dismantle the system of graft. This system is based on laws and arrangements, and only politicians can put forward and approve bills to change them. Political will is also needed because without it we cannot resist corruption. Most corruption cases in Tunisia involve administration, broadly speaking, and concern politicians and government bureaucrats, because Tunisia has a highly centralized system where the government plays an outsized role—the state is the top employer, exporter, and importer. Corruption was rampant within the political scene, as a marriage of convenience took place between money and politics in Tunisia. The state's weakness allowed corrupt ringleaders to enhance their grip over the primarily smuggling-based parallel economy, which in turn requires graft to survive. The parallel economy now makes up about half of the Tunisian economy, giving an idea how rampant corruption is. Tunisia's economy is fairly modest in size, with a GDP of around $50 billion. Corruption has an outsized impact on such resource-poor economies, and our GDP is based largely on corruption-prone sectors such as services, tourism, industry, and foreign investment.[53]

Moreover, Tunisia's former colonial master, France, has stepped up its economic and security support for the country. In addition to providing intelligence and security assistance following terrorist attacks in post-revolution Tunisia, France has also "pledged a $1.1 billion aid package over five years to enrich Tunisia's poorest areas and promote job creation."[54] Such assistance is desperately needed in Tunisia, as it bears high debts and deficits. The fiscal deficit "reached 6.1 percent of GDP in 2017, 1 percentage point of GDP above the initial budget, due mainly to higher wage bill spending. The current account deficit reached a record 10 percent of GDP in 2017 as export growth remained low compared to import growth, despite a gradual depreciation of the Dinar. Consequently, public and external debt reached respectively 73 and 80 percent of GDP (compared to 40 and 52 percent of GDP in 2010)."[55] The current account deficit has expanded, and foreign direct investment (FDI) has plummeted, while "gross international reserves have continued to decrease, reaching 3.1 months of import by end-2017 (US $5.7 billion) and dropped below 90 days in February 2018."[56]

Economic Reforms Race Against Time

Tunisia has turned to the International Monitory Fund (IMF) and other international lenders to assist in its economic reforms. The IMF demands that Tunisia trim its subsidies to "cut a budget deficit estimated to have hit 6.8 percent of national output last year. But the cuts will raise fuel and food costs and may spark further discontent among Tunisians,"[57] and that prediction has rang true. As of early 2014, the IMF had yet to allocate $500 million out of its $1.5 billion loan to Tunisia.[58]

These numbers and debts are not comforting for Tunisia's economic health, and, in fact, economic stagnation threatens to fester. More protests have burst on to the scene intermittently, demanding faster and more effective economic improvements. Throughout most of 2017, the country still suffered from 15.3 percent unemployment rate, "up from a pre-revolution rate of 13 percent."[59] Plus, the problem of highly educated youth comprising the bulk of the unemployed demographic continues to plague Tunisia. Political analyst Youssef Cherif says, "Tunisia is trapped in a vicious circle. 'It is a tricky situation, a chicken-or-egg scenario: Tunisians are in the streets protesting the economic stagnation that is, in part, caused by lack of investment,' he told FRANCE-24. 'But as long as this unrest continues, other countries will look elsewhere to spend their money'."[60] Given that Tunisia's second economic partner happens to be Libya, the 2011 campaign that overthrew Colonel Muammar Qaddafi and precipitated the country into violent chaos also negatively affected Tunisia's economy and security due to the porous border. The flow of terrorists, traffickers, weapons, and migrants have inundated Tunisia and seriously challenge its national security and economic health.

The 2015 terrorist attacks on the Bardo Museum and the Sousse resort beachgoers "crippled the tourist industry, a major source of income for the North African state."[61] These attacks have further obstructed Tunisia's economic development and progress. However, the environment in which these economic woes continue to anger the masses has changed, since "Tunisians can now engage freely in public discourse and use social media to share their views"[62] without the kinds of consequences they would have faced under the Ben Ali regime.

It is not only tourism that has suffered from economic malaise in Tunisia. The agriculture sector is also facing formidable challenges, including politicians tending to frustrate farmers by failing to meet their needs. The interior and southern regions of Tunisia are not the only ones that feel neglected. Tunisia's agricultural sector in the northwest contains villages and vast plots of land that generations of farming families have cultivated. These farming families feel increasingly neglected by the powers that be in Tunis.

Tunisia's Agriculture Sector

Tunisia's arable land yields some of the best produce in the region. However, despite this reality, Tunisia has been importing agricultural products for the last 20 years. Tunisia imports corn, soybeans, sugar, vegetable oils, and barley, while it exports dates, olive oil, citrus, and fish.[63] Olive oil is a product of Tunisian pride, as it serves as "the world's top four exporters of olive oil; … About 70% of Tunisia's olive oil production is destined for export, mainly in bulk, with 14% exported in bottles."[64]

However, the neoliberal system in the era of globalization has not been kind to the traditional Tunisian farmer. Tunisian scholar and geographer Habib Ayeb has shined a light on the plight of the Tunisian farmers in the northwest Tunisian-Algerian border region. His documentary film, "Couscous: Seeds of Dignity" (2017), "deals with issues relating to food sovereignty in Tunisia from the ground up – from the point of view of the small farmer, whose expertise and physical bond with the land have been rejected and violated at every turn by corporate-capitalist agricultural policies designed to wrest as gigantic a profit as possible from the human need to consume food."[65] The right to one's land and what to do with it are at stake in this part of Tunisia.

According to the documentary, "while the vast majority of Tunisian farmers own less than 10 hectares of land, three percent of farmers own 36 percent of the total agricultural area and one percent owns 22 (percent)."[66] Big corporations pressure the small farmers to produce crops with the companies' seeds, which are inferior in quality compared to the indigenous seeds; and these pressures bear down on the farming communities in order to produce for-export crops, rather than for domestic consumption. These business-oriented pressures have angered Tunisian farmers, and they feel frustrated because they contend that the politicians are not listening to their complaints.

Farmers are forced to use imported seeds for watermelon, wheat, and other crops, which "proved far less resilient to climate disruptions as well as inferior in numerous other ways. Complaints include subpar harvests, less flavor and nutritional value, a proliferation of seeds with nonrenewable traits – meaning, for instance, that watermelon seeds can't be replanted and instead have to be continually repurchased from the supplier – and a toxic reliance on pesticides and chemicals, also imported from abroad."[67]

The farmers profiled in the documentary film blame the Tunisian government for being "inattentive to their needs, instead favoring large producers and other agricultural profiteers. Case in point: a 2016 dispatch at the Open Society Foundation's website discusses how Tunisian small farmers relying on springs and wells have 'been undermined by investors who are able to drill more wells for their large-scale irrigation schemes', while the Tunisian 'government exempts large farmers from water and irrigation taxes' but forces small farmers to pay them."[68]

Moreover, according to Habib Ayeb, "olive oil is prohibitively expensive for many Tunisian families despite being a staple of the national diet and despite the saturation of much of the country with olive trees. A liter of olive oil can cost 10 dinars (approximately $4) in southern Tunisia – the equivalent of a 'good' daily salary for a Tunisian agricultural worker."[69] Farmers want to be able to produce crops for the domestic market and not be told how to do their jobs, as they have been doing agricultural work for centuries. Until now, the agricultural sector provided abundant produce to the domestic market, then the large agribusinesses and their investors have taken the reins. In the documentary film, the Tunisian farmers consider these new methods imposed on them as a "neocolonial" tool to undermine the country's self-sufficiency.

At the end of the film, a farmer says, "I don't want my children, my grandchildren and future generations to be dependent on Western or other countries who decide what they eat."[70] Once again, the farmers' sentiments convey their strong desire and right for dignity.

Tunisia's Energy Sector

Tunisia does not possess much hydrocarbon, and in fact its petroleum production has been "steadily declining from its peak of 120,000 barrels per day (bbl/d) in the mid-1980s to 60,000 bbl/d in 2013. Tunisia produced 66 billion cubic feet of dry natural gas in 2012."[71] Tunisia's government bureaucracy has delayed approval of gas and oil projects, and foreign investors are frustrated due to the red tape.[72] The British BG Group, Austrian OMV, and Italian ENI are the "main foreign companies operating in Tunisia."[73]

Tunisia has a single oil refinery, but "it is not enough [production] to meet domestic demand, which averaged 90,000 bbl/d in 2013. As a result, Tunisia imports a majority of the petroleum projects it consumes."[74] There are plans to construct another refinery in Skhira. Investors for that refinery include "the Tunisian government, Qatar Petroleum, and the Libyan government. However, given the unrest and political uncertainty in Libya, it is unlikely that the Libyan government will take part in the project anytime soon."[75]

Recently, vast shale reserves have been discovered in the Ghadames Basin, which could potentially provide oil resources. According to the Energy Information Administration (EIA), the Trans-Mediterranean Pipeline passes through Tunisia, for which Tunisia "receives natural gas as a royalty."[76] Tunisia has also been "committed to be part of the DESERTEC 'super-grid' that will connect African and European countries."[77]

Overview and Outlook for Tunisia's Economy

In post-revolution Tunisia, the pervasive economic demands still stem from "massive youth unemployment, the proliferation of marginal jobs in the informal sector, and increasing income inequality."[78] According to the Carnegie Endowment for International Peace, Tunisia's 2018 unemployment rate "remains high at 15.5 percent. And young university graduates now face an even greater level of unemployment (29 percent), which continues to be the principal driver of social discontent."[79] Specifically,

> One problem is the long-standing mismatch between Tunisia's educated labor force and the relatively low number of qualified job openings. In 2015, it was estimated that, on average, it takes graduates six years to find a stable job, and half are still unemployed by age thirty-five. Unwisely, the government has responded by further increasing public sector hiring and wages. At about 14 percent of the gross domestic product (GDP), spending on public sector salaries in Tunisia is now higher than anywhere else in the world. Not only is this costly, it also does not adequately address the underlying employment problem and leaves little room in the budget for investment.

> … The government has failed to enact much-needed reforms—including streamlining the bureaucracy, fighting corruption and nepotism, reforming customs, and establishing comprehensive tax regimes—and has instead prioritized political change. Economic challenges were deferred while political leaders focused on their own internal disputes, and few actors were willing or able to stand up to the powerful trade unions who have consistently blocked the implementation of key reforms. While it would be nearly impossible to tackle all the political and economic reforms simultaneously, the decision to postpone necessary economic reforms created the challenging economic situation the country is now in.
>
> As a result, an increasing number of Tunisians are joining the informal economy, which now accounts for about half of the country's GDP. Moreover, following the guidance of international lenders, including the European Union and International Monetary Fund (IMF), Tunisia has adopted painful austerity measures at the expense of meeting a high demand for jobs, leading to increased taxes and prices. In October 2018, Tunisia's annual inflation rate rose to 7.4 percent, the highest in twenty years.[80]

Poverty is persistent in some parts of Tunisia; in fact, 26 percent of Tunisians "indicated that they have trouble feeding [themselves] and [their] family and buying even the most essential things for survival – a figure that has fluctuated from 32 percent in March 2011 down to 15 percent in May 2016 and back up in recent years."[81] Therefore, dignity based on fundamental human development and security factors, like food, water, and job security, is paramount in Tunisia today and for its future economic health.

What is working in favor of Tunisia's socioeconomic progress and sets it apart from the other MENA actors is the outreach to European partners for job training, employment opportunities, and innovations in foreign direct investment (FDI) and job creation. Tunisia's post-revolution determination to stay on course for democratization and economic liberalization also sets the country apart from other MENA countries that have experienced Arab Awakening uprisings. Most of the latter countries have either collapsed into violent civil conflict, like in Libya and Syria, or they have retrenched themselves in the old guard status quo scenario. On the other hand, Tunisia continues to fight against the few remnants of the old guard status quo forces. Tunisian institutions' cooperation with each other through negotiations and dialogue also sets the country apart from the rest of the MENA region.

Also, Tunisia has immunized itself from the extremely sensitive conflicts and rifts that pervade in the MENA region. Distancing itself from these powder kegs in both geopolitical and ideological terms has, for the most part, shielded Tunisia from economic and humanitarian catastrophes arising from conflicts, wars, and terrorist attacks. If Tunisia were to get involved in supporting proxy militias fighting against Syria's Assad regime, then it would fail to focus on domestic socioeconomic development and progress. The latter constitutes the priority for Tunisia, and its detachment from MENA regional conflicts contributes to Tunisian leaders' focus on improving the domestic economy. This, too, sets Tunisia apart from the rest of the region, which is extremely preoccupied with purchasing weapons, building up their militaries, and engaging in regional geopolitical power competitions. Given this reality, Tunisia fares better than the rest of the regional actors in political economy terms.

Since the 2011 Arab Awakening began in Tunisia, the onus has been on the country's transitional leadership, institutions, and political system to ensure effective reforms and uphold the commitment to dialogue, negotiations, and agreements. These aspects of post-revolution transitions make Tunisia's case unique. The commitment of various political actors and institutions to remain on a non-violent track of negotiations and consensus-building is unheard of in the MENA region. Yet, Tunisia has kept the promise to stay the course along those lines of non-violent dialogue and negotiations.

The Political Economy of the Middle East and North Africa: A Comparative Analysis

Comparing Tunisia's case to the overall political economy of the Middle East and North Africa (MENA) region, several crises, dilemmas, financial downturns, and economic deficiencies are noticeable. Even the oil-rich countries have not exhibited sound economic policies. Government decision-making concerning economic activities and resource allocation, for the most part, have been counterproductive, if not wholly unwise.

First, examining the poorest country in the region, Yemen, it will be surprising to see if it survives at all from the conflict and humanitarian crises that the Saudi-led coalition as well as the Houthi rebels have perpetuated and inflicted on the country. In addition to poverty, Yemen is now suffering terrible conflict-caused diseases, like cholera, severe malnutrition, high mortality rates, general human insecurity, and a stagnant economy. Plus, Yemen is predicted to run out of water very soon. This will trigger yet another wave of humanitarian crisis.

Clearly, the Saudi-allied forces and Iran's proxies, with Al Qaeda in the Arabian Peninsula (AQAP) and the Islamic State (IS) cells operating within vacuums in Yemen, all vying for power and trying to undermine each other, there is no respite for the Yemeni civilians. Western powers are culpable in this genocide, since they are supplying the Saudis and its coalition forces with weapons and military assistance for the failed, disastrous campaign.

Second, related to the first point, in recent years oil prices have plummeted and shocked the oil-export-dependent economies in the region. Saudi Arabia and the other Gulf Cooperation Council (GCC) countries—the six Arab monarchies in the Persian Gulf region—have been scrambling to compensate for the decline in oil prices. Many are trying to diversify their economies by expanding their investments abroad and inviting more investors into their countries; reforming some subsidies, even in energy; and initiating social reforms specially to liberalize—albeit gradually and not holistically—restrictive codes imposed on women. Saudi Arabia, the most restrictive misogynist society, intends to initiate these social reforms because this is meant to appear as intending to modernize Saudi society with hopes that the country would be more palatable to Western businesses and investors. It is also part of the Saudi plan to open the kingdom to tourism, which is extremely challenging, given the country's strict Wahhabi rules and codes that the religious police enforce vigilantly. Plus, this begs the question, what is there for tourists to see in Saudi Arabia? How viable are these proposed reforms and initiatives remain to be seen.

However, despite the decline in oil prices, Saudi Arabia and its coalition have continued to purchase weapons and equipment and receive training from Western powers. The money for these purchases could be used to reinvest in various sectors of the countries' economies and research and development (R&D), rather than allocate resources to needlessly destroy a fellow Arab country, Yemen, in the most brutal, genocidal manner.

Saudi Arabia also locked up a number of top royal family members in the Ritz Carlton in Riyadh: "more than 30 of Saudi Arabia's most senior figures, among them blood relatives of senior rulers, were locked inside the hotel, accused of corruption. Their ignominious arrests were the talk of the country, and so too was the fact that they were far from a prison cell, where most citizens facing similar charges could expect to find themselves."[82] This was an attempt to corner and squeeze the 30 or so senior figures to get them to release huge sums of money that the authorities alleged originated from corruption. The Saudi leadership realized that the kingdom's coffers are low, because of the oil price crisis, and so they decided that the best way to refill the coffers is by demanding hundreds of millions of dollars from the top royal family members in the façade of an anti-corruption campaign. With all this drama and palace intrigue, in the end the Saudis still decided to continue the catastrophic military campaign in Yemen, with no clear objectives, and no apparent strategy. These realities illustrate one of the most pervasive problems in governance throughout the region: confused priorities at the domestic and regional levels, all of which directly affect the economic health and status of the regional actors.

Third, the propensity for regional actors to remain preoccupied with conflicts, rivalries, and strategic advantages to undermine one another has rendered terrible costs in human security terms to the people caught in conflict zones. This pervasive regional competition, particularly between Saudi Arabia and Iran by means of proxies, is also affecting Iran's economic health and status. The bottom line is that both Saudi Arabia and Iran have been pursuing agendas and strategies for respective regional hegemony at the expense of their domestic economic health. Rather than allocating resources to strengthen their economies, each country is more focused on competing against each other at the regional level, and neither considers conflict resolution as a viable option.

All of the Persian Gulf Arab states have large youth demographics, as does Iran. If the national economies of these countries fail to meet the needs of the masses of unemployed youth, this could be a recipe for disaster. Setting domestic economic priorities is crucial for these countries' future and security. Anything else is counterproductive, especially in the absence of long-term sustainable conflict resolution.

In terms of domestic economic policies, the MENA countries do not fare well. Even the oil-rich Gulf Arab states face "profound economic challenges."[83] According to scholars Joseph Bahout and Perry Cammack:

> The rentier model and its redistribution mechanisms, upon which Arab economies were built, have unraveled.
>
> In a rentier system, the state uses rents—payments received for the use of fixed factors of production—to fund vast networks of patronage and provide social services to its people. For years, rentierism derived from oil sales or other sources maintained the political and economic status quo in the Middle East.

But lower oil prices, increased global competition, and growing populations have rendered this model unsustainable. This becomes even more apparent when compared with geographic regions that have experienced sustained, dynamic economic growth in recent decades, such as Southeast Asia.

As the old systems collapse, there has been no clear articulation of what will replace them. Besides the unescapable macroeconomic reorientations, constructing a new order requires states to begin confronting the patronage system and crony networks that distort economic outcomes and suppress job creation. The economic challenge is thus not merely technical, but profoundly political as well.[84]

The patronage and clientelist systems have led to immense, multi-level corruption. According to Transparency International, which measures corruption, the Corruptions Perceptions Index for 2017 shows that 16 of the 21 Arab countries surveyed "scored below the global mean of 43 (on a 0–100 scale)."[85] Moreover, "with growing perceptions of corruption, festering poverty and underemployment, and continuing political stagnation, the explosion of public discontent was likely inevitable."[86] The 2017 Corruption Perceptions Score (0–100 scale)[87] for the MENA countries are as follows (the lower the number, the more corrupt):

Algeria	33
Bahrain	36
Egypt	32
Iran	30
Iraq	18
Israel	62
Jordan	48
Kuwait	39
Lebanon	28
Libya	17
Morocco	40
Oman	44
Qatar	63
Saudi Arabia	49
Sudan	16
Syria	14
Tunisia	42
Turkey	40
UAE	71
Yemen	16

Also, in recent years, the declining oil prices have negatively affected the oil-exporting economies in the MENA region. Combined with rising population growth, the economies of Oman, Bahrain, and Saudi Arabia, in particular, have been extremely strained. In addition, the UAE, Bahrain, and Saudi Arabia "have responded to the ongoing regional turmoil with increased repression against any form of political dissent."[88] Yemen and Syria "were formerly oil exporters, but revenues have collapsed amid a combination of war, dwindling production, and declining prices."[89] Specifically, the oil-exporting countries' revenues "have been disproportionately spent on repression and the military as well as captured by cronyism and corruption. The results are underperforming economies and particularly grievous failures in governance."[90]

The non–oil-exporting economies, like Egypt, Palestine, Lebanon, Morocco, and Jordan, have growing populations, with which their economic growth and development cannot keep up. Egypt's population has reached almost 100 million. Most importantly, "[These states] contain more than half of the region's population but account for only one-quarter of its GDP."[91] They have operated on the rentier system since independence. Yet, the MENA region has not exemplified sound macroeconomic policies, focusing heavily on defense spending and supporting proxy wars in Syria, Iraq, and Yemen, but failing in other essential economic improvements. Annually, Saudi Arabia spends $56.7 billion on defense, ranking number 3 in the world, coming third after China, ranking 2, and the United States, ranking number 1; the United Arab Emirates spends $14.3 billion on defense, ranking number 16 in the world; Israel spends $20 billion, ranking 14; Algeria and Turkey spend $10 billion, ranking 21 and 22, respectively; Egypt spends $4.4 billion, ranking 45; Libya spends $3 billion, ranking 54; Bahrain spends $730 million, ranking 79; and Tunisia spends $550 million, ranking 84.[92]

Two economic challenges in the MENA region are prominent: "the urgent and related needs for job creation – especially among the burgeoning number of unemployed youth – and for sustained, equitable macroeconomic growth."[93] Rentier systems will not suffice in dealing with these challenges. The MENA governments need to adopt sound macroeconomic policies, which encompass: "supporting macroeconomic stability, building human capital, promoting international trade, and encouraging private enterprise."[94]

- *Supporting macroeconomic stability* includes controlling government deficit and debt levels and maintaining low inflation and stable interest rates. Oil-exporting countries have the added challenge of responsibly managing government spending across boom-and-bust commodity cycles. Several of the region's poorer countries, including Egypt, Jordan, and Lebanon, rank among the most indebted countries in the world, hampering their long-term growth prospects.
- *Building human capital*, first and foremost, is about providing citizens with the tools to compete in the twenty-first-century knowledge economy, through the creation of dynamic education systems. Qatar, the UAE, and Tunisia, for example, are pursuing noteworthy improvements in education. Ensuring adequate legal protection for workers, including migrant workers across the region, is also critical.
- *Promoting international trade* can be accomplished through policies that expand the export-oriented segments of the economy, manage the exchange rate effectively, and remove obstacles to trade, such as tariffs, duties, licenses, and quotas. Oman and Lebanon impose low import tariffs and are relatively open to foreign investment. While Morocco has made progress integrating itself into global supply chains to European consumer markets, the Maghreb subregion remains one of the least economically integrated in the world.
- *Encouraging private enterprise* is critical if job creation is to reach its potential. This ultimately requires shifting the economy from oil-based and state-dominated to non-oil-based and private sector–oriented. Steps that have been articulated to generate private sector job creation, especially among small and medium-sized firms, include reducing onerous bureaucratic impediments to private enterprise; enacting flexible hiring and firing practices; reducing subsidies for politically connected and state-owned firms; increasing the transparency of procurement standards to reduce corruption; and expanding access to the 70 percent of Arab citizens who lack bank accounts through financial technology and microfinance. The UAE scores highest among Arab countries in the World Bank's Ease of Doing Business ranking—21st out of 190 countries—which considers variables such as permitting, infrastructure, credit access, and legal environment. No other Arab country ranks in the top 60, highlighting the detrimental impact of protectionist policies, rentierism, and crony capitalism.[95]

Implementation of these reform-oriented policies would be very difficult for the MENA economies. Economic reform "is no mere technocratic exercise but a political process that gets to the heart of the division of spoils in a society."[96] However, Arab economies, in particular, have failed in reform efforts over the last few decades. Moreover, MENA economies need to integrate women and youth demographics into "modernization projects," as they "account for roughly two-thirds of the populations of most Arab societies. Yet, they do not have significant political influence in any Arab society."[97]

Unfortunately, the MENA region harbors substantial impediments to economic reform, and transcending them "may require that Arab states and their reformers embrace new models that emphasize inclusive growth and give more responsibility, as well as more rights, to participating citizens."[98] These steps require the political will of governments to adopt and implement progressive reforms along with building institutions that can handle, and perhaps even transcend the challenges of the global economy. Currently, the political will of MENA governments seem focused on the status quo, which is the reason for arrested development and quashed optimism.

Conclusion

While eating lunch at a Tunis restaurant on July 13, 2017, I attempted to pay with Tunisian currency I had with me from prior travels to Tunisia. The waiter looked at it and said, "You have Ben Ali money." I had not realized that following the 2011 revolution, Tunisia introduced new currency and rendered the one from the Ben Ali dictatorship obsolete. That is a good sign.

No one denies that Tunisia faces a formidable set of challenges that simultaneously pummel and bruise diverse sectors of the country's politics, economics, society, sectors, industries, finances, and national security, of which economic health is a vital part.

Tunisia continues to face economic challenges, including protests and strikes, like the November 2018 public workers strike numbering 650,000, "to protest the government's refusal to raise wages," which the IMF dictated as a reform measure.[99] Economic forecasters for Tunisia predict steady growth (about 2.6 percent in 2019) with strengthening of and support from the tourism industry.[100] Nevertheless, "the country's elevated fiscal and trade deficits, high youth unemployment, public unrest, and growing political instability all represent downside risks to its economic outlook."[101]

Change is gradual in a society like Tunisia, where bureaucratic obstacles pose hurdles to economic reforms and improvements. These realities and gradualism test the patience of the masses, especially the unemployed youth.

Overall, Tunisia has shown resilience, and Tunisians have conveyed the message in the strongest and most vocal terms that the essence of the country is in its people's determination to set it on the democratic track with aims to codify liberalism as its core principle. Safwan Masri summarizes this important track that Tunisians have committed themselves to progress forward, rather than regress back to the Ben Ali status quo in failure. He says, "It is a new story in that so little was known about Tunisia and its specificities until it became the lone success story of the Arab Awakening. But it is an old story in that democratic and liberal Tunisia had been in the making for a long, long time."[102] The other actors in the MENA region have a lot to learn about non-violent transitions from the Tunisia model.

Tunisia's progress, albeit gradual, in its economic and political health will stay on course as long as freedoms and rights, particularly for personal choices, as Amartya Sen's Social Choice Theory stipulates, are insured and preserved. The Tunisian leadership and people will also have to stay the course for engaging in peaceful dialogue and negotiations, which will immunize the country from violent conflict, despite the challenges the country continues to endure.

Notes

1. "Tunisia: Percent Agricultural Land," *The Global Economy* (Source: The World Bank), 2018: https://www.theglobaleconomy.com/Tunisia/Percent_agricultural_land/
2. "Country Profile Tunisia," *International Trade Centre (ITC)*, UNCTAD/WTO, 1994–2015: http://www.intracen.org/exporters/organic-products/country-focus/Country-Profile-Tunisia/
3. "Countries and Regions: Tunisia," *European Commission*, May 24, 2018: http://ec.europa.eu/trade/policy/countries-and-regions/countries/tunisia/
4. Ibid.
5. Ibid.
6. "Tunisia Trade, Exports and Imports," *Economy Watch*: http://www.economywatch.com/world_economy/tunisia/export-import.html

7. Ibid.
8. Ibid.
9. Ibid.
10. "Tunisia," *The Observatory of Economic Complexity (OEC)*, 2018: https://atlas.media.mit.edu/en/profile/country/tun/
11. "Tunisia GDP," *Trading Economics*, 2018: https://tradingeconomics.com/tunisia/gdp
12. "Tunisia," *Focus Economics*, Economic Forecasts from the World's Leading Economists, November 27, 2018: https://www.focus-economics.com/countries/tunisia
13. "Tunisia – Research and Development Expenditure (% of GDP)," *Trading Economics*, 2018: https://tradingeconomics.com/tunisia/research-and-development-expenditure-percent-of-gdp-wb-data.html
14. "R&D Spending by Country," *UNESCO*, 2018: http://uis.unesco.org/apps/visualisations/research-and-development-spending/
15. "Norway," *OECD Data*, 2018: https://data.oecd.org/norway.htm
16. "Research and Development Expenditure," Office of National Statistics, UK, 2018: https://www.ons.gov.uk/economy/governmentpublicsectorandtaxes/researchanddevelopmentexpenditure
17. "R&D Spending by Country," UNESCO.
18. "Tunisia: Fourth Review Under the Extended Fund Facility Arrangement and Request for Modification of Performance Criteria-Press Release; Staff Report; and Statement by the Executive Director for Tunisia," IMF Staff County Reports, *International Monetary Fund (IMF)*, October 8, 2018: https://www.imf.org/en/Publications/CR/Issues/2018/10/08/Tunisia-Fourth-Review-Under-the-Extended-Fund-Facility-Arrangement-and-Request-for-46285
19. Ibid.
20. "Rising Food and Energy Prices in Europe and Central Asia," *The World Bank*, 2011: http://www-wds.worldbank.org/external/default/WDSContentServer/WDSP/IB/2011/04/14/000333037_20110414015110/Rendered/PDF/610970WP0P1262171World1Bank1Combine.pdf, "Summary," p. 1.
21. Thanassis Cambanis, "The Arab Spring was the Revolution of the Hungry," *The Boston Globe*, August 23, 2015: https://www.bostonglobe.com/ideas/2015/08/22/the-arab-spring-was-revolution-hungry/K15S1kGeO5Y6gsJwAYHejI/story.html
22. Ibid.
23. Ibid.
24. Ibid.
25. Ibid.
26. "Freedom in the World 2002, 2007, and 2010: Tunisia," *Freedom House*: http://www.freedomhouse.org/report/freedom-world/2002/tunisia

27. Interview with Radwan Masmoudi, March 2012, Tunis, Tunisia.
28. "Tunisia Country Fact Sheet," *International Fund for Agricultural Development (IFAD)*, 2011 Governing Council: http://www.ifad.org/events/gc/34/nen/factsheet/tunisia.pdf
29. Ibid.
30. "Profile: Zine el-Abidine Ben Ali," *BBC News*, June 20, 2011: https://www.bbc.com/news/world-africa-12196679
31. Safwan M. Masri, *Tunisia: An Arab Anomaly* (New York: Columbia University Press, 2017), p. 34.
32. Ibid.
33. "The World Bank in Tunisia," *The World Bank*, April 18, 2018: https://www.worldbank.org/en/country/tunisia/overview
34. Ibid.
35. Ibid.
36. Ibid.
37. Interview with Radwan Masmoudi.
38. "Tunisia Country Fact Sheet," *IFAD.*
39. "Poverty in Central Tunisia a Ticking Time Bomb," *Gulf News*, March 4, 2016: https://gulfnews.com/news/mena/tunisia/poverty-in-central-tunisia-a-ticking-time-bomb-1.1683702
40. Ibid.
41. Ibid.
42. Ibid.
43. Ibid.
44. Ibid.
45. Ibid.
46. Masri, p. 35.
47. Ibid.
48. Tristan Dreisbach, and Robert Joyce, "Revealing Tunisia's Corruption under Ben Ali," *Al Jazeera*, March 27, 2014: https://www.aljazeera.com/indepth/features/2014/03/revealing-tunisia-corruption-under-ben-ali-201432785825560542.html
49. Ibid.
50. Ibid.
51. Sarah Chayes, "How a Leftist Labor Union Helped Force Tunisia's Political Settlement," *Carnegie Endowment for International Peace*, March 27, 2014: https://carnegieendowment.org/2014/03/27/how-leftist-labor-union-helped-force-tunisia-s-political-settlement-pub-55143
52. Ibid.
53. "Tunisia's Fight against Corruption: An Interview with Chawki Tabib," *Sada Journal*, Carnegie Endowment for International Peace, May 11, 2017: http://carnegieendowment.org/sada/69939

54. Marc Rivett-Carnac, "France Strengthens Support for Tunisia in the Face of Islamist Threats," *Time*, March 17, 2016: http://time.com/4262329/tunisia-france-aid-security-ben-guerdane-isis-islamist/
55. "The World Bank in Tunisia," https://www.worldbank.org/en/country/tunisia/overview
56. Ibid.
57. Patrick Markey, and Aziz El Yaakoubi, "Tunisian Premier Resigns for Caretaker Government," *Reuters*, January 9, 2014: https://www.reuters.com/article/us-tunisias-pm-idUSBREA080MY20140109
58. Ibid.
59. Owen Barnell, "Seven Years after Arab Spring Revolt, Tunisia's Future Remains Uncertain," *France24*, December 18, 2017: https://www.france24.com/en/20171217-tunisia-seven-years-after-arab-spring-revolution-protests-economic-uncertainty
60. Ibid.
61. Ibid.
62. Ibid.
63. "Tunisia – Agricultural Sector," Country Commercial Guide, U.S. *Export.Gov*, June 22, 2017: https://www.export.gov/article?id=Tunisia-Agricultural-Sector
64. Ibid.
65. Belen Fernandez, "Couscous, Capitalism and Neocolonialism in Tunisia," *Middle East Eye*, June 28, 2017: https://www.middleeasteye.net/columns/couscous-capitalism-and-neocolonialism-tunisia-1659688403
66. Ibid.
67. Ibid.
68. Ibid.
69. Ibid.
70. Ibid.
71. "Tunisia," *Energy Information Administration (EIA)*, October 2014: https://www.eia.gov/beta/international/analysis.php?iso=TUN
72. Ibid.
73. Ibid.
74. Ibid.
75. Ibid.
76. Ibid.
77. Ibid.
78. Sarah Yerkes, and Zeineb Ben Yahmed, "Tunisians' Revolutionary Goals Remain Unfulfilled," *Carnegie Endowment for International Peace*, December 6, 2018: https://carnegieendowment.org/publications/77894
79. Ibid.
80. Ibid.

81. Ibid.
82. Martin Chulov, "How Saudi Elite Became Five-Star Prisoners at the Riyadh Ritz Carlton," *The Guardian*, November 6, 2017: https://www.theguardian.com/world/2017/nov/06/how-saudi-elite-became-five-star-prisoners-at-the-riyadh-ritz-carlton
83. Joseph Bahout, and Perry Cammack, "Arab Political Economy: Pathways for Equitable Growth," Arab Horizons, *Carnegie Endowment for International Peace*, 2018: https://carnegieendowment.org/2018/10/09/arab-political-economy-pathways-for-equitable-growth-pub-77416
84. Ibid.
85. Ibid.
86. Ibid.
87. "Corruption Perceptions Index 2017," Surveys, *Transparency International*, February 21, 2018: https://www.transparency.org/news/feature/corruption_perceptions_index_2017
88. Bahout and Cammack, "Arab Political Economy: Pathways to Equitable Growth."
89. Ibid.
90. Ibid.
91. Ibid.
92. "Defense Spending by Country," *Global Fire Power (GFP)*, 2018: https://www.globalfirepower.com/defense-spending-budget.asp
93. Bahout and Cammack, "Arab Political Economy: Pathways to Equitable Growth."
94. Ibid.
95. Ibid.
96. Ibid.
97. Ibid.
98. Ibid.
99. "Tunisia," *Focus Economics.*
100. Ibid.
101. Ibid.
102. Masri, p. 295.

CHAPTER 6

Secularism Versus Political Islam: The Case of Tunisia

In the midst of the competition between secularists and Islamists, Tunisia has tried to engage in a balancing act between these forces since the 2011 Jasmine Revolution toppled the Ben Ali dictatorship. The attempts to balance the opposing interests and values of the secularists and Islamists, respectively, have been formidable and extremely challenging for the Tunisian government and people, to say the least. However, given that secularism has served as Tunisia's inherent legacy since its independence from France in 1956, appeasing the Islamists becomes a dangerous prospect for politicians, which could lead to political suicide. Equally, appeasing the secularists and tipping the balance in their favor also poses significant challenges for the government. Since the 2011 Jasmine Revolution, Tunisia has opened religious freedoms to the masses, and Tunisians have embraced their newly found freedoms and rights. Those who are religious conservatives see secularism and its values as oppositional to religious values and principles. The very national character, identity, and ideology of the country are at stake, and both sides are competing for securing the ideological mantle at the national level.

The original version of this chapter was revised. The flags of Turkey and Tunisia were reversed and the same has been corrected in this revised version. A correction to this chapter can be found at https://doi.org/10.1007/978-3-030-17050-9_8

H. Alvi, *The Political Economy and Islam of the Middle East*, Political Economy of Islam,
https://doi.org/10.1007/978-3-030-17050-9_6

For Tunisia, several essential national principles of secularism since independence are at stake if the balance tips in favor of Islamism. Since the post-colonial era, and the republic's founding father, Habib Bourguiba, placed Tunisia on a solid path toward secularism, modernization, and Westernization, the idea of entertaining "Political Islam" in its government is extremely threatening to countless Tunisians. In particular, feminists and human rights activists fear any implementation of Islamic principles and laws at the national level. Moreover, in the minds of secularists, Islamism connotes "regression," rather than "progression," for the country's future, directly affecting its economic, political, educational, sociocultural, and institutional sectors. Devout secularists vow to maintain Tunisia on Bourguiba's path toward secularism and preserve it into the future.

Conversely, it is wrong to assume that throughout the period of nation-building during the post-colonial era religion had been rendered obsolete in Tunisian society. While Bourguiba and later Ben Ali's platforms remained steadfastly in the secular camp, Tunisian society's religious groups, organizations, and citizens found other means to preserve their belief system and practices, but it was not always easy. Prisons overflowed with religious activists, but that is where they tended to harden, rather than soften, in their religious orthodoxy. Many others were exiled, often to parts of Western Europe, where, as intellectuals, they learned about Western political ideals, values, and structures, like liberalism and democracy. This is where and how many religious Tunisian intellectuals began to address the discourse about Islam's compatibility with liberal democracy.

The new stage for that debate has been Tunisia following the 2011 Jasmine Revolution. Many Islamists, like Rachid al-Ghannouchi, returned from exile, and promoted their ideas about an Islamist-oriented democracy. Al-Ghannouchi set up the Ennahda Party, which won the first post-revolution election in Tunisia. However, Ghannouchi and Ennahda quickly found themselves locked in heated debates with secularists, feminists, and human rights activists.

The struggle for Tunisia's national identity and values is not a new one. The conflict and disputes between secularism and Islamism are not new either, especially for the Middle East and North Africa (MENA) region. The debate about the relationship between Islam and politics is as old as the religion itself. Throughout the colonial era and the rise of diverse anti-colonial ideologies, the MENA region experienced the push and pull of secular and religious ideologies alike. The world's two theocracies are in the MENA region today: Saudi Arabia and Iran. The former is a Sunni-Wahhabi theocracy, while the latter is a Twelver-Shi'ite theocracy since the

Iranian Revolution (1979). However, even governments in the "secular republics" in the MENA region have had to pay lip service to the religious establishment; otherwise, they would lose a degree of legitimacy and potentially face harsh backlash from the public, the majority of whom, after all, are Muslim throughout the region. Hence, often there are knee-jerk reactions to the concept of secularism as well as political Islam. Both of these concepts need to be understood specifically in the Tunisian context in order to assess their impacts on the country's government, public, institutions, and society.

Political Islam and Democracy

Scholars John Esposito and John Voll remind us that, "The relationship between Islam and democracy in the contemporary world is complex. The Muslim world is not ideologically monolithic. It presents a broad spectrum of perspectives ranging from the extremes of those who deny a connection between Islam and democracy to those who argue that Islam requires a democratic system. In between the extremes, in a number of countries where Muslims are a majority, many Muslims believe that Islam is a support for democracy even though their particular political system is not explicitly defined as Islamic."[1] Presently, Tunisian society is torn apart about this issue of secular democracy versus Islamism (or political Islam) governing a progressive, generally secular country.

Esposito and Voll further explain the sensitivities and controversies involved in the secularism versus Islamism scenario:

> The participation of self-identified Islamically oriented groups in elections, and in democratic processes in general, aroused considerable controversy. People who believe that secular approaches and a separation of religion and politics are an essential part of democracy argue that Islamist groups only advocate democracy as a tactic to gain political power. They say Islamist groups support 'one man, one vote, one time.' In Algeria and Turkey, following electoral successes by parties thought to be religiously threatening to the existing political regimes, the Islamic political parties were restricted legally or suppressed.
>
> A relatively neutral starting point for Muslims is presented in a 1992 interview in the London Observer with the Tunisian Islamist leader and political exile, Rashid Ghanoushi: 'If by democracy is meant the liberal model of government prevailing in the West, a system under which the people freely choose their representatives and leaders, in which there is an alternation of

> power, as well as all freedoms and human rights for the public, then Muslims will find nothing in their religion to oppose democracy, and it is not in their interests to do so.' Many Muslims, including Ghanoushi himself, go beyond this and view democracy as an appropriate way to fulfill certain obligations of the faith in the contemporary world.[2]

On March 2, 2012, I sat in the audience during a public talk that Rachid al-Ghannouchi gave in Tunis, where the press and cameramen and Tunisian intellectuals gathered in a crowded room. Ghannouchi spoke (in Arabic) for about 45 minutes at the podium, and then he answered questions. Some from the audience even came to the podium and spoke into the microphone to emphasize their comments and questions. In his speech, Ghannouchi's main message conveyed that there is harmony between Islamism and democracy, and there are no contradictions therein. He tried to alleviate tensions and fears in the secular camp about the intentions of Tunisian Islamism. Ghannouchi cited the existence of religion and religious elements in Western societies, including in the United States. He pointed out that the Prophet Muhammad was both a religious and a political leader, and he listed examples of rule and governance by Muslim empires in Islamic history. Therefore, according to Ghannouchi, the philosophy of mixing religion and politics is sound. He contended that the essence of Islam is freedom; he said, "Ennahda will not require *salat* (praying) and fasting, etc. People will have their full freedoms."[3] Then, he ended his talk by reminding everyone that, after all, Tunisia's religion is Islam.

However, the sensitivities still persist, and in terms of public perceptions there is a tendency to describe Islamism as having a fine line between its democratic ideals and aspirations and those of supposed hidden agendas that would transform a country into a totalitarian religious fascist state. Tunisia's Ennahda Party strives to distance itself from extremism, describing itself as "moderate" and pro-democracy. On the other hand, Tunisia's secularists and feminists are totally against religion in politics. They are far from convinced that political Islam would be fair and equitable when it comes to human rights, women's rights, and minority rights. All this said, the consensus among the Islamists, secularists, and feminists is to engage in national dialogue, which is seen as the ideal political process for negotiations and compromise. This is the reason why Tunisia is viewed as the regional model of successful democratic process, which has been committed to non-violent dialogue, negotiations, and transitions. This is also why Tunisia is remarkable, and it is a source of tremendous pride for all Tunisians.

Following the 2011 revolution, the new political ideals floating in Tunisia's orbit constitute a new experiment for the country. Never before has Tunisia experienced real democracy, nor has it seen Islam introduced, or one might say *injected*, into politics. Upon setting itself on a new path toward democracy, Tunisians have been compelled to play a delicate balancing act. The 2011 Jasmine Revolution has demanded dignity, rights, and freedoms, which include an end to detentions without due process, an independent judiciary, rule of law, and no more torture. During the Ben Ali dictatorship, the Islamists had been the main targets for detentions and torture. Now, Tunisia has found itself in a difficult position of trying to reconcile new religious freedoms—which were not permitted during the Bourguiba and Ben Ali regimes—and the secular legacy of the country. Today, Tunisia must engage in the democratic process allowing for political discourse between religious and secular groups without violence and/or repression. Also, Tunisia has to ensure that women's rights and freedoms, and gender equality in general, all of which have been embodied in its secular legacy, will not be violated or undermined.

In the minds of many, once political Islam is empowered, women's rights will be the first to erode. In addition, if we consider the importance of Amartya Sen's Social Choice Theory, wherein socioeconomic progress cannot take place without individuals' rights and freedoms to make choices, then the arguments against political Islam harden, because it is assumed that, by nature of religious laws and principles, various restrictions on individuals are likely to be imposed.

However, it is not correct to assume that political Islam, by nature, equates with jihadism and/or terrorism. Following are some issues that Esposito and Voll specifically address:

> The Turkish experience reflects the fact that many Muslims, whether living in formally secular or formally Islamic states, see democracy as their main hope and vehicle of effective political participation. One important dimension of this participation is that despite conservative Muslim opposition to the idea of rule by a woman, the three largest Muslim states in the world – Indonesia, Bangladesh, and Pakistan – have had or now have elected women as their heads of government. None of these women was explicitly Islamist and one was directly opposed by an Islamist party. In this complex context, it is clear that Islam is not inherently incompatible with democracy. 'Political Islam' is sometimes a program for religious democracy and not primarily an agenda for holy war or terrorism.[4]

There exists another argument for modern Islamism that supposedly harmonizes democracy and its principles. In their book, *Reformation and Development in the Muslim World: Islamicity Indices as Benchmark*, scholars Hossein Askari, Hossein Mohammadkhan, and Liza Mydin posit the theory that if Muslims implement "true" Islamic principles in society based on the Quran and Hadith (sayings of the Prophet Muhammad), then social justice, economic equality, institutional effectiveness, the rule of law, and sound political processes will prevail. These scholars developed "Islamic indices," which "assess which societies reflected the teachings of the Quran and to gauge their performance relative to this benchmark. In other words, which societies practiced what Islam preached in the Holy Quran and through the practice of the Prophet?"[5]

In many respects, their theory aligns with Rachid al-Ghannouchi's beliefs, and how he may envision the role and responsibilities of Ennahda in Tunisia. The book authors point out that, "In light of conditions in many Muslim countries – dictatorial and autocratic governance, little or no personal freedoms, massive abuse of human rights, sub-par economic performance, social and cultural stagnation, economic and social injustice, and virulent rhetoric of a few thousand Muslim extremists – there can be no doubt Muslim countries need reform."[6] These descriptions fit the former Ben Ali regime's rule over Tunisia, and, of course, still more work needs to be done to improve quality of life in the country.

According to Askari, Mohammadkhan, and Mydin, Muslims are obligated to fight against corruption, injustices, and inhumane treatment of others. The "capstone rule in Islam assigns Muslims the duty to collectively enjoin the good and forbid what is evil, or any wrongdoing as outlined in Surah Al-Imran, Verse 104 of the Quran: 'And from among you there should be a party who invite to good and enjoin what is right and forbid the wrong, and these it is that shall be successful'."[7] The authors further contend that, "The Quran provides a comprehensive and complete guide to achieving successful development. It provides the framework, scaffolding, and rules that stress justice, coordination, cooperation, trust, and sharing to manage resources for the benefit of all members of society."[8] Islam provides the prescription for socioeconomic development, according to the authors. These prescriptions involve self-development (*rushd*), physical development of the earth (*isti'mar*), and the development of human collectivity "covering both the self and the physical dimensions."[9]

The authors concede that the Muslim collective, as symbolized in the Organization of Islamic Conference (OIC), have failed in the most fundamental areas of development and social justice. For the authors, this is all the more reason to abide by the teachings of the Quran and the Prophet Muhammad to achieve development, prosperity, equality, social justice, and righteous leadership that would be accountable to the citizenry. These are all very noble thoughts and ideas.

However, the actual interpretation of Islamic principles, as in all religions, is highly subjective and lacks consensus, except for basic moral concepts such as "murder is wrong." Islamic hermeneutics and exegeses are primarily conducted by male clerics and/or Islamic jurists. That alone is problematic, because of the gender ratio disparity. Women are not usually included, or even accepted in clerical establishments, which means that they are not represented in the interpretation processes. That, in turn, means that religious interpretations of Islamic texts, scripture, and laws are predominantly done by men, and as human beings they cannot do so without viewing Islam through their own biased lenses. This is not accounted for in the Askari, Mohammadkhan, and Mydin text. Plus, no male Muslim religious figure, even Rachid al-Ghannouchi, is likely to concede this aspect of hermeneutical deficiency.

Furthermore, Askari, Mohammadkhan, and Mydin also do not address the issue of lack of consensus within and between Sunni and Shia religious establishments. Again, Islam is not monolithic, and in today's world it consists of sectarian divisions and even subsets within a particular sect. Each one fervently believes that it is following the "true" interpretation of Islam. Moreover, the Muslim world contains the world's two official theocracies: Saudi Arabia and the Islamic Republic of Iran. Saudi Arabia's brand of ultra-orthodox Sunnism, called Wahhabism, has one of the worst track records in terms of development, human rights, women's empowerment, wealth distribution, equality, justice, and due process. Iran is a Twelver Shia theocracy, and it also has a terrible record when it comes to these important human development variables. Yet, both theocracies insist that they follow and implement the "true" Islam.

Also, with the majority of the world's Muslims being Sunni, it is imperative to mention that Sunnism consists of four main schools of law: Hanafi, Hanbali, Maliki, and Shafi'i. How would they be reconciled in the implementation of a global mainstream "true" Islam, which is also applied at the state level? This needs significant assessments and explanations.

The Quran and Hadith address countless issues and discuss institutions that would be anachronistic in the modern era. For example, polygamy, inheritance issues, and women's status and rights do not meet modern standards. These issues, among others, would also need to be addressed and reconciled, and that begs the question about how there could be consensus about these issues, particularly in the context of socioeconomic and political reforms.

Although Ghannouchi and Ennahda have made some concessions pertaining to women's rights, gender equality, and the like, most experiments in political Islam during modern history have been disastrous failures. Examples include the Taliban, Hamas, and the theocracies of Saudi Arabia and Iran (as mentioned), to name a few. The preponderance for religious and political authoritarianism eventually overtakes even the sincerest efforts for "enjoining what is right and forbidding the wrong."

Finally, the uncomfortable reality in the world today is that Islamist terrorists, and especially their leaders, not only claim to follow and implement the "true" Islam, but they proliferate and enforce their interpretations of Islam by force and brutality. They, too, claim that they operate in the effort to bring justice to the world, but their brand of Islamic justice is far from desirable.

In addition, scholar Mehdi Mozaffari offers an opposing view to the ideal of political Islam, contending that "sacredness and equality are also directly interrelated. In situations in which the political regime is based on faith, discrimination between the citizens will be inevitable. Individuals who have the same faith as those in power will be given far more rights and privileges than those who do not share the religious or ideological persuasions that form the basis of the regime."[10] Regarding freedoms, Mozaffari compares Islamism and secularism, quoting Bassam Tibi saying, "Freedom is a secular project."[11] Mozaffari explains that, "Instead, the concept of justice (*'adl/'adala*) is the keyword in Islam. For example, the Shias believe in five fundamental principles (the Unity of God, the true prophecy of Muhammad, Judgment Day, the Imamate, and Justice), while the Sunnis only believe in the first three principles. However, there is nothing about freedom – which is, after all, a new notion for Muslims."[12]

Mozaffari further explicates the concept of secularization in relation to Islamism in the context of a democracy. He says,

> While secularization stands as the necessary condition for freedom of expression, democracy represents the sufficient condition. By democracy, I mean a pluralist and participative regime that allows a peaceful transmission of power from one group of citizens to another. Rawls takes at least one more step towards deepening the sense of democracy when he writes that a 'modern

democratic society is characterized not simply by pluralism of comprehensive religious, philosophical, and moral doctrines but by a pluralism of incompatible yet reasonable doctrines.'

Democracy in this sense is only a system, an instrument that is itself a product and consequence of a specific state of mind and an intellectual position. In this connection, the Muslim attitude towards democracy is divided into two main trends: the moderates and the radicals, or fundamentalists. The partisans of the moderates claim from its beginning that Islam is compatible with democracy. They argue that Islam from its beginning has possessed some institutions and procedures of a democratic character. In this respect, the *shura* and *bay'at* are often mentioned as examples. The *shura*, which is recommended by the Quran and was used by the Prophet himself, is a 'consultative body' that assisted the Leader in decision making. Its members were not elected and its opinions were not executed. Similar institutions existed in China, India, Persia, and even in Mongolia, where the *quriltai*, the assembly of Mongol-Tartar nobles and clan chiefs, gathered to elect a new khan.

However, this kind of institution has nothing to do with democracy, neither in essence nor form. *Bay'at* means 'the act by which a certain number of persons recognize the authority of another person.' This is also alien to democracy, in which the recognition of authority is decided by free elections and not by co-optation, designation, or seizing power by force, which has happened so often in Islamic history. Thus, the tension between Islam and democracy is not only institutional, but predominantly philosophical. Democracy is based on citizens' rights, which is unknown in Islam. The only right that exists is God's right. How is it possible to reconcile these two rights with each other, especially when they contradict each other?

Islamists, whatever their sectarian belonging may be – Shia, Sunni, Wahhabi, Salafi, Jihadi, and so on – seem to be closer to the essence of Islam both as value and as fact. None of them has ever claimed that Islam is compatible with democracy.[13]

Mozaffari emphasizes that in Islamic history we see periods "when tolerance was relatively high, with dynamic flourishing intellectual debates, i.e., under Al-Mamun and during the Andalusian Epoch. Then, slowly, successive periods of stagnation began, later to be followed by Western dominance and colonization, until the rise of Islamism with its nostalgia for the 'glorious' epochs in the history of Islam. Therefore, in reality, it is not Islam that is challenging the West, but rather the idea of modernity that is challenging Islam. Freedom of expression is an inherent part of modernity and perhaps its most vulnerable dimension."[14]

Furthermore, where secularization identifies diversity of racial/ethnic groups, genders, and economic status of people as constituting a country's demographics, Islamism classifies individuals in society according to the Quran. The categorization of people "into different groups, and in particular the designation of enemies, is therefore made according to the attitude of each individual and each group vis-à-vis the compulsory requirements of the Quran. Either you are with us or against us! – in the Quran, this was the guiding principle for categorization of people."[15]

In addition, within Islam and Islamism, sectarian identities and ideologies present yet another set of categories, which reinforces the fact that Islam is not monolithic. Mozaffari makes some crucial points about these identities and ideologies:

> Islamism is divided into three main branches: Sunni, Shia, and Wahhabi. This classification is neither perfect nor exhaustive, but it is useful. For instance, Wahhabi is a Sunni sub-sect, but it is so different from other Sunni sub-sects that it may be treated as an autonomous entity. Sunnism is divided into four theological and juridical schools: Hanafi, Malaki, Shafii, and Hanbali. Wahhabi is a derivative of the Hanbali School, with a particularly dogmatic interpretation of Islam.
>
> The Sunni Islamists represent the vast majority of Islamists. Sunni movements embrace the geographical space reaching from Mali to Bali; from the Somalian desert to the Pakistani Himalayas. Chronologically, Sunni Islamism is older than both Shia and Wahhabi Islamism … Contemporary Islamism, as a movement and as an organization, is a phenomenon of the 20th century. It emerged with the creation of the Muslim Brotherhood by Hassan al-Banna in Egypt in 1928.[16]

Mozaffari specifically notes Tunisia's special circumstances and choices. "The Islamist movement of Ennahda in Tunisia has made difference choices. Ennahda decided to join the democratic process."[17] However, Ennahda did not last long in Tunisia's seat of power. Nonetheless, it continues to play a major role in Tunisian politics.

The danger lies in the cycle of repression that even secular democracy potentially facilitates in such complex scenarios as in the Middle East and North Africa. When the floodgates are opened for pluralist political processes that permit both secular and religious parties to seek power, the opposing elements of secularism and Islamism are likely to compel one to undermine the other, particularly when either is perceived as attempting to repress the other. In other words, empowerment of one vis-à-vis freedoms and rights, democratic processes, and elections allow for open dialogue and negotiations (see Chart 6.1). Once empowered, there is a danger of the empowered party to undermine, and even repress, the other, especially if the parties involved refuse to engage in dialogue and negotiations.

However, the moment the party in power appears to tip the sociopolitical and legal scales in favor of its own ideological agenda, the risks of violent repression rise even in a democracy—in fact, that is the case *especially* in a fragile democracy just now developing and emerging from its embryonic stage (see Chart 6.2).

In Tunisia's case, the sociopolitical system has only seen violent repression at the hands of the secular Ben Ali regime. As the flow Chart 6.2, "The Cycle of Repression," indicates, the granting of freedoms, rights,

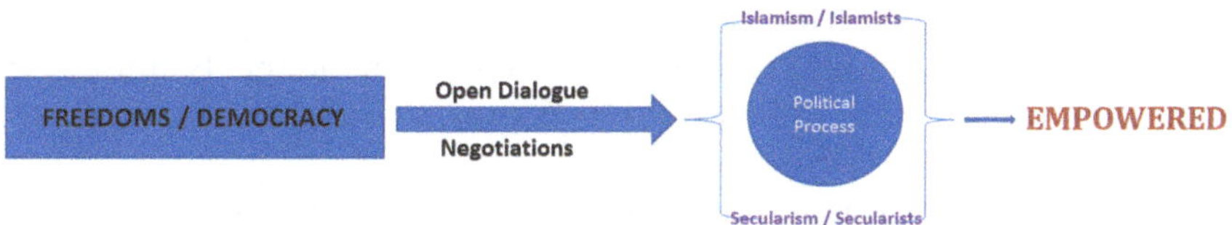

Chart 6.1 Empowerment process in Tunisia

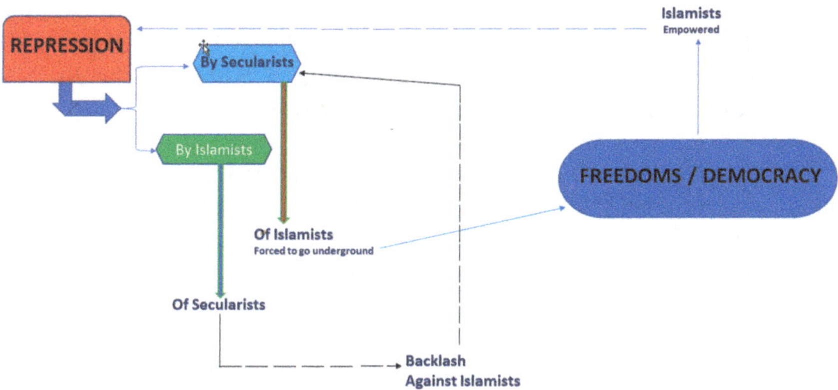

Chart 6.2 The cycle of repression

and political participation to everyone, including Islamists, leads to the empowerment of Islamists, specifically Ennahda. Once empowered, the Islamists could have repressed the secularists in the future, but Ennahda stepped down before such charges against them could arise. Usually, in numerous examples in modern history, the empowerment of Islamists has led to repression of secularism and secularists (e.g., Gaza under Hamas; Afghanistan under the Taliban—although the Taliban empowered themselves through warfare and not democracy; Egypt under the Muslim Brotherhood, that is, the short-lived presidency of Mohamed Morsi; and many allege that what is currently happening in Turkey under the ruling Justice and Development Party, the AKP, and Recep Tayyip Erdogan is yet another example).

Ultimately, such repression at the hands of Islamists could result in a backlash against them, as seen in Egypt against President Morsi and in Tunisia against Ennahda, but in two very different contexts. In the case of Egypt, it has constituted violence, whereas, in Tunisia Ennahda volunteered to step down in order to avoid violent conflict. The cycle of repression indicates that the backlash against the Islamists usually results in the re-empowerment of the secularists and repression of the Islamists yet again. The cycle is likely to repeat itself, although Tunisia so far has proven to be an exceptional case.

It is equally important to understand the nuanced differences between secularism, political Islam (or Islamism), and violent extremism (or Jihadism).

According to Table 6.1, secularism pursues a platform that separates religion from politics; usually embraces democracy, although in the MENA region it has mainly been a façade of pseudo-democracies governed by autocratic rulers; usually secularism promotes non-violence, but there have been many exceptions to this especially in the modern history of the MENA region; secularism is supposed to allow for political dialogue; usually feminism flourishes in a secular political system, but once again, the MENA region has exceptions to this because many secular republics still have to pay lip service to the religious establishment, or body of Islamic scholars called the *'ulama*. Most often, the 'ulama reject feminism. In secular societies, religious practices are usually observed in private. In the MENA region, two countries stand out for having deeply embedded post-colonial secular legacies: Turkey under Mustafa Kemal Ataturk, and Tunisia under Habib Bourguiba. Also, secularism generally implies good relations with the West, because the secular legacies are attempts to orient a given society toward Western values, ideals, and political systems, at least on the surface.

Table 6.1 The differences between Secularism, Islamism, and Extremism in the Modern MENA

Secularism	*Political Islam/Islamism*	*Violent Extremism/Jihadism*
No religious parties	Religious parties participate	Only religious parties allowed, usually one ruling religious ideology rules over everyone
Pro-democracy	Empowered through democracy (by choice, depending on circumstances)	Rejects democracy
Usually non-violent (image)—but could be violently repressing Islamists and other opposition groups	Prefers non-violent change—but could splinter into violent groups	Violent
Usually permits political dialogue	Could permit political dialogue	No dialogue
Feminism flourishes	Feminism marginalized	No compromise on gender issues—embraces patriarchy
Prefers a secular society where religion is practiced in private	Religion influences politics and society	Religious fascism and totalitarianism are imposed on society
Secular legacy in the post-colonial era	Tried to influence using soft power—previously operated underground	Actively recruits operatives
Usually good relations with the West	Hot and cold relations with the West, depending on situation	Extremely anti-West

In Islamism, or political Islam, if Islamist parties are allowed to participate in politics, then they are likely to seek empowerment through democratic processes, as seen in Egypt following the Tahrir Square Revolution and Tunisia after the Jasmine Revolution. Islamists have traditionally suffered from repression throughout modern history, and often their responses were in the form of violent attacks against the regimes. However, in recent decades, it is more acceptable for Islamists to pursue empowerment through non-violent soft power means, such as democratic processes. Those within such parties who reject these non-violent means of empowerment tend to break off into splinter groups, usually in small numbers, and embrace violent extremism.

In Tunisia, we see that Ennahda quickly embraced the democratic process, and the Islamists succeeded for a time. Now, even though they are unseated, albeit non-violently, Ennahda members continue to engage in politics, participate in parliament, and operate numerous offices proliferating throughout the country. Ennahda is proactive in presenting itself as a "moderate" Islamist party, and as of May 2018 it won in significant municipal elections,[18] the first for the country. Thus, Ennahda remains active in Tunisia's democratic system, and has remained committed to non-violent change in Tunisian politics. That is an anomaly in the legacy of Islamism.

According to journalist Lotfi Hajji, "Tunisian Islamists are different, in that, they seem to accept democracy based on civil laws, as opposed to theocratic laws. Islamists in Tunisia are more open-minded,"[19] in his view.

While Islamists generally tend to reject feminism, Ennahda has allowed for a degree of flexibility, at least initially, when it comes to women's rights and freedoms that have been embodied in Tunisia's secular legacy. At times, however, Ennahda seems unclear about its true platform concerning these issues. Ennahda

> entered the new era with a flexible political discourse, seeking to turn over a new page and provide reassurance that it is committed to the values of democracy, human rights, non-violence, and the personal status code, which bans polygamy and provides for gender equality. *Le Temps* reported on February 6, 2011 that Ghannouchi stated that the personal status code is derived from shari'a (Islamic law), polygamy has been determined to be illegal, the hijab (headscarf) is a personal choice, and stoning and amputation cannot be carried out as punishments. There are some indicators, however, that Ennahda's stance is not so clear, including a February 17 interview in which Ennahda spokesman Hamadi Jebali denied having aims to implement shari'a law [sic] on one hand then went on to confirm the party's adherence to it during the same conversation.[20]

By definition, Islamism, or political Islam, requires that religion influence politics and the legal codes and framework of the country. This is one of the reasons why secularists are extremely skeptical, if not outright suspicious, of the Islamists' intentions and agendas. This is also the reason why Islamists and Western countries have hot and cold relations, and in fact, in the case of democratic elections in Algeria and Gaza that brought Islamists to power, the West has been manifestly opposed to, and even hostile toward them. Western powers repeatedly label Gaza's Hamas-led democratically elected government as a terrorist group,[21] and they also callously turned a blind eye to the bloody Algerian civil war (1991–2002). Algeria's civil war began

> after an era of unprecedented openness in the late 1980s. Personal freedoms blossomed and dozens of new political parties were created. But when Islamist parties appeared ready to sweep to victory in the early [19]90s, the government canceled legislative elections. The Islamists fought back, initially targeted the army and police — but then they began attacking civilians; artists, teachers, judges and journalists were slain. State security forces, trying to root out the insurgency, often killed indiscriminately. By the end of the 1990s, an estimated 200,000 Algerians had died.[22]

When Islamists resort to violence, it is generally in the context of "jihadism," and, depending on the degree of orthodoxy of a given Islamist ideology, the extremism therefrom could embody totalitarian religious fascism, like in the case of the Islamic State (IS), also called the Islamic State of Iraq and Syria (ISIS). In such scenarios, there is no dialogue, no compromises, no democracy and human rights, and utter contempt for feminism, the West, and secularism. This is a case of the Islamist extremist pendulum swinging far beyond the spectrum of extremism, particularly in its depth of brutality and lust for violence against civilians and combatants alike. As bizarre as it sounds, it can be described as "*extreme* extremism."

The rise of ISIS does not happen overnight, but in stages and evolving phases that produce the right opportunities, environments, and conducive leadership. However, now that the world is alert to the potentials of Islamism evolving into a brutally violent, fascist entity like ISIS, the secular public becomes leery of Islamist parties emerging and seeking power. The moment an Islamist party and leadership entertain policies that affect dress codes and family law (e.g., divorce, inheritance, and polygamy), and outwardly counter secular ideals, the public begins to feel apprehensive, especially in societies with long-held secular legacies (e.g., Tunisia and Turkey).

In the case of the post–Arab Awakening 2011 revolution and elections in Egypt that empowered Mohamed Morsi of the Muslim Brotherhood (MB), when policies that resembled religious priorities rather than pressing economic and institutional priorities, the public reacted angrily, to the extent that the Tamarod movement called on the Egyptian military to step in and remove Morsi and MB from power. This resulted in violent repression at the hands of the Egyptian military and a coup engineered by

General Abdel Fattah el-Sisi, leaving Morsi languishing in prison today. Tunisians have been determined not to allow the same to happen in their country. Moreover, Tunisians are equally determined not to allow their country's commitment to women's rights to be derailed, particularly by Islamists.

Tunisia Leads in Women's Rights

The revolutionaries in Tunisia's 2011 Jasmine Revolution included women in the frontlines. Tunisia has long been considered among the most liberal countries, and that is especially true in the MENA region. In 2011, the Tunisian parliament "consisted of 27.6% seats reserved for women; that is 58 women out of 217 seats, which is considerably progressive compared to other Arab countries. Still, women in Tunisia continue to protest especially potential constitutional changes that would infringe on women's rights. The Islamist Ennahda party faced pressures from the Salafists calling for implementation of Islamic law on the one hand, and on the other hand, the secularists who demand secular liberal democracy ensuring rights and freedoms to all."[23] In 2012, the Ennahda-led government challenged gender equality when revising the constitution, adding a stipulation that "considers women to be 'complementary to men.' Tunisian activists protested, demanding that a 1956 law granting women full equality with men to remain unchanged. Thousands of activists protested in Tunis in August 2012."[24] One of the protestors is quoted as saying,

> 'Normally, more important issues ought to be tackled like unemployment, regional development. Ennahda seems bent on making steps backwards but we are here to say that Tunisian women will not accept that. I fear for the future of my daughters who may grow up in a totally different Tunisia.'
>
> Ennahda representatives denied that the draft constitutional amendment would render regressive policies for women. The chair of the assembly's human rights and public freedoms panel, Farida al Obeidi, explains that the draft stipulates: 'sharing of roles and does not mean that women are worth less than men.' However, many Tunisians worried that passing this draft would lead to future policies and laws that threaten gender equality, which would be a significant reversal for women's rights. In Tunisia, the struggle for preserving women's rights and freedoms has continued, as activists feared an agenda of greater Islamization on the horizon. They are determined not to give up or let up on the pressure to maintain the long tradition of women's equality in Tunisia.

> Eventually, secular activists succeeded in not only overturning the offensive language, but also in paving the way for drafting a new constitution.[25]

Tunisia has "been a standard-bearer in the Muslim world for women's rights."[26] As a gesture of recognizing this fact and sustaining its legacy, Tunisian President Beji Caid Essebsi created a commission in August 2017 to examine national reforms pertaining to gender equality. This has been done in accordance with the January 2014 Tunisian Constitution. The commission published the final report in June 2018, entitled the Colibe Report, standing for "The Committee on Individual Liberties and Gender Equality." The 300-page Colibe Report also addresses other pressing human rights issues, including a proposal "to end the death penalty and legalize homosexuality, which the current penal code outlaws and punishes with three years in prison."[27]

In June 2017, Tunisia's parliament passed a new law "criminalizing domestic violence against women. Two months later, President [Beji Caid] Essebsi overturned a law that banned women from marrying non-Muslim men."[28] The 2014 constitution "codified equality for women."[29] Tunisian women –

> are better represented in the Tunisian Parliament, at 31 percent, than in legislative bodies in the United States, Britain, and Canada. Perhaps more significantly, Tunisian women exceed 31 percent representation in the economic and foreign affairs committees, and 34 percent in the power committees, arguably the most influential legislative committees. In the United States, comparatively, less than 14 percent of members in the foreign affairs committees and less than 23 percent of members in the armed services committees are women. Many identify Tunisia as a 'pioneer' in the region for women's rights due to its progress.[30]

Still, Tunisian women face significant challenges, as "progressive laws on the books may have little to no impact without consistent enforcement across all of Tunisia. Going forward, reform initiatives by Tunisia's political leaders will need to be met with sustained outreach and dialogue with the public … Therefore, recent reforms on women's rights should be met with cautious optimism as well as a sustained effort at a dialogue with all elements of society–both men and women–that makes the case for these necessary reforms. Ultimately, these reforms present Tunisian civil society with an opportunity and momentum to engage with the whole of Tunisian society to further the women's rights agenda in a region long-criticized for inequality."[31]

This encompasses a battle for Tunisia's soul and national identity. It is also a battle that exists under the umbrella of the broader *secularism* versus *Islamism* competition that continues to take place in the country and illustrates one of many challenges pervading Tunisian society and politics. Women's rights issues become the central points of contention in this ideological and identity competition. Often, women's rights, freedoms, and choices turn into the primary objects of *regressive* change once Islamists come to power, and they force the hands of the secularists to readjust society and politics toward a *progressive* direction. Women, then, become the pawns in these socio-political and legal battles between Islamists and secularists.

So far, Tunisia's feminists and secularists have maintained leverage pertaining to women's rights over the Islamists, who continue to influence Tunisians to accept their religious identity as the cornerstone of the country's national ideology. Religion requires conformity, and that begs the question of whether Islamism would be conducive to the principles of liberalism, which places value on the individual and the rights of individuals to make personal choices. Tunisian society is divided about the tensions between secular liberalism and Islam.

Furthermore, Ennahda's historical positions pertaining to women's rights have not always been liberal or progressive. Julia Clancy-Smith reminds us that in the 1980s Ennahda, then called the *Harakat al-Ittijah al-Islami* (Islamic Tendency Movement), "became politically active, advocating for the needs of the most underprivileged. But in 1985 the party also demanded a national referendum on the 1956 Personal Status Code (PSC), part of a state-driven secularization of society, which had conferred equal rights in law upon Tunisian women."[32] According to the Islamists, "the PSC not only violated Islamic principles, notably the religiously-sanctioned existence of different, though complementary, spheres for man and woman, but also promoted female equality in the job force, which had deprived men of employment."[33] As a result, Islamist parties in general have much to prove when it comes to their supposed claims of accepting liberalism and gender equality.

Presently, Ennahda has learned how to play the gendered political game. Julia Clancy-Smith explains that, "As the big winner in the October 23, 2011 elections, Ennahda sent the largest single bloc of female lawmakers to the 217-member Constituent Assembly, although only 53 percent of the eligible electorate had exercised its right to vote. The question now is how Ennahda women will govern."[34] Rachid al-Ghannouchi's daughter and Ennahda's spokeswoman, Soumaya Ghannouchi, "a British newspaper columnist and a scholar at the School of Oriental and African Studies in London, maintains that Ennahda is the most progressive Islamic party in North Africa or the Arab world."[35] However, Julia Clancy-Smith wonders "how well someone who was raised in England can understand the stakes and complexities of the 'woman question,' which currently constitutes the single most important issue facing Tunisian state and society."[36]

Both Tunisia and Turkey face similar challenges pertaining to women's rights and freedoms coming at the heels of decades of secularism, while at the same time allowing for some experimentation with political Islam, albeit in varying degrees. There is much more to the common denominators between Tunisia and Turkey, which deserve deeper examination. A comparative analysis of both countries illuminates the complexities and potentialities of rising models of "Islamic democracy."

The Tunisia-Turkey Nexis: Models of "Islamic Democracy"?

When Tunisia gained independence in 1956, its new leader Habib Bourguiba placed the newborn republic on a distinct path of secularism. Bourguiba admired Turkey's Ataturk and wanted to replicate his secular ideals and policies in Tunisia. The Republic of Tunisia even borrowed symbols from Turkey's flag as inspiration, and the irony is that the star and crescent in Tunisia's flag represents the Ottoman Empire (Fig. 6.1).

The Tunisian flag is "red with a white disk in the center bearing a red crescent nearly encircling a red five-pointed star; resembles the Ottoman flag (red banner with white crescent and star) and recalls Tunisia's history as part of the Ottoman Empire; red represents the blood shed by martyrs in the struggle against oppression; white stands for peace; the crescent and

Fig. 6.1 Image of Tunisian flag. (Source: The World Factbook. Central Intelligence Agency, 2019)

star are traditional symbols of Islam. Note [that] the flag is based on that of Turkey, itself a successor state to the Ottoman Empire."[37] The symbolic linkages to the Ottoman Empire and modern-day Turkey have parallels with Tunisia's post-colonial sociopolitical track toward secularism, that is, the "Young Tunisians" movement that specifically followed the "Young Turks" model; and the orientation toward the West and modernization, while at the same time preserving—often in the periphery—the country's Islamic identity, principles, and historic legacy, just as in Turkey.

Starting with the Bourguiba era, Tunisia placed itself on the path toward secularism, very similar to Turkey under Mustafa Kemal Ataturk. Both leaders severely restricted the religious establishment, public displays of religious dress and symbols, outlawed polygamy, and reformed their countries' education system by incorporating secular sciences, mathematics, and other disciplines into the curricula. The fact that Tunisia historically fell under the Ottoman Empire's jurisdiction is yet another direct linkage to Turkey. Therefore, the Tunisian flag speaks volumes about the country's feelings pertaining to Turkey, including a similar star and crescent logo of Islam appearing on the flag, again mirroring Turkey's flag (Fig. 6.2).

The fact that Islam is represented on the flag indicates the dual identity of Tunisia, which embodies both secularism and Islamic history and its significance for the republic. All dictators in the MENA region have had to recognize Islam's undercurrents and the need for significant segments of society to identify with Islam as *a way of life*. Although dictators have routinely repressed Islamism in their respective countries, they have been cognizant about not crossing certain red lines that could lead to public protests and mass mobilizations that would threaten the regimes. Consequently, Islam and politics in the MENA region need to be viewed as two sides of the same coin, even in self-proclaimed highly secularized

Fig. 6.2 Image of Turkish flag. (Source: The World Factbook. Central Intelligence Agency, 2019)

societies. Regimes have sought to repress other avenues of political checks and balances and dissent, including civil society. Tunisia's civil society has been thriving since the 2011 Arab Awakening, which has fervently tried to facilitate the democratization process, and it has a historical legacy even in the face of violent repression. Ennahda has participated in civil society activism as well.

Fast forward to the post–Arab Awakening 2011 era, and there is talk of a "Turkish model" for Islamists to follow. However, the positive reputation of the Turkish model has not survived. The Turkish model, as scholar Monica Marks describes it, "began losing its luster following the AKP's complicity in the politicization of the judiciary, its support for widespread military purges, and its crackdowns on media freedom – trends that had become visible by 2010."[38] In fact, the AKP and Erdogan's reputation worsened with the repression of civil society protests, specifically the Gezi Park crackdown in 2013.[39] In Tunisia, the fact that Ennahda has stepped down and earned global respect for preventing a violent conflict, as witnessed in Egypt, Libya, Syria, Bahrain, and Yemen, has led to a new moniker, the "Tunisian model," which has replaced the Turkish model. According to Marks, "As the AKP's star faded … another party of self-proclaimed Muslim democrats was on the rise. Tunisia's Ennahda party – brutally oppressed during the twenty-three-year rule of dictator Zine al-Abidine Ben Ali – earned well-deserved plaudits for its leadership in advancing Tunisia's post-revolutionary transition."[40] Ennahda initially led the three-party coalition, the "Troika," and

> Deftly negotiated through Tunisia's post-revolutionary waters. Through canny maneuvering in mid-2013, for example, Ennahda's leaders defused a soft coup attempt known as the Bardo Crisis that could easily have derailed Tunisia's transition. To stave off such threats, Ennahda's leaders adopted a pragmatic approach focused on securing the long-term survival of the party itself and of Tunisia's nascent democracy.
>
> … In response, the party's leaders held countless regional and local-level meetings to persuade grassroots members that forgiveness of, and even compromises with, their former oppressors represented the best way forward.[41]

By 2016, the term "Tunisian model for Turkey" could be heard "as opposed to 'Turkish model for Tunisia'."[42] In addition, both the AKP and Ennahda have communicated and interacted with each other. Turkey under the AKP has expressed support for the Muslim Brotherhood in Egypt, and "opened [its] doors to political asylum seekers from the Egyptian Brotherhood,"[43] following the military coup. Similarly, Turkey has taken in millions of Syrian refugees. This gesture has been seen as a "humanitarian act, approved by Erdogan at a time of Western waffling and hypocrisy on the issue of Syria, bolstered his image as a man of principle who placed Muslim solidarity over self-seeking political gain."[44] Ennahda has applauded these decisions on the part of Erdogan and AKP.

At the same time in Tunisia, after the party stepped down, Ennahda has been compelled to separate the practice of preaching (*da'awa*) from politics (*siyasa*) and "eased membership regulations to facilitate the entry of non-Islamists."[45] Yet, the most controversial issue "during Ennahda's national congress concerned the party's internal structures,"[46] based on three proposals, as Marks explains:

> Three proposals were presented regarding the election of the party's *maktab tenfidhi* (Executive Board). The first, supported by party president Ghannouchi, proposed retaining the existing system, according to which the president appointed all board members and the elected 150-member *majlis shura* (Shura Council) then confirmed them. The other two proposals aimed to give the Shura Council greater say over the Executive Board's appointment. One, proposed by long-time Ennahda leader Abdellatif Mekki, called for the Shura Council to elect the members of the Executive Board. The second, put forward by Abdelhamid Jelassi, called for a mixture of the two models (election of one-third of the Executive Board by the Shura Council).
>
> … The delegates then voted to maintain the current system.[47]

This episode illustrates that Ghannouchi does not enjoy absolute power within Ennahda. Those who are members of Ennahda, the *nahdawis*, explain that because "the party was formed during and in opposition to dictatorship, and that institutionalized governance – as opposed to the personalization of power – is a core part of its identity,"[48] Ennahda is committed to decentralization and compatibility with democracy. In contrast, Turkey's Erdogan seeks the personalization of power, and the ruling AKP tolerates this reality, and, to some extent, benefits from it. "The AK Party has only one leader," according to the Turkish Justice Minister Bekir Bozdag, "and that is our president, Recep Tayyip Erdogan."[49]

Rachid al-Ghannouchi, on the other hand, is often described as a philosopher and idealist; he is "described by his supporters as a subdued philosopher-politician – a grandfatherly yet often quite cunning thinker whose rhetoric is measured, not hostile, and who has been surprisingly free of paranoia or egoism."[50]

Moreover, the Ennahda-AKP relationship is strategic. As Marks aptly concludes, "In a region where Islamists have few friends, and in a context where Western democracies still seem prone to accept Gulf-supported critiques of Islamist parties, Ennahda would have good reason to cultivate a friend and strategic partner in Turkey."[51] After all, Tunisia's homage to the Ottoman Empire symbolized in its flag is a nod to the reality that the Tunisian people are Muslims, even if since independence the constitution has called the country a "secular republic." In that regard, Turkey shares a similar history, in that, despite Ataturk's efforts in enforcing secularization, many Turkish citizens have managed to preserve their religious identity and practices. Today, the religious segment of Turkish society enjoys more religious freedoms and rights than in the past. That is yet another common denominator with Tunisia in the post–Arab Awakening era.

Rached al-Ghannouchi's Treatise on Islam and Democracy

Rachid Ghannouchi had to cancel his keynote address to the Ninth Assembly of the World Movement for Democracy in Dakar, Senegal, on May 9, 2018, due to municipal elections taking place in Tunisia. However, Ghannouchi still delivered his speech, but Dr. Radwan Masmoudi, head of the Center for the Study of Islam and Democracy (CSID), read it on his behalf. The text of the speech has been published in the July 2018 edition of the *Journal of Democracy*. In his speech, Ghannouchi emphasizes the importance of upholding democracy, and he explains how and why Islam and democracy are compatible. According to Ghannouchi:

> Elections are not enough to sustain democracy. Especially in a country that is still a nascent democracy, where the culture of democracy and the institutions of democracy are still weak, we must all learn the art of governing by compromise, negotiation, and consensus.
>
> I believe that decentralization will pave the way for deepening the roots of democracy in Tunisia and for much greater involvement of citizens in decision making at the local and regional levels.

> There is full compatibility between Islam and democracy … The government is and must be of the people, by the people, and for the people – not in the name of God, who is sovereign and watching over all of us.
>
> There should be no compulsion in religion … there is no real democracy without freedom and human rights, including and especially women's rights and minority rights. That is why in Tunisia we are very proud of our new constitution, which mandates equal rights for women, including parity between men and women on all electoral lists.
>
> We are very happy with our progress in the fight against violence and extremism in Tunisia, where we have had more than three years of peace and tranquility … violence is not the answer and is against the values of Islam.
>
> In order for state institutions to be strong, they must enjoy legitimacy, which means they must reflect the society they serve. Tunisians have managed to preserve their democratic transition, despite all the challenges and threats, by insisting on constant dialogue between all parties, NGOs, and religious leaders and institutions.
>
> We must understand that the sources of terrorism are dictatorship and bad governance … The solution to extremism is more freedom (not less), more democracy (not less), more debate and dialogue, and more moderate religious teachings that confront this extremist ideology.
>
> We cannot forget the importance of economic development and growth – these are key to having a stable, and strong democratic state; … A strong state must ensure economic and social inclusion, enabling people to enjoy opportunities, prosperity, and security.
>
> Our second goal and priority [is] strengthening democratic culture and institutions; we are working on civic-education, voter-registration, and citizenship initiatives across the country.[52]

Despite Ennahda and Ghannouchi's insistence that the new Tunisia will be a shining example of peaceful democratization that embodies a mutually compatible mix of Islamism and liberal democracy, many Tunisians have turned to radicalism and extremism.

Religious Extremism in Tunisia

Tunisia has suffered numerous high-profile terrorist attacks in the post-2011 revolution era. The impact of these terrorist attacks has hit the tourism industry the hardest, and that has been by design. Terrorist groups, like Ansar al-Sharia and ISIS, deliberately target the tourism industry because they want to hurt Tunisia's economy. In addition, the terrorist attacks have negatively affected Tunisia's national security, damaging the public's trust in the government's ability to protect them. The 2011 revolution "created a combustible mix of rising and unmanaged social expectations and declining institutional capacity, in a climate of persistent socioeconomic grievances."[53] That describes one among many reasons for the phenomenon of religious extremism in Tunisia.

Soon after the 2011 revolution, Ansar al-Sharia, the Al Qaeda-affiliated cell in North Africa, regularly held protests and demonstrations in Tunis, and specifically targeted the US embassy after Friday prayers with boisterous demonstrations and anti-American chants. Violent extremists have attacked cinemas, art exhibits, and other public events and gatherings to protest what they view as "un-Islamic" behavior and gender mixing, which they consider as serious transgressions. ISIS has followed with high-profile attacks at the Bardo Museum in March 2015, where three terrorists killed 21 people. Then, in June 2015 the city of Sousse suffered an attack when a gunman killed 38 people relaxing at beach resorts on the Mediterranean coast (Fig. 6.3).

Indirectly, the attacks have caused the jittery public to intensify its distrust of the Islamists in Tunisian politics. It has comprised, to some extent, guilt by association of the common ideology of political Islam, wherein Ennahda, viewed as a branch of the Muslim Brotherhood, has been the object of distrust in the eyes of the secularists. Also, these attacks, along with a remarkably high number of Tunisian recruits joining ISIS in Syria and Iraq, highlight a particular problem with Tunisian education, which has traditionally focused on secular curricula. Therefore, religious knowledge and education have been severely marginalized during the secularist eras of Bourguiba and Ben Ali, and these deficiencies in religious education presumably have led to a religiously uneducated populace, especially the youth. The terrorist groups like ISIS have exploited this lack of religious knowledge and education, and successfully recruited thousands of Tunisian males and females into their ranks. In 2015, "an estimated seven-thousand Tunisians had gone to join ISIS in Syria and Iraq. This was a very sizable contingent, especially given that Tunisia's population as a whole is only about eleven million."[54]

What has made violent extremism appealing to many Tunisians? There is a list of factors: upon the 2011 Jasmine Revolution, countless Islamist political prisoners were released from Tunisia's prisons, flooding the pub-

Fig. 6.3 Photo of Bardo Museum Memorial. (Source: Photo taken by author)

lic sphere with newfound freedoms and rights to practice their religion and openly preach to the masses. Many of them have been eager to counter Tunisia's secular legacy and grounded secularism. In addition, many Islamists returned after years in exile, adding to the pool of religious actors in society. In the past, Ben Ali's security services actively monitored Tunisia's mosques, scaring religionists into private and underground domains. After the revolution, mosques have been flourishing with congregations and clerics who are no longer policed.

Another reason why violent extremism has been appealing to many Tunisians is, simply, continuous economic hardships, which again the terrorist groups are effective in exploiting. The Tunisian youth—many of them participant revolutionaries in 2011—have been anxiously awaiting recourse in the form of economic health, welfare, and opportunities. These economic factors have not been delivered, or they have been painfully slow in materializing. Hence, the allure of terrorist groups sometimes becomes too hard to resist, especially if one is desperate.

The Tunisian people have been "feeling cruelly let down. Public services remain spotty, jobs scarce, and government at all levels rife with corruption. Disillusionment and even despair have been on the rise. Within this governance vacuum, the violent religious extremism preached by ISIS and other jihadist groups seems to some to offer a sense of identity and opportunity."[55]

A number of European countries and the United States have been providing counterterrorism assistance to Tunisia, especially since the high-profile attacks in Bardo and Sousse. However, "governance deficiencies and susceptibility to grievance-driven radicalism remain widespread."[56] The governance deficiencies factors contrasted against the Tunisian people's high expectations for fast positive changes following the revolution have led to what is being described as the "expectations-versus-reality gap," which, according to some scholars, "makes some among [Tunisians] prone to choose violent extremism, for reasons both ideological and material."[57]

This is more pronounced in remote inland areas of the country, like Beja, located about 70 miles west of the capital, Tunis. Beja, in particular, "has seen an alarming number of its residents leave to join ISIS or other extremist groups."[58] Scholars Geoffrey Macdonald and Luke Waggoner have conducted research in Tunisia and Beja specifically, and found that "during times of transition elected officials, constitutional designers, and the international community should take special care to ensure inclusive and efficient governance while properly managing sociopolitical and economic expectations. Doing these things will give the fledgling democratic order its best chance of keeping violent ideologies at bay."[59]

Macdonald and Waggoner formed and interviewed focus groups in Beja, and they discovered that, "Those who sympathize with ISIS fighters are more likely than others to feel intense hopelessness and powerlessness, to have negative interactions with police, and to find justifications for violence within Islamic texts."[60] Moreover, the scholars found that, "for those vulnerable to extremist appeals, this sense of powerlessness and despair was often closely tied to poor governance."[61] This means that the coastal-interior wealth gap and government negligence of the remote, rural, and inland areas are continuing today, and this negligence poses a serious threat to Tunisia's future health and outlook. The Tunisian government and businesses need to rectify these problems immediately.

However, the factors described above are not the only ones affecting the proliferation of religious extremism in Tunisia. Additionally, the Tunisian-Libyan border has simultaneously caused serious problems for Tunisia's national security. Following the NATO campaign in Libya that led to Colonel Qaddafi's downfall and demise, the country has collapsed into violent chaos, which is still ongoing. The flow of weapons and people across the extensive and often porous borders has exacerbated Tunisia's security woes. Tunisia's nascent democracy faces serious threats stemming from Libya's turmoil, where a hodgepodge of Islamist militias and terrorist groups, including ISIS and Ansar al-Sharia, operate and proliferate. Simmering security problems also persist at the Tunisian-Algerian border, where violent extremists are active.

Finally, if the risks of Tunisia reverting back to an autocratic system persist, or at a minimum if the Ben Ali-era institutions and corruption remain unchanged, that will account for further malaise that the terrorist groups could exploit. The three major causal factors of the 2011 Jasmine Revolution—corruption, youth unemployment, and the regional wealth gap between the coastal and interior areas of the country—could pose serious problems for the country's political economy and national security if they remain unrectified.

> A lack of infrastructure and jobs has also raised fears that Tunisia's interior could become a breeding ground for extremism.
>
> The country is facing a growing terrorist menace, with security forces coming under periodic attack and a young shepherd beheaded in November near Sidi Bouzid by extremists allied to the Islamic State group.
>
> Residents of Kasserine have warned that the town's youth, short of work or education prospects, could become a target for extremist recruiters.
>
> 'We are in such a state of despair that one might even follow the devil out of misery,' one protester said during January's demonstrations.[62]

Recognizing the daunting risks and threats that Tunisia's fragile democracy faces, France and other Western European countries have offered Tunisia security support. France provides Tunisia with a security package "that includes intelligence and $22 million for equipping special forces, according to *Reuters*. It has also pledged a $1.1 billion aid package over five years to enrich Tunisia' poorest areas and promote job creation."[63]

Nonetheless, the onus remains on the Tunisian government to "provide adequate services and opportunities for many of their constituents,"[64] which so far it has failed to achieve, especially for residents of the inland areas who feel desperate and neglected. This is not to say that democratization in Tunisia is a failure, because it has not failed; and the non-violent processes for political transitions deserve praise, recognition, and emulation in the MENA region. But the pace and efficiencies of socioeconomic changes, which are supposed to improve quality of life for all, urgently need to accelerate. As Macdonald and Waggoner point out, "In the wake of a democratic revolution, expectations regarding what the state could deliver rose dramatically, only to be met with crushing disappointment."[65]

Tunisia has been fortunate to see a decline in terrorist attacks in recent years. This is attributed to the Tunisian government's counterterrorism efforts using security forces and assistance from Western countries. However, this decline in terrorism in Tunisia does not translate into the elimination of extremist ideologies all together, as "the circumstances that breed extremism are still in place."[66] Those circumstances that pertain to governance, socioeconomic improvements, and wealth distribution in all regions of the country need to be addressed. After all, "democracy is more than just elections."[67]

Implications for the Political Economy in the MENA Region

The health of the MENA region's actors in political economy terms depends directly on national and regional security; freedoms and rights; diversified economic and educational opportunities; technology innovation and transfer; women's empowerment; and pluralist political participation. Regional and national security challenges have existed for decades, and they stem from not only state-based conflicts, insecurity, and instability, but non-state actors have constantly been threatening state actors as well as each other. The MENA region has suffered from conflicts and wars for a very long time, and if long-term, sustainable conflict resolution does not take root in the region, then the political economy will further stagnate. These factors rely on government decisions, as well as public reactions. If poor governance and/or authoritarianism—whether secular or Islamist—persists, then freedoms and rights, economic opportunities, women's empowerment, and pluralism will deteriorate, if not succumb to complete repression.

The groundbreaking *2002 Arab Human Development Report (AHDR)* published three major findings from the analysis of the political economy of the region. Both secular and religious/Islamist decision-makers have yet to heed all three findings, which emphasize the deficiencies in the MENA Arab countries in: (1) building a knowledge-based society; (2) establishing democratic governmental systems, complete with rights and freedoms; and (3) ensuring women's empowerment. Given the presumed religious restrictions that political Islam would likely impose on the masses, there is reasonable cause to infer that the three deficiencies that the *2002 AHDR* identifies will persist in an Islamist government and society. Moreover, given the track record of secular governments in the region, there is equally reasonable cause to infer that the MENA region still harbors an aversion to (liberal) democracy, gender equality, and women's empowerment and, at a minimum, a woeful neglect of improvements in education in the process of building a knowledge society. In particular, the latter poses substantial threats to authoritarian monarchies as well as secular autocratic governments, because increased education, knowledge, and information are likely to motivate the masses to challenge the regimes and the status quo. Also, the latter is equally threatening to political Islam, because increased education, knowledge, and information are likely to engender questions and doubts about religious absolutism.

Muslim secularists and formerly Muslim atheists in Muslim-dominated countries are under grave threats and socially ostracized, and a number have been brutally killed in recent years. Control of the public has been the top priority of regimes in the region. Clearly, it has not been in the interest of secular and Islamist decision-makers to allow (liberal) democracy, education, and knowledge, and women's empowerment to flourish in the MENA region in modern history.

Therefore, the likelihood of secular or Islamist governments to initiate dynamic reforms to reverse the deficiencies articulated in the *2002 AHDR* is not promising. Tunisia has been the exception in this scenario.

A greater danger is the ongoing capability of various non-state actors, including terrorist organizations, to operate in the vacuums that exist in MENA countries. In fact, groups like Hezbollah and the Muslim Brotherhood have perfected the art of fulfilling the needs and demands of the public, and especially the lower economic classes, by offering much needed social services, health care, education, and financial assistance. These services have effectively popularized such groups at the expense of the respective governments. Islamism in the form of these services and actors has learned how to use the tools of soft power to improve local political economies. Although Islamists have the potential to bring such services to the national level, without full freedoms, rights, and choices granted to the public—including minority groups and women—their efforts to develop and advance political economies will not bear fruit. As Amartya Sen's theory stipulates, in order for the political economy and socioeconomic health of a country to progress, the people must be given freedoms, rights, and choices and opportunities. Constraints imposed by either secular or religious regimes are counterproductive to their own political economy and overall socioeconomic health.

The fact that not much has improved in the MENA region's political and economic health since the *2002 AHDR* was published indicates that secular and Islamist decision-makers alike have failed to embrace the ways and means for holistic modernization, development, and progress. The 2011 Arab Awakening uprisings and revolutions provided hope for overturning the previously harmful trends in the MENA region, but, thus far, only Tunisia has illustrated a steadfast determination to stay the course, despite many challenges the country faces in improving its political economy.

Conclusion

Tunisia's 2011 revolution cast off the yoke of dictatorship and its violent repression. The revolutionaries demanded freedoms and rights along with dignity in their aspirations for placing Tunisia on the path toward democracy, something it has never experienced in the past. These newfound freedoms and rights have allowed Islamist political groups to enter the governmental process and system without suffering the violent repression they experienced in the days of the Ben Ali dictatorship. Tunisia has heralded a new era with new ideas, competing ideologies, and political groups. Given its long legacy of secularism, it is particularly challenging for Tunisians to wholly embrace political Islam.

However, at the same time, it is foolish to forget that the majority of Tunisia's population is Muslim, and the Islamists are well organized and capable of mobilizing effectively. Moreover, they have been there all along, a point that Tunisia scholar Kenneth Perkins underscores, saying,

> Despite the efforts of Ben Ali, and of Bourguiba before him, to minimize the role of Islam in Tunisian national life, the end of the dictatorship and the rejuvenation of Ennahda were, for all intents and purposes, *simultaneous.* Enthusiasm for a party advocating for the values and traditions of Islam at this specific juncture fits neatly into the warp and weft of contemporary Tunisian history. Between the purge of the Islamists in the 1990s and the revolution in 2011, disgust with the culture of rampant consumerism, greed, dishonesty, and selfishness that flourished seemingly everywhere and that ordinary Tunisians felt powerless to change, proliferated unchecked. Many such persons reacted by reviving their engagements with the rituals and practices of daily Islam, which comforted and strengthened them. They did so spontaneously, not at the urging of an organized political or religious leadership, which had already been broken or co-opted by the regime. Since the authorities made clear their distaste for such pursuits, they also offered one of the very few ways Tunisians could, more or less safely, thumb their noses at the government.
>
> When the revolution came, *these pious souls joined it,* generally not as members of a part of an organized movement, but *as individuals.* Inevitably, *they became a vanguard for a resuscitated Ennahda, most of whose principles they already embraced.*[68]

The experience of Tunisia's Ennahda Islamist party is "indicative of the push and pull between religion and secularism in Tunisian politics. In 2016, the party declared it would separate Islam and politics, announcing that, 'There is no longer any justification for political Islam in Tunisia.' Since 2011, Ennahda has exhibited a pattern of political compromise and survival at the possible expense of grassroots support."[69]

That being said, Ennahda remains proactive throughout Tunisia, and Tunisians continue to contemplate their identities, affinities, loyalties, and ideological persuasions in the modern era. At the same time, the MENA region in general is grappling with the idea of political Islam in a post-Bin Laden, post-ISIS, and post–Arab Awakening era. The term "liberal Islamists" has emerged to compensate for the negative image of Islamism, which has radical and extremist elements rooted in parts of its evolutionary history. As Mark Haas and David Lesch point out, "The tension between democracy, especially liberal democracy that respects minority rights and protects political pluralism, is great for hardline Islamists, but not nearly as much for pragmatic conservatives and, particularly, liberal Islamists."[70]

The forces for liberalization "will obviously be even stronger the more power secular liberals possess. Such individuals were instrumental in creating and sustaining the protests that ultimately toppled authoritarian governments. Their challenge will be organizing in such a way that allows them to compete against well-established Islamist parties in competitive political processes."[71] That rings true in today's Tunisia, which, to some extent, has become the MENA region's metaphoric petri dish for the liberal Islamist experiment.

Notes

1. John L. Esposito, and John O. Voll, "Islam and Democracy," *Humanities*, Vol. 22, No. 6, November/December 2001: http://www.artic.ua.es/biblioteca/u85/documentos/1808.pdf
2. Ibid.
3. Rachid al-Ghannouchi, public speech in Arabic, topic: "Secularism: The Relationship of Religion and Politics from the Perspective of the Ennahda Movement" (*al-Eilmania: ʿilaaqa al-deen bi-l al-dawla min manzoor harakat al-Nahda*), Tunis, Tunisia, March 2, 2012.
4. Esposito and Voll, "Islam and Democracy."
5. Hossein Askari, Hossein Mohammadkhan, and Liza Mydin, *Reformation and Development in the Muslim World: Islamicity Indices as Benchmark* (Palgrave, 2017), p. viii.
6. Ibid., p. vii.
7. Ibid., pp. 3–4.
8. Ibid., p. 14.
9. Ibid.
10. Mehdi Mozaffari, *Islamism: A New Totalitarianism* (London: Lynne Rienner, 2017), pp. 169–170.
11. Ibid., p. 176.
12. Ibid., p. 177.
13. Ibid., pp. 179–180.
14. Ibid., p. 215.
15. Ibid., pp. 243–244.
16. Ibid., pp. 252–253.
17. Ibid., pp. 264–265.

18. See Tarek Amara, "Tunisia's Ennahda Claims Victory in Landmark Local Elections," *Reuters*, May 6, 2018: https://www.reuters.com/article/us-tunisia-election/tunisias-ennahda-claims-victory-in-landmark-local-elections-idUSKBN1I708Q
19. Interview with Lotfi Hajji, Tunis, Tunisia, July 19, 2017.
20. Rajaa Basly, "The Future of Ennahda in Tunisia," *Sada, Carnegie Endowment for International Peace*, April 20, 2011: https://carnegieendowment.org/sada/43675
21. The Hamas Charter refuses to recognize Israel's right to exist, and it identifies all of Palestine as the future Palestinian state. The Charter refers to Israel as "the Zionist enemy." See: http://avalon.law.yale.edu/20th_century/hamas.asp
22. Eleanor Beardsley, "Algeria's Black Decade Still Weighs Heavily," *National Public Radio (NPR)*, April 25, 2011: https://www.npr.org/2011/04/25/135376589/algerias-black-decade-still-weighs-heavily
23. Hayat Alvi, "Women's Rights Movements in the 'Arab Spring': Major Victories or Failures for Human Rights?" *Journal of International Women's Studies (JIWS)*, volume 16, issue 3, July 2015, https://vc.bridgew.edu/cgi/viewcontent.cgi?article=1828&context=jiws, p. 306.
24. Ibid.
25. Ibid.
26. Bouazza Ben Bouazza, "Tunisian Fundamentalists Protest Report on Sexual Equality," *US News and World Report*, August 11, 2018: https://www.usnews.com/news/world/articles/2018-08-11/tunisian-fundamentalists-protest-report-on-sexual-equality
27. Ibid.
28. Andrea Taylor, and Elissa Miller, "How Legal Reform Can Drive Social Change for Women in Tunisia," *The Atlantic Council*, March 8, 2018: http://www.atlanticcouncil.org/blogs/menasource/how-legal-reform-can-drive-social-change-for-women-in-tunisia
29. Ibid.
30. Ibid.
31. Ibid.
32. Julia Clancy-Smith, "From Sidi Bou Zid to Sidi Bou Said: A *Longue Durée* Approach to the Tunisian Revolutions," in *The Arab Spring: Change and Resistance in the Middle East*, edited by Mark L. Haas, and David W. Lesch (Boulder: Westview Press, 2013), p. 15.
33. Ibid.
34. Ibid., p. 25.
35. Ibid.
36. Ibid., pp. 25–26.
37. Clancy-Smith, p. 15.
38. Monica Marks, "Tunisia's Islamists and the 'Turkish Model'," *Journal of Democracy*, vol. 28, no. 1, January 2017, p. 103.

39. Ibid.
40. Ibid.
41. Ibid.
42. Ibid., p. 104.
43. Ibid.
44. Ibid., p. 107.
45. Ibid., p. 108.
46. Ibid.
47. Ibid., pp. 108–109.
48. Ibid., p. 109.
49. Ibid., p. 110.
50. Ibid., p. 111.
51. Ibid., p. 114.
52. Rached Ghannouchi, "Islam and Democracy in Tunisia," *Journal of Democracy*, vol. 29, no. 3, July 2018, pp. 5–8.
53. Geoffrey Macdonald, and Luke Waggoner, "Dashed Hopes and Extremism in Tunisia," *Journal of Democracy*, vol. 29, no. 1, January 2018, p. 127.
54. Ibid.
55. Ibid.
56. Ibid.
57. Ibid.
58. Ibid.
59. Ibid., p. 128.
60. Ibid., p. 130.
61. Ibid.
62. "Poverty in Central Tunisia a Ticking Time Bomb," *Gulf News*, March 4, 2016: https://gulfnews.com/news/mena/tunisia/poverty-in-central-tunisia-a-ticking-time-bomb-1.1683702
63. Marc Rivett-Carnac, "France Strengthens Support for Tunisia in the Face of Islamist Threats," *Time*, March 17, 2016: http://time.com/4262329/tunisia-france-aid-security-ben-guerdane-isis-islamist/
64. Macdonald and Waggoner, p. 137.
65. Ibid.
66. Ibid.
67. Ibid.
68. Kenneth Perkins, *A History of Modern Tunisia*, second edition (New York: Cambridge University Press, 2014), p. 259. Emphasis added.
69. Taylor and Miller, "How Legal Reform Can Drive Social Change for Women in Tunisia," *The Atlantic Council.*
70. "Introduction," in *The Arab Spring: Change and Resistance in the Middle East*, edited by Mark L. Haas, and David W. Lesch (Boulder: Westview Press, 2013), p. 6.
71. Ibid.

CHAPTER 7

Conclusion

The hypothesis of this analysis has been sufficiently proven, ascertaining that because Tunisia's civil society and political system have engaged in inclusive dialogues and negotiations, democratic transition processes have been non-violent, hence providing the Middle East and North Africa (MENA) region with a positive example, or model, of post-revolution evolution and transformations. This accounts for a major milestone in the entire region, because no other country has been able to sustain the post-2011 Arab Awakening revolutionary momentum, changes, reforms, and non-violent political discourse in the same manner as Tunisia. That is why Tunisia is considered a cautionary success story, and, as such, it serves as the model of democracy in the MENA region.

The dependent variable, commitment to national dialogue for non-violent conflict resolution, has underscored Tunisia's success in preventing civil conflict during political transitions and institutional transformations following the revolution. Tunisia has remained committed to democratization, even though it has been painfully gradual and intense, and Tunisia has embraced inclusiveness in sociopolitical and economic activities. These are the independent variables that this analysis has tested. Of course, the Tunisian government still has a long way to go to root out corruption—another independent variable—and expand the inclusiveness to equitable wealth distribution and, most importantly, job creation throughout the country. Efforts in these areas are ongoing, but the results have been slow,

H. Alvi, *The Political Economy and Islam of the Middle East*, Political Economy of Islam,
https://doi.org/10.1007/978-3-030-17050-9_7

which has tested the patience of the masses, particularly the educated unemployed youth.

Overall, though, the hypothesis has been proven, due to the commitment of the Tunisian people to peaceful negotiations and reconciliation between parties. The Tunisian people are determined not to allow their country to collapse into violent chaos as seen in Libya, Egypt, Syria, Iraq, Bahrain, and Yemen. According to the sociologist Asef Bayat,

> If we look carefully to all of these experiences, all of the protests, including those in Libya, Syria, and Yemen, they were at first remarkably peaceful and civil. In both Syria and Libya, the regimes' reaction was brutal and extraordinary. The protests suffered a lot of casualties, but they were still non-violent until the foreign forces got involved: NATO and Qatar in Libya and a host of countries ranging from Saudi Arabia, Turkey, and the United States to Iran, Hezbullah, al-Qaeda and then Russia.
>
> Their involvement militarized the bulk of the uprisings, turning these countries into a theatrical stage for settling geopolitical accounts. It is remarkable that despite the brutality and violence by the regime and the armed opposition, the ordinary Syrians have shown that they still wish to protest peacefully when opportunities arise as we have seen in recent episodes.
>
> … in many ways the prospect in Tunisia looks better. In Tunisia, the army has been far less aggressive than that in Egypt. Ennahda has been much more inclusive, tolerant, and wise in its perspective than the Egyptian Muslim Brotherhood; and in Tunisia, there has been a powerful labor movement organization, UGTT, which mediated between Ennahda and the secular liberal forces. The Tunisian Constitution is a remarkable achievement. But the political class (both secular and Islamic) has basically bought into the neoliberal economy, and social justice has remained, as in Egypt, a key unfulfilled claim of the revolution. Inequality, unemployment, exclusion largely remain, and they are likely to come and haunt the post-revolution governments.[1]

Tremendous credit goes to Tunisia's Islamist party, Ennahda, for volunteering to step down from power, rather than stubbornly prolonging the political crisis and allowing the situation to spiral into violent civil conflict. This book has articulated how these events unfolded, and how the Tunisian political leadership and prominent stakeholders, such as civil society, have steadfastly remained committed to national dialogue and consensus building for the sake of peace, stability, and national security.

This analysis has also shed light on the MENA region's political economy trends and statuses, which have shown little improvement since the *2002 Arab Human Development Report (AHDR)* was published. Because the political and economic variables are interdependent at the national, regional, and international levels, especially in the era of globalization, the health of the MENA region's political economy presupposes good governance and sound policy-making. However, the MENA region unequivocally illustrates the direct opposite, that is, the preponderance of violent conflicts and wars, which perpetuate cycles of humanitarian crises; poor domestic economic policies; poverty and glaring economic class gaps; prevalence of corruption; propensity for authoritarianism; marginalization, if not wholesale suppression, of women's rights and empowerment; and persistent deficiencies in education, knowledge, and information.

Moreover, this analysis has applied the paramount theory of Amartya Sen to illustrate the importance of individual freedoms, rights, choices, and agency for socioeconomic development and progress. Dr. Sen's Social Choice Theory promotes the free agency of people; gender equality; human rights for socioeconomic outcomes; and, most importantly, these factors presuppose the "removal of repressive states." The *2002 Arab Human Development Report* (AHDR) has direct interconnectedness with Dr. Sen's theory, in that, even following the 2011 Arab Awakening, authoritarianism still pervades in the MENA region—something that the *AHDR* emphasizes in its findings as one of three major deficiencies in Arab states. Tunisia has remained as the outlier in this regard. The Tunisian people and political leadership have been determined to engage in national and local dialogues, negotiations, and compromises leading to collective agreements to uphold non-violent transitions and democratic changes. This is why Tunisia is viewed as an exceptional case in the MENA region.

The *AHDR* further lists deficiencies in building a knowledge society and women's empowerment throughout the region. Tunisia has been committed to gender equality, and the Tunisian people have reaffirmed this commitment, despite ideological competition and significant sociopolitical challenges, following the 2011 Jasmine Revolution. They have been mindful of the fact that gender equality and women's rights are part and parcel of the demands for dignity and human rights. This is yet another reason why Tunisia is an outstanding case for the region to follow. The MENA region is not only known for authoritarianism, but also for strict patriarchal structures, systems, and institutions that continuously repress women. In fact, I prefer to use the term "patriarchal despotism" to describe the severity of misogyny in the region. Tunisia stands out as a beacon of hope in the MENA region for advancing a model for women's rights, agency, and empowerment.

Comparative democratization in the MENA region is an easy assessment, since Tunisia stands out in this regard compared to all the rest. The other countries in the region, even those who have experienced Arab Awakening uprisings, revolutions, and changes, have fallen into violent chaos and upheavals and/or counterrevolutions. The Persian Gulf Arab states openly express contempt for democracy and civil and human rights, particularly as Tunisia has embraced and implemented them. Egypt has undergone a counterrevolution that has resulted in a repressive military dictatorship. Libya and Syria are engulfed in violent civil conflicts. In the latter, the Bashar al-Assad regime has slaughtered half a million Syrians since 2011. Yemen is suffering a brutal slow genocide at the hands of the Saudi-led coalition and the Houthi rebels. Revolutions have not been successful in the MENA region, but Tunisia has been the only "success story" in the post–Arab Awakening era.

Furthermore, democratization presupposes the *will* to democratize from the bottom-up and top-down, including the political leadership. A historical example of this is India starting from the anti-colonial movement with Mahatma Gandhi's leadership. By independence in 1947, the vast majority of Indians had accepted and supported India's future path toward democracy. In the case of the MENA region, only Tunisia has the attributes of this conviction to democracy. Given that democracy encompasses freedoms and rights, the political economy outlook for democratic systems is deemed as promising.

Referring back to Schmitter and O'Donnell's precepts about democracy, we are reminded that change in regime implies a "complete change of elite personnel and structure." And, "the ensuing governing elite (or non-elite) is expected to pursue different policies benefitting different segments of the population."[2] In addition, democracy is "in perpetual crises, because it is "constantly redirecting its citizens' gaze from a more or less unsatisfactory present toward a future of still unfulfilled possibilities ... The capacity for hope is the great capacity of democracy, one which under the right circumstances can and should nourish other, more specific capacities that may promote improvements in democratic quality."[3]

The bottom line for all of the MENA region's political leaders is that governance determines successes and failures in the overall political economy of a given country. Good governance, sound economic policies, elimination of corruption, and equitable wealth distribution are required for socioeconomic progress. But good governance is not exactly a characteristic of the MENA states. In fact, they have failed to heed the findings and warnings of the 2002 *AHDR*, even after the 2011 Arab Awakening. Authoritarianism is still painfully pervasive in the region. Coincidingly, the MENA region's regimes continue to repress people, which counters the fundamental tenets of Amartya Sen's Social Choice Theory. When freedoms, rights, and choices are repressed, society will ultimately face arrested development. It seems that the MENA regimes have yet to comprehend that simple point.

Tunisia is a regional model to follow for many reasons. Underneath the surface of Tunisia's post-revolution democracy is an intricate matrix of political groups, parties, institutions, and constituents competing ideologically and politically. Among the two major competitive streams are those of the secularists and the Islamists. Elizabeth Shakman Hurd has described Tunisia's political blend as a "bizarre concoction between secularism and Islamism."[4] Even within Tunisia's feminist movements we see two streams: secular feminism versus Islamic feminism.

However, the common denominator in all these political contexts is a commitment to consensus building through non-violent dialogue. Tunisians are proud of this display of non-violent collective agreements in light of deep, and at times very tense, ideological and political divisions among diverse groups and organizations, as well as individuals. Tunisia has proven resilient even following a few political assassinations and high-profile terrorist attacks.

Sarah Chayes, a specialist on corruption and civil society, summarizes the case of Tunisia with these profound thoughts:

> Westerners, while acknowledging the persistence and ultimate flexibility of Tunisian political actors in reaching consensus, should not draw the wrong lesson from this remarkable story. As they think about how Tunisia's experience might usefully be applied to other contexts, they should be sure to give appropriate weight to the mediating role of powerful and legitimate external institutions. After all, as LTDH (Tunisia League of Human Rights) Vice President Ali Ziddini puts it, 'just as our revolution was a model, we want our National Dialogue to be a model for other countries.'[5]

On July 13, 2017, I revisited Dr. Radwan Masmoudi at his office in Tunis. He is the director of the Center for the Study of Islam and Democracy (CSID), and he plays a significant role in facilitating the national dialogue in Tunisia.

Dr. Masmoudi tells me that the revolution in Tunisia was *for* two things and *against* two things. It was a revolution for freedom and dignity (in Arabic, *thawra al-hurriyya wa-al-karaama*); and it was a revolution against corruption and dictatorship (in Arabic, *thawra did al-fasaad wa-al-diktaatoria*). He emphasizes that the youth unemployment crisis and the wealth distribution disparities between the coastal and poorer interior region of Tunisia have been the results of the Ben Ali era's gross corruption and dictatorship. He assures me that "We are working on that," that is, rooting out all elements of corruption.

Moreover, in post-revolution Tunisia, the fight for preserving the nascent democracy and the fight against corruption require diligence and persistence. Dr. Masmoudi says, "We think that by removing the dictatorship and corruption and having a democratic system, we can address all the needs of the youth and regional disparities. The problem is that that takes time, it's not going to be done overnight."

Youth unemployment continues to tear at Tunisia's seams, and the desperation of the Tunisian youth often boils over and manifests itself even today. Dr. Masmoudi mentions that occasionally young men continue to burn themselves, like Mohammed Bouazizi did in December 2010. "So, the problem of youth anger and frustration and disenchantment is still a big problem," he says.

However, he adds, "What we have achieved in the last six years since the revolution is mostly building a new democracy. On the political side, we have a new constitution as well as new freedoms and institutions that protect freedoms, that protect elections and human rights, and all that. We have a very strong and thriving civil society, we have the media; so, we have a lot achieved on the political front. In that respect, what we were able to achieve is a miracle – that we were able to build all these democratic institutions. And, that required, in the political sphere, a lot of dialogue, especially between Islamists and secularists." Dr. Masmoudi contends, "That is the real achievement in Tunisia on the political front, is finding common ground between Islamists and secularists." He ends the conversation by saying, "When people want democracy, no one can stop them."

A prominent Tunisian civil society activist, Souad Goussami Hajji, is relieved to see Tunisia on a solid path toward democracy today. She sees freedom of the press flourishing, and while she is optimistic about Tunisia's future, she is still cognizant of what remains to be achieved at the local and national levels. I asked her what she believes are Tunisia's top three priorities today. She responded, "first, national security; second, economic development and fighting corruption; and, third, reforms in education."[6] She elaborated that security is the responsibility of the state, and the state must continue the fight against corruption and bring in investors, develop infrastructure, and close the regional wealth gap between the wealthier coastal areas and the poverty-stricken interior region.

In the education sector, Ms. Hajji mentioned the need for curriculum reforms. She said that many proposals and initiatives for education reforms have begun, including a call for forming a new commission on education.[7] She added that Tunisia needs to make Arabic the official language of the sciences and research. Ms. Hajji emphasized the important role of civil society activism in revising the progressive Tunisian Constitution following the 2011 Jasmine Revolution.[8] However, there is still tremendous work to be done, especially pertaining to the country's top priorities, as she has articulated.

Tunisia has come full circle in a positive sense, because, after decades of repressive dictatorship and authoritarianism, Tunisians have returned to the fundamental principles of one of their own great historical figures, Ibn Khaldun, the father of sociology. As mentioned in Chap. 2, Ibn Khaldun posits the concept of a governmental *social contract*, which translates into good governance practices that meet the needs of the people.

Tunisia has not only striven to change the status quo in the effort to cement the social contract, but its people have also illustrated their commitment to the priority of non-violence at the highest levels. As Safwan Masri says:

> Powers were handed over – peacefully – multiple times during the nascent era of democratic rule, and for the first time in the Arab world, an Islamic party, Ennahda, 'voluntarily' ceded control to a secular one.
>
> In each and every event, entity, and process during the Tunisian spring – Kasbah, Troika, and Quartet, for inspiration – there is strong evidence of a Tunisian way, *tunisianité*.
>
> This is the story of Tunisia.[9]

Although this sounds very simple, the governments in the MENA region have failed miserably with respect to their social contract concerning the masses. Cammett, Diwan, Richards, and Waterbury, in their book, *A Political Economy of the Middle East* (2015), emphasize these failures:

> MENA governments have long been either incapable of responding to the demands of their populations or unwilling to do so. Middle Eastern states have been 'fierce,' particularly in their coercive control over society, but as Nazih Ayubi (1996, 449) points out, such states are neither strong nor capable when it comes to delivering shared growth and development.
>
> And now, in the aftermath of massive street protests of 2011–2012, the situation in much of the region has become more unsettled and chaotic. So far, the Arab uprisings have not ushered in a more inclusive polity or more effective state institutions. At this juncture, many countries in the region face the serious risk of falling into deep violence traps.[10]

Perhaps everyone in the MENA region would benefit from reading Ibn Khaldun and taking his concept of the social contract to heart. Tunisia is doing its best in this grand ambition.

Notes

1. Ozgur Gokmen, "Five Years after the Arab Uprisings: An Interview with Asef Bayat," *Eutopia On Middle East, Islam, Diversity and Democracy*, May 3, 2016: http://www.eutopiainstitute.org/2016/05/five-years-after-the-arab-uprisings-an-interview-with-asef-bayat/
2. Philippe Schmitter, "Democratization and Political Elites or Political Elites and Democratization or The Process of Democratization and the Role of Elites or the Role of Elites in Democratization or Democratization: The Role of Elites," European University Institute, p. 1: https://www.eui.eu/Documents/DepartmentsCentres/SPS/Profiles/Schmitter/DEMOCRATIZATION-AND-POLITICAL-ELITES.REV.pdf
3. Guillermo O'Donnell, "The Perpetual Crises of Democracy," *Journal of Democracy*, vol. 18, January 2007 (pp. 5–11): https://www.journalofdemocracy.org/article/perpetual-crises-democracy
4. See Elizabeth Shakman Hurd in Chap. 1.
5. Sarah Chayes, "How a Leftist Labor Union Helped Force Tunisia's Political Settlement," *Carnegie Endowment for International Peace*, March 27, 2014: https://carnegieendowment.org/2014/03/27/how-leftist-labor-union-helped-force-tunisia-s-political-settlement-pub-55143
6. Interview with Souad Goussami Hajji, Tunis, Tunisia, July 17, 2017.
7. Ibid.
8. Ibid.
9. Safwan M. Masri, *Tunisia: An Arab Anomaly* (New York: Columbia University Press, 2017), p. 295.
10. *A Political Economy of the Middle East*, fourth edition. Edited by Melani Cammett, Ishac Diwan, Alan Richards, and John Waterbury (Boulder: Westview Press, 2015), p. 515.

Correction to: Secularism Versus Political Islam: The Case of Tunisia

CORRECTION TO:

Chapter 6 in: H. Alvi, *The Political Economy and Islam of the Middle East*, Political Economy of Islam, https://doi.org/10.1007/978-3-030-17050-9_6

In this chapter the flags of Turkey and Tunisia were reversed and the same has been corrected in this revised version.

The updated original online version of this chapter can be found at https://doi.org/10.1007/978-3-030-17050-9_6

H. Alvi, *The Political Economy and Islam of the Middle East*, Political Economy of Islam,
https://doi.org/10.1007/978-3-030-17050-9_8

Correction to: The Political Economy and Islam of the Middle East

Correction to:

H. Alvi, *The Political Economy and Islam of the Middle East*, Political Economy of Islam, https://doi.org/10.1007/978-3-030-17050-9

This book was inadvertently published without updating the following corrections:

Chapter 1: An error had been introduced in this chapter that Ghannouchi was the first president of Tunisia after the revolution. It was, in fact, Moncef Marzouki. The same has been corrected in this revised version.

Chapter 3: An error had been introduced in this chapter that Tunisia follows the Hanafi school of law in Islam. It's been verified that Tunisia follows the Maliki school of law in Islam. Hence, the related text has been edited on page 70 in this revised version.

The updated versions of the chapters can be found at
https://doi.org/10.1007/978-3-030-17050-9_1
https://doi.org/10.1007/978-3-030-17050-9_3

H. Alvi, *The Political Economy and Islam of the Middle East*, Political Economy of Islam,
https://doi.org/10.1007/978-3-030-17050-9_9

Bibliography

Interviews

Interview with Fatma Kamoun. Tunis, Tunisia, July 17, 2017.
Interview with Hatem Abidi. Sousse, Tunisia, July 15, 2017.
Interview with Kamal Ben Younes. Tunis, Tunisia, February 29, 2012.
Interview with Lotfi Hajji. Tunis, Tunisia, July 19, 2017.
Interview with Meherzia Labidi. Tunisian Parliament, Bardo, Tunis, July 18, 2017.
Interview with Radwan Masmoudi. Center for the Study of Islam and Democracy (CSID), Tunis, February 29, 2012.
———. Center for the Study of Islam and Democracy (CSID), Tunis, July 13, 2017.
Interview with Souad Goussami Hajji. Tunis, Tunisia, July 17, 2017.

Speech

Rachid al-Ghannouchi, Public Speech in Arabic, Topic: "Secularism: The Relationship of Religion and Politics from the Perspective of the Ennahda Movement," (*al-Eilmania: 'ilaaqa al-deen bi-l al-dawla min manzoor harakat al-Nahda*), Tunis, Tunisia, March 2, 2012.

H. Alvi, *The Political Economy and Islam of the Middle East*, Political Economy of Islam,
https://doi.org/10.1007/978-3-030-17050-9

Books

A Political Economy of the Middle East. 4th ed. Ed. Melani Cammett, Ishac Diwan, Alan Richards, and John Waterbury. Boulder: Westview Press, 2015.

Alexander, Christopher. 2010. *Tunisia: Stability and Reform in the Modern Maghreb*. New York: Routledge.

Clancy-Smith, Julia. 2013. From Sidi Bou Zid to Sidi Bou Said: A *Longue Durée* Approach to the Tunisian Revolutions. In *The Arab Spring: Change and Resistance in the Middle East*, ed. Mark L. Haas and David W. Lesch. Boulder: Westview Press.

Masri, Safwan M. 2017. *Tunisia: An Arab Anomaly*. New York: Columbia University Press.

Mozaffari, Mehdi. 2017. *Islamism: A New Totalitarianism*. London: Lynne Rienner.

Oxford Atlas of the World. 17th ed. New York: Oxford University Press, 2010.

Perkins, Kenneth J. 2004. *A History of Modern Tunisia*. New York: Cambridge University Press.

———. 2014. *A History of Modern Tunisia*. 2nd ed. New York: Cambridge University Press.

Sen, Amartya. 1999. *Development as Freedom*. New York: Alfred A. Knopf.

The Arab Spring: Change and Resistance in the Middle East. Ed. Mark L. Haas and David W. Lesch. Boulder: Westview Press, 2013.

Wolf, Anne. 2017. *Political Islam in Tunisia: The History of Ennahda*. London: Hurst and Company.

Wright, Robin. 2012. *Rock the Casbah: Rage and Rebellion Across the Islamic World*. New York: Simon and Schuster.

Journal Articles

Alvi, Hayat. 2015a. The Post-Secular Republic: Turkey's Experiments with Islamism. *Air & Space Power Journal (USAF)*. 2nd Quarter, 6 (2): 22–39. http://www.au.af.mil/au/afri/aspj/apjinternational/aspj_f/article.asp?id=151

———. 2015b. Women's Rights Movements in the 'Arab Spring': Major Victories or Failures for Human Rights? *Journal of International Women's Studies (JIWS)* 16 (3). https://vc.bridgew.edu/cgi/viewcontent.cgi?referer=https://www.google.com/&httpsredir=1&article=1828&context=jiws

Basly, Rajaa. 2011. The Future of Ennahda in Tunisia. *Sada Journal, Carnegie Endowment for International Peace*, April 20. https://carnegieendowment.org/sada/43675

Cafer Karatas, Selim. 2006. The Economic Theory of Ibn Khaldun and the Rise and Fall of Nations. *Muslim Heritage*. Foundation for Science, Technology and

Civilization, April. http://www.muslimheritage.com/article/economic-theory-ibn-khaldun-and-rise-and-fall-nations

Chayes, Sarah. 2014. How a Leftist Labor Union Helped Force Tunisia's Political Settlement. *Carnegie Endowment for International Peace*, March 27. https://carnegieendowment.org/2014/03/27/how-leftist-labor-union-helped-force-tunisia-s-political-settlement-pub-55143

Cherif, Youssef. 2017. Tunisia's Fledgling Gulf Relations. *Carnegie Endowment for International Peace*, January 17. http://carnegieendowment.org/sada/67703

Daniele, Giulia. 2014. Tunisian Women's Activism After the January 14 Revolution: Looking Within and Towards the Other Side of the Mediterranean. *Journal of International Women's Studies (JIWS)* 15 (2): 18. https://vc.bridgew.edu/cgi/viewcontent.cgi?referer=https://www.google.com/&httpsredir=1&article=1750&context=jiws.

Dhaouadi, Muhammad. 2006. The Concept of Change in the Thought of Ibn Khaldun and Western Classical Sociologists. *Ýslâm Araþtýrmalarý Dergisi*, Sayý 16: 68. http://www.isam.org.tr/documents/_dosyalar/_pdfler/islam_arastirmalari_dergisi/sayi16/043_087.pdf

Esposito, John L., and John O. Voll. 2001. Islam and Democracy. *Humanities* 22 (6). http://www.artic.ua.es/biblioteca/u85/documentos/1808.pdf

Hirschkind, Charles. 2015. What Is Political Islam. *Middle East Research and Information Project (MERIP)*, Winter. http://www.merip.org/mer/mer205/what-political-islam

Tunisia's Fight Against Corruption: An Interview with Chawki Tabib. *Sada Journal*. Carnegie Endowment for International Peace, May 11, 2017. http://carnegieendowment.org/sada/69939

Reports

Ayed, Jaloul. 2011. Quoted in Conference Report, *Tunisia's and Egypt's Revolutions and Transitions to Democracy: What Is the Impact on the Arab World? What Lessons Can We Learn?* ed. Thomas W. Skladony, Peter Winston Fettner, and Alexandra Tohmé. Center for the Study of Islam and Democracy (CSID). 12th Annual Conference, Washington, DC, April 15.

Masmoudi, Radwan. 2011. Quoted in Conference Report, *Tunisia's and Egypt's Revolutions and Transitions to Democracy: What Is the Impact on the Arab World? What Lessons Can We Learn?* ed. Thomas W. Skladony, Peter Winston Fettner, and Alexandra Tohmé. Center for the Study of Islam and Democracy (CSID). 12th Annual Conference, Washington, DC, April 15.

Rising Food and Energy Prices in Europe and Central Asia. *The World Bank*. 2011. http://www-wds.worldbank.org/external/default/WDSContentServer/

WDSP/IB/2011/04/14/000333037_20110414015110/Rendered/PDF/610970WP0P1262171World1Bank1Combine.pdf

The World Bank in Tunisia. *The World Bank*, April 18, 2018. http://www.worldbank.org/en/country/tunisia/overview

Media and Online Resources

Abouzei, Rania. 2011. Bouazizi, the Man Who Set Himself and Tunisia on Fire. *Time Magazine*, January 21. http://content.time.com/time/magazine/article/0,9171,2044723,00.html

Adel, Hayam. 2018. Egypt Struggles to End Female Genital Mutilation. *Reuters*, March 8. https://www.reuters.com/article/us-womens-day-egypt/egypt-struggles-to-end-female-genital-mutilation-idUSKCN1GK1ZL

Amara, Tarek. 2012. Thousands Rally in Tunisia for Women's Rights. *Reuters*, August 14. http://af.reuters.com/article/worldNews/idAFBRE87C16320120814

———. 2018. Tunisia's Ennahda Claims Victory in Landmark Local Elections. *Reuters*, May 6. https://www.reuters.com/article/us-tunisia-election/tunisias-ennahda-claims-victory-in-landmark-local-elections-idUSKBN1I708Q

An Assassination in Tunisia. *The New York Times*, February 8, 2013. http://www.nytimes.com/2013/02/09/opinion/the-assassination-of-chokri-belaid-in-tunisia.html?_r=0

Asabiyyah. *Oxford Islamic Studies Online*. 2018. http://www.oxfordislamicstudies.com/article/opr/t125/e202

Badran, Margot. 2002. Islamic Feminism: What's in a Name? *Al-Ahram Weekly*, January 17–23. http://weekly.ahram.org.eg/2002/569/cu1.htm

Barnell, Owen. 2017. Seven Years After Arab Spring Revolt, Tunisia's Future Remains Uncertain. *France24*, December 18. https://www.france24.com/en/20171217-tunisia-seven-years-after-arab-spring-revolution-protests-economic-uncertainty

Beardsley, Eleanor. 2011a. Algeria's Black Decade Still Weighs Heavily. *National Public Radio (NPR)*, April 25. https://www.npr.org/2011/04/25/135376589/algerias-black-decade-still-weighs-heavily

———. 2011b. In Tunisia, Women Play Equal Role in Revolution. *National Public Radio (NPR)*, January 27. https://www.npr.org/2011/01/27/133248219/in-tunisia-women-play-equal-role-in-revolution

Ben Bouazza, Bouazza. 2018. Tunisian Fundamentalists Protest Report on Sexual Equality. *US News and World Report*, August 11. https://www.usnews.com/news/world/articles/2018-08-11/tunisian-fundamentalists-protest-report-on-sexual-equality

Biography of Zine al-Abidine Ben Ali. *Africa Success*, January 23, 2011. http://www.africansuccess.org/visuFiche.php?id=964&lang=en

Bremmer, Ian. 2017. Top 5 Countries Where ISIS Gets Foreign Recruits. *Time Magazine*, April 14. http://time.com/4739488/isis-iraq-syria-tunisia-saudi-arabia-russia/

Cambanis, Thanassis. 2015. The Arab Spring Was the Revolution of the Hungry. *The Boston Globe*, August 23. https://www.bostonglobe.com/ideas/2015/08/22/the-arab-spring-was-revolution-hungry/K15S1kGeO5Y6gsJwAYHejI/story.html

Cherif, Youssef. 2015. Tunisia's Foreign Policy: A Delicate Balance. *Atlantic Council*, March 23. http://www.atlanticcouncil.org/blogs/menasource/tunisia-s-foreign-policy-a-delicate-balance

Chulov, Martin. 2017. How Saudi Elite Became Five-Star Prisoners at the Riyadh Ritz Carlton. *The Guardian*, November 6. https://www.theguardian.com/world/2017/nov/06/how-saudi-elite-became-five-star-prisoners-at-the-riyadh-ritz-carlton

Constructivism in International Relations. InternationalRelations.org. 2018. http://internationalrelations.org/constructivism_in_international_relations/

Dreisbach, Tristan, and Robert Joyce. 2014. Revealing Tunisia's Corruption Under Ben Ali. *Al Jazeera*, March 27. https://www.aljazeera.com/indepth/features/2014/03/revealing-tunisia-corruption-under-ben-ali-201432785825560542.html

Economic Theory, Freedom and Human Rights: The Work of Amartya Sen. ODI Briefing Paper, *Overseas Development Institute (ODI)*, November 2001. http://www.odi.org.uk/resources/docs/2321.pdf

Egypt: A Year After 'Virginity Tests', Women Victims of Army Violence Still Seek Justice. *Amnesty International*, March 9, 2012. https://www.amnesty.org/en/latest/news/2012/03/egypt-year-after-virginity-tests-women-victims-army-violence-still-seek-justice/

Eltahawy, Mona. 2018. Seven Years After the 'Arab Spring,' Tunisia is Leading in Another Revolution – on Women's Rights. *The Washington Post*, January 31. https://www.washingtonpost.com/news/global-opinions/wp/2018/01/31/seven-years-after-the-arab-spring-tunisia-is-leading-another-revolution-on-womens-rights/?noredirect=on&utm_term=.7062213b5ccf

Freedom in the World 2002, 2007, and 2010: Egypt. *Freedom House*. http://www.freedomhouse.org/report/freedom-world/2002/egypt

Freedom in the World 2002, 2007, and 2010: Libya. *Freedom House*. http://www.freedomhouse.org/report/freedom-world/2002/libya

Freedom in the World 2002, 2007, and 2010: Tunisia. *Freedom House*. http://www.freedomhouse.org/report/freedom-world/2002/tunisia

Friedman, Thomas. A-Z Quotes. http://www.azquotes.com/quote/1573822?ref=tunisia

Gall, Carlotta. 2013. Second Opposition Leader Assassinated in Tunisia. *The New York Times*, July 25. http://www.nytimes.com/2013/07/26/world/middleeast/second-opposition-leader-killed-in-tunisia.html?pagewanted=all&_r=1&

Gasciogne, Bamber. History of Tunisia. *HistoryWorld*. From 2001 ongoing. http://www.historyworld.net/wrldhis/PlainTextHistories.asp?historyid=ac93

Habib Bourguiba: Father of Tunisia. *BBC News*, April 6, 2000. http://news.bbc.co.uk/2/hi/obituaries/703907.stm

Hilleary, Cecily. 2011. Return of Islamic Leader Worries Some Tunisian Women. *Voice of America (VOA)*, February 4. http://www.voanews.com/english/news/middle-east/115291829.html

Hodge, Carl Cavanaugh. 2014. Imperialism. *Oxford Bibliographies*, September 19. Accessed 12 June 2018, from http://www.oxfordbibliographies.com/view/document/obo-9780199743292/obo-9780199743292-0010.xml

Hurd, Elizabeth Shakman. 2012. Tunisia: Democracy After Secularism: The Rise of So-Called Islamist Parties in the Wake of the Arab Spring Is a Product of Democracy, Not an Obstacle. *Al Jazeera*, April 11. http://www.aljazeera.com/indepth/opinion/2012/04/20124795440442662.html

Iran's Currency Plunges to Record Low as US Sanctions Loom. *Al Jazeera*, July 29, 2018. https://www.aljazeera.com/news/2018/07/iran-currency-plunges-record-sanctions-loom-180729135733789.html

Islamist-backed Candidate Becomes First Woman Mayor of Tunis. *France24*, July 3, 2018. http://www.france24.com/en/20180703-islamist-backed-candidate-abderrahim-first-woman-mayor-tunis-tunisia

Laurence, Michael. 2018. Democratic Theory. *Oxford Bibliographies*, February 22. Accessed 15 June 2018, from http://www.oxfordbibliographies.com/view/document/obo-9780199756223/obo-9780199756223-0162.xml

Lewis, Aidan. 2011. Profile: Tunisia's Ennahda Party. *BBC News*, October 25. http://www.bbc.com/news/world-africa-15442859

Luck, Taylor. 2018. Islamist and Feminist: A New Generation Stakes Its Claim. *The Christian Science Monitor (CSM)*, June 18. https://www.csmonitor.com/World/Middle-East/2018/0618/Islamist-and-feminist-A-new-generation-stakes-its-claim

Malsin, Jared. 2017. Why Tunisians Are Testifying About Horrific Tortures by the State. *Time Magazine*, January 13. http://time.com/4634622/tunisia-truth-dignity-commission-zine-al-abidine-ben-ali/

Markey, Patrick, and Aziz El Yaakoubi. 2014. Tunisian Premier Resigns for Caretaker Government. *Reuters*, January 9. https://www.reuters.com/article/us-tunisias-pm-idUSBREA080MY20140109

Miller, Andrew. 2018. Tunisia Is One of the Arab World's Biggest Success Stories. The Trump Administration Doesn't Seem to Care. *The Washington Post*, March 15. https://www.washingtonpost.com/news/democracy-post/wp/2018/03/15/tunisia-is-one-of-the-arab-worlds-biggest-success-stories-the-trump-administration-doesnt-seem-to-care/?utm_term=.b7093a8b7040

Milne, Seumas. 2013. Tunisian Government Has No Hidden Agendas, Says New Prime Minister. *The Guardian*, April 2. http://www.guardian.co.uk/world/2013/apr/02/tunisia-government-agenda-prime-minister

Obama, Barack, and Beji Caid Essebsi. 2015. Helping Tunisia Realize Its Democratic Promise. *The Washington Post*, May 15. https://www.washingtonpost.com/opinions/us-helping-tunisia-to-make-sure-democracy-delivers/2015/05/20/05b029e4-fe75-11e4-833c-a2de05b6b2a4_story.html?noredirect=on&utm_term=.54b0e439037f

Osman, Tarek. 2013. Why Border Lines Drawn with a Ruler in WWI Still Rock the Middle East. *BBC News*, December 14. http://www.bbc.com/news/world-middle-east-25299553

Poverty in Central Tunisia a Ticking Time Bomb. *Gulf News*, March 4, 2016. https://gulfnews.com/news/mena/tunisia/poverty-in-central-tunisia-a-ticking-time-bomb-1.1683702

Profile: Zine el-Abidine Ben Ali. *BBC News*, June 20, 2011. https://www.bbc.com/news/world-africa-12196679

Prominent Saudi Women Activists Arrested. *Human Rights Watch (HRW)*, August 1, 2018. https://www.hrw.org/news/2018/08/01/prominent-saudi-women-activists-arrested

Rivett-Carnac, Marc. 2016. France Strengthens Support for Tunisia in the Face of Islamist Threats. *Time Magazine*, March 17. http://time.com/4262329/tunisia-france-aid-security-ben-guerdane-isis-islamist/

Steele, Jonathan. 2001. Food for Thought –The Guardian Profile: Amartya Sen. *The Guardian*, March 30. http://www.guardian.co.uk/books/2001/mar/31/society.politics

Taylor, Andrea, and Elissa Miller. 2018. How Legal Reform Can Drive Social Change for Women in Tunisia. *The Atlantic Council*, March 8. http://www.atlanticcouncil.org/blogs/menasource/how-legal-reform-can-drive-social-change-for-women-in-tunisia

The 2011 Time 100: El Général, Tunisian Rapper. *Time Magazine*. 2011. http://www.time.com/time/specials/packages/article/0,28804,2066367_2066369_2066242,00.html

The State, Policy-Making and Political Economy. School of Oriental and African Studies. Political Economy of Public Policy. No date. Accessed 12 June 2018, from https://www.soas.ac.uk/cedep-demos/000_P527_PEPP_K3736-Demo/unit1/page_13.htm

Tunisia. *CIA World Factbook*, July 2, 2018. https://www.cia.gov/library/publications/the-world-factbook/geos/ts.html

Tunisia – Economy. *CIA World Factbook*, June 10, 2013. https://www.cia.gov/library/publications/the-world-factbook/geos/ts.html

Tunisia – Politics. GlobalSecurity.org. 2018. https://www.globalsecurity.org/military/world/tunisia/politics.htm

Tunisia Country Fact Sheet. *International Fund for Agricultural Development (IFAD)*. 2011. Governing Council. http://www.ifad.org/events/gc/34/nen/factsheet/tunisia.pdf

Tunisia: Islamist-Led Government Steps Down. *Wilson Center*, January 9, 2014. https://www.wilsoncenter.org/article/tunisia-islamist-led-government-steps-down

Tunisia: Military Hunts Militants Near Algerian Border. *The New York Times*, August 2, 2013. http://www.nytimes.com/2013/08/03/world/africa/tunisia-military-hunts-militants-near-algerian-border.html

Tunisia: People and Society. *CIA World Factbook*, August 20, 2018. https://www.cia.gov/library/publications/the-world-factbook/geos/ts.html

Tunisia's Nobel Prize-Winning Trade Unions Are Holding the Country Back. *The Economist*, December 14, 2017. https://www.economist.com/middle-east-and-africa/2017/12/14/tunisias-nobel-prize-winning-trade-unions-are-holding-the-country-back

Willsher, Kim. 2011. Leila Trabelsi: Tunisia's Lady MacBeth: Tunisia's First Lady Was Said to Be Manipulative and Ruthless. *The Guardian*, January 18. http://www.guardian.co.uk/world/2011/jan/18/leila-trabelsi-tunisia-lady-macbeth

Wisner, Frank G., and W. Bowman Cutter. 2015. Why the United States Should Act Quickly to Help Tunisia. *The Washington Post*, August 6. https://www.washingtonpost.com/opinions/why-we-should-act-quickly-to-help-tunisia/2015/08/06/f5d27f8c-324e-11e5-8353-1215475949f4_story.html

Women in National Parliaments. June 30, 2012. http://www.ipu.org/wmn-e/classif.htm

Worstall, Tim. 2013. Paul Krugman on the Inevitable Decline of Apple and Microsoft. *Forbes*, August 25. http://www.forbes.com/sites/timworstall/2013/08/25/paul-krugman-on-the-inevitable-decline-of-apple-and-microsoft/

Yerkes, Sarah. 2017. Young People Are Staying Away from Tunisian Politics – Here's Why. *Brookings*, March 20. https://www.brookings.edu/blog/markaz/2017/03/20/young-people-are-staying-away-from-tunisian-politics-heres-why/

Index

H. Alvi, *The Political Economy and Islam of the Middle East*, Political Economy of Islam,
https://doi.org/10.1007/978-3-030-17050-9

Zeitfracht Medien GmbH
Ferdinand-Jühlke-Straße 7
99095 Erfurt, Deutschland
produktsicherheit@kolibri360.de